What People Are Say[...]

Chicken Soup fo[...]

TWINS and More

"*Like the song says, 'I'm So Excited' that* Chicken Soup for the Soul: Twins and More *is here! I have always been excited about our twin boy, Conor, and girl, Ali. They are everything and more when it comes to raising both genders. They are the other music in my ears and my heart. They bring me life-changing melodies. Raising twins is a song I'm still learning to sing.*"

~**Ruth Pointer**, The Pointer Sisters

"*As a journalist covering breaking news around the globe and mother of two young daughters, I thought I was juggling a lot—until I had twin boys!* Chicken Soup for the Soul: Twins and More *is funny and moving, insightful and inspiring. Life with twins is a chaotic, wonderful, joyful experience—and this book captures it perfectly!*"

~**Soledad O'Brien**, CNN journalist

"*What a blessing* Chicken Soup for the Soul: Twins and More *is to our family. With Tom being on the PGA Tour, we don't always have the gift of time to pause and count our blessings. Our two sets of twins sure do keep us hopping! When I do find the time to cuddle up and read, this is the book I grab. It allows me to laugh, cry and reflect on the beautiful gifts that twins give so effortlessly. Thank you for speaking for us all.*"

~**Tom Purtzer**, PGA Tour Professional, and his wife, **Lori Purtzer**

"In countless nations, we have witnessed an insatiable fascination for twins. Even we, being identicals, marvel at the God-given uniqueness of our twinship. Dive into these intriguing first-hand accounts in Chicken Soup for the Soul: Twins and More. *You will laugh. You will cry. Your heart will be stirred. Read and be doubly blessed."*

~**Janice and Faye Rostvit**, international singers, composers, recording artists, and co-authors of *Twin Reflections*

"As a mom of twins and owner of a greeting card line for twins, I can't get enough of the subject of twins! So I was the first in line when I heard that Chicken Soup for the Soul: Twins and More *was coming out! This is a wonderful read, and an excellent addition to the growing line of products available for families of twins and multiples."*

~**Angelice Tyson**, founder, Gemini Greetings

"As a child development specialist, I thought I knew all about bonding by studying the beautiful mother/child bond. But when I became the mother of identical twin girls, I learned about a bond that is unlike any other. I'm continually amazed by the unique connection shared by my girls. Chicken Soup for the Soul: Twins and More *is filled with stories that showcase this mysterious and wondrous relationship between twins."*

~**Holly Engel-Smothers**, coauthor,
Boosting Your Baby's Brain Power

Chicken Soup for the Soul®

Twins and More

Chicken Soup for the Soul: Twins and More
101 Stories Celebrating Double Trouble and Multiple Blessings
by Jack Canfield, Mark Victor Hansen, Susan M. Heim

Published by Chicken Soup for the Soul Publishing, LLC www.chickensoup.com

The publisher gratefully acknowledges the many publishers and individuals who granted Chicken Soup for the Soul permission to reprint the cited material.

Front cover photo courtesy of Stockbyte. Back cover photo courtesy of Rob Sweeten of Rob Sweeten Photography. Interior photograph courtesy of iStockphoto.com/ ImageMediaGroup/© Scott Kochsie

Cover and Interior Design & Layout by Pneuma Books, LLC
For more info on Pneuma Books, visit www.pneumabooks.com

Distributed to the booktrade by Simon & Schuster. SAN: 200-2442

Publisher's Cataloging-in-Publication Data
(Prepared by The Donohue Group)

Chicken soup for the soul : twins and more : 101 stories celebrating double trouble and multiple blessings / [compiled by] Jack Canfield, Mark Victor Hansen [and] Susan M. Heim.

p. ; cm.

ISBN-13: 978-1-935096-32-0
ISBN-10: 1-935096-32-X

1. Twins--Literary collections. 2. Multiple birth--Literary collections. 3. Twins--Anecdotes. 4. Multiple birth--Anecdotes. I. Canfield, Jack, 1944- II. Hansen, Mark Victor. III. Heim, Susan M. IV. Title: Twins and more

PN6071.T83 C45 2009
810.8/02/0306875 2008944058

PRINTED IN THE UNITED STATES OF AMERICA
on acid∞free paper
17 16 15 14 13 12 10 09 01 02 03 04 05 06 07 08

Chicken Soup for the Soul®

Twins and More

101 Stories Celebrating Double Trouble and Multiple Blessings

Jack Canfield
Mark Victor Hansen
Susan M. Heim

CSS
Chicken Soup for the Soul Publishing, LLC
Cos Cob, CT

Chicken Soup for the Soul

www.chickensoup.com

Contents

3

~Seeing Double~

4

~A Special Bond~

5

~Twin Trials~

6

~It's Triplets!~

7

~Grandparenting Twins~

8

~A Different Path to Parenthood~

9

~Double Trouble, Double Fun~

10

~Lessons Learned~

Chicken Soup for the Soul

Foreword

I was completely shocked when I found out I was expecting twins. There was no family history of multiples. Growing up, I knew only one family with twins, and they had two sets! (One set of boys was fraternal; the other twin boys were identical.) But other than that, I'd never really thought about twins very much. All that changed one morning in the spring of 2003 in my doctor's office. Since then, I've learned that I tend to be in the minority when it comes to thinking about twins. Everywhere I go with my family, the twins get all of the attention. And look how much press celebrities receive when they're expecting twins!

But this love of twins is nothing new. In fact, twins have fascinated people for thousands of years. Throughout history, certain cultures have actually considered it a curse or a bad omen to be a twin or give birth to twins! Other cultures have revered twins and seen them as a sign of good fortune.

Ancient mythology is riddled with tales of twins. In Greek mythology, it was believed that twins were conceived when a woman had relations with both a mortal man and a god on the same day. When twins resulted, one of them would have godlike qualities and the other would be an ordinary mortal person. This was true for Heracles, known as Hercules in Western cultures, son of the god

Zeus and the human Alcmene, who also conceived Iphicles, a twin for Heracles, with her mortal husband, Amphitryon.

And, of course, there were the famous "Gemini twins," Castor and Pollux. In Greek and Roman mythology, the twins were born of the same mother, but had different fathers. Pollux was an immortal god, while Castor was mortal. However, when Castor died, Pollux was so grieved that he asked Zeus to keep them together, so Castor and Pollux were made into the Gemini constellation that we see among the stars.

Twins were often cited in various mythologies to explain the dualistic nature of the universe. For example, Greek gods Apollo and Artemis were known as the sun god and the moon goddess, respectively. In the Xingu myths of Brazil, twin brothers Kuat and Iae represented the sun and the moon. To the Fon people in Benin, West Africa, the god Liza is representative of the sun, while his twin Mawu is associated with the moon.

Twins have also been seen as the polar forces of good and evil. In Zoroastrian myths, good and evil were represented by the twins Ahriman and Ahura Mazda. A Native American myth tells the story of Gluskap, a god of creation, who must defeat Malsum, his evil twin, who ruled the demons. Even the Biblical twins, Jacob and Esau, were completely different. It was said that they struggled with each other even in their mother's womb, and their competitiveness and animosity continued throughout their lives.

Long ago, the Yoruba tribe of Nigeria would kill twins, and sometimes their mother, because they believed the twins were evil or the result of their mother's liaison with two men. However, in today's times, the Yoruba see twins as a good sign, a welcome change of perspective considering that the Yoruba have an exceptionally high incidence (5%) of twin births. Scientists are not sure if it's because the villagers eat a lot of yams (which contain a natural hormone called phytoestrogen that may stimulate the ovaries to produce more eggs) or whether it's genetics (in which Yoruban women inherit the tendency to release more eggs).

In Native American cultures, women were sometimes advised

not to eat foods that were thought to increase the likelihood of conceiving twins, such as bananas and double almonds, because twins were viewed negatively. However, other Native American tribes saw twins in a positive light.

Fortunately, in today's modern world, twins and multiples are seen as a blessing, despite their reputation for "double trouble" and "multiple mischief." Who cannot be moved by the sight of twin babies snuggled together in a crib, holding hands as they begin their lives together? Who hasn't dreamed of having an identical twin with whom one could switch places when it comes to a dreaded exam or a conflicting appointment? Twins themselves tell of the great blessing of always having a confidant by their side. It somehow makes the difficulties of life much easier to digest. And for parents who have struggled with infertility, the arrival of twins, triplets or more signifies the joyous end to many years of tears and dashed hopes.

The stories in *Chicken Soup for the Soul: Twins and More* explore the many joys and challenges of being twins and raising multiples. The special bond they share, the challenges they face together, the trouble they get into, and the mysteries surrounding twins are all evident in these tales submitted by twins, parents of multiples, and friends and relatives of these special siblings. Just like the people of ancient times, we're still fascinated by twins—and you're certain to be inspired and delighted by the stories in *Chicken Soup for the Soul: Twins and More*!

~Susan M. Heim

It's Great to Be a Twin!

Now I'm a twin as you can see,
For as you look, there's two of me,
And that's a fact that no one can deny,
When we're together we're aware,
That people often stop and stare,
Now could that be an indication why,

Twins are a fascination,
All across the nation,
With twins there's no mistake,
People do a "double take."

Which is which? And who is who?
I am me, and you are you,
I can say, "It's great to be a twin."

Now I am glad that I am two,
God chose to make me just like you,
For our genetic makeup is the same,
I was born the new creation,
I must be the duplication,
We wouldn't have it any other way,

It's fun to cause confusion,
We are no illusion,
We are simply two of a kind,
A better friend we cannot find,

Just like two peas in a pod,
Our creator we applaud,
I can say, "It's great to be a twin."

It's double pleasure, double fun,
To be a twin, we're two in one,
The mirror image is no accident,
Though others tend to scrutinize,
Eventually they'll realize,
The bond we share is no coincidence,

Twins are a dual creation,
Not a freak mutation,
Twins have not been cloned by man,
They are made by God's own plan,

We give God double praise,
To Him our voices raise,
We are glad that God has made us twins.

Thank you, God, it's great to be a twin!

~Song written by international singers and identical twins, Janice and Faye Rostvit

Chapter 1

Twins and More

Expecting Multiples

Pregnancy is a disease from which you recover in eighteen years and nine months.

~Carrie Latet

1

Chicken Soup for the Soul

The Journey

Life's a journey, not a destination.
~Aerosmith

"How would you like to go to California?" my pilot husband, Bill, asked as he bounded in the door on his return from a trip.

"Sure. You know I love it there."

"I don't mean to visit," he interrupted. "I mean to live."

"Move? You must be kidding!" I responded in disbelief. "You know I can't move now. I can't leave my doctor."

He stared at me and nodded. "I guess not."

I was thirty-one, and five months pregnant with twins, which was definitely considered high risk in 1972. We had been waiting for an opportunity to move to California for five years as we shoveled snow in Chicago, and finally here was our chance.

"Oh, why not?" I exclaimed. "With my luck, the doctor won't even be here. He'll be fishing or vacationing in some exotic out-of-the-way place since my due date is Labor Day. Let's do it."

At my next appointment, the doctor stammered in utter disbelief when we told him. "You can't move at this stage of your pregnancy." Then he looked at me, took a breath and said, "Oh, well, planes land for emergencies all the time."

"Oh, we're driving," I told him. "We're pulling a trailer and taking the dog."

"You'll never make it. You'll go into labor in the middle of the desert."

But we packed the car and set out for the West eight weeks before my due date, with doctor's orders to stop every hour to stretch and walk. We did that for the first two days. Then we hit Oklahoma and saw the temperature in Tulsa: 102 degrees. We weren't even to the desert yet.

Our Fiat station wagon had no air conditioning, just wing-vent windows I could turn toward me for air. The only clothes I could wear at that point were "tents," loose dresses that provided space and comfort. I pulled up my skirt to feel the rush of air, even though it was HOT. Oncoming truck drivers stared in horror as they tried to keep their rigs on the road while looking at me and my ballooning dress.

Roadside "rest stops" were nothing more than a bench and a trash can at a wide spot beside the road. "Ready to walk a bit?" Bill asked, as we saw the sign for the next one a mile ahead.

"If you stop, I'll kill you!" I almost screamed. "Keep moving—it's the only way to get any air. I'll do isometric exercises here in the car," I said, flexing my feet and knees as I spoke.

Right behind our seats was an aluminum cooler full of ice and cold drinks. Our clever cocker spaniel found it to be the coolest spot in the car and was sprawled across it. He growled when I reached back to get a cold drink. "Come on, Buff. I just want to get something to drink," I said as I gently shoved him off. He glared and jumped back on the top before I could close the lid.

When we got to Flagstaff, with its trees and cooler temperatures, it felt like a true oasis. Heavenly. I didn't want to leave.

"It's only one more day, honey," Bill tried to encourage me.

We poured ourselves into the car early the next morning to complete the drive. And, finally, there was California. We'd made it!

First thing the next morning was a visit to my new doctor. He took one look at me and said, "You have to lie down."

"I can't. Our furniture arrives in the morning and..."

"Your babies are going to arrive, too, if you don't lie down. Let your husband unpack."

"He has to fly a trip."

"Then lie down, unpack the boxes, and let him put things away when he gets home." It was tedious, but I managed to unpack enough for us to live.

Our new home's yard was nothing but dirt, and the dog's feet had to be washed every time he came in from outside. The air conditioning hadn't yet been installed, so lying down on our black leather sofa was not comfortable. Nothing was comfortable.

Bill fashioned a sling that went around my neck and held up my tummy to ease the load because I was carrying our babies all in front. From the back, I still had a waistline, but from the side... well, people would stare in shock when they saw my profile. Men, in particular, would turn pale, certain I was going to drop the babies at their feet. They hurried to do whatever business they had to do with us so as to be free of perceived danger.

When we went for our new California drivers' licenses, I was whisked from the line and told to take the driving part of the test immediately. It consisted of little more than driving around the block and parallel parking the car on my return. The examiner said, "You passed. Now go home."

"I can't. My husband is in line over there." I pointed.

"Get him over here," I was ordered. Bill had the same modified driving test and was told to take me home immediately. We went to dinner instead.

It was a charming place, but I couldn't fit into a booth, so they pulled up a chair for me. When my food arrived, the plate held beautiful kosher dill pickle wedges, which had been my favorite before pregnancy and all through my life. When we were dating and would buy big pickles in bags, we'd get understanding smiles from clerks. Now that I was finally pregnant, the sight of them made me feel ill. It was ironic.

"Could you remove these, please?" I asked.

"I thought people in your condition loved dill pickles," the waitress commented, looking a bit confused.

"I did, but don't now. Please." I handed her my plate, and she rushed to the back with it, bringing me lettuce instead. It didn't matter—I couldn't eat much. There was no room. I just drank milk, often milkshakes. An interesting diet, as it turned out; the babies gained, and I lost weight.

One night, my mother phoned and announced that they were tired of waiting. My parents were heading to California to be with us for the exciting event. The day they arrived, we took them to Laguna Beach for an ocean view dinner, then home to plan for a visit to the summer art festival the next day.

"Never mind," Mother said. "You'll have the babies tomorrow."

"They're not due for two weeks," I protested.

"Well, I'm going on up to bed now to be ready," she said.

At 4:00 A.M., my water broke.

I knocked on the guest room door. "It's time," I said.

"Told you," she answered.

"I changed my mind. I don't want to do this," I muttered, as we headed to the hospital.

Fourteen hours later, we had two beautiful, perfect little girls who weighed almost six pounds each. As I soaked in the miracles in my arms, I realized that people wouldn't stare in shock at the sight of me anymore. They'd be staring at our precious little ones instead.

~Jean H. Stewart

2

The Power of Brotherly Prayer

Be thankful that God's answers are wiser than your answers.
~William Culbertson

When he was seven years old and the second of six children, our son Teddy began adding a special request to family bedtime prayers: "And, God, please send us identical twin babies, and please bless them if you do."

It wasn't too long before I was pregnant, and Teddy insisted these were the twins he'd been praying for. But my doctor, who had extensive experience with my pregnancies and their outcomes, assured us it was a singleton. He was a rare gem, this doctor, a family practitioner who also did obstetrics, but as a GP he didn't have ultrasound equipment in his office. And without seeing "shadow pictures" to prove that there was only one, Teddy refused to relinquish his dream of twin babies. Every night, we heard the same thing: "And, God, please send us..."

The rest of the children were frankly excited about a single new baby because he or she would break the tie between our three boys and three girls. They took turns talking to my belly, encouraging the life within to "C'mon, be a boy!" or crooning, "Girl... girl... you know you want to be a girl."

Whichever sex, the baby was big... but the others had been big, too. I asked the doctor again, "Are you sure there's only one?" He spent an extra fifteen minutes palpating before giving me his answer. "Yes, there's only one. See? Here's the back and the head. No room for anyone else."

Still, Teddy's faith in God's answer never wavered. And my faith in our doctor never wavered... until one night, at thirty-six weeks, I was driving down the interstate and felt the baby hiccupping under my rib cage. Then I felt the baby hiccupping against the base of my spine. At the same time. In a different rhythm.

Yes, one baby can fool a mom and her doctor by being especially big or especially active. But one baby cannot hiccup in two different places in two different rhythms.

My doctor was out of town, but he arranged for a high-risk OB to give me a sonogram at the hospital the next week. For almost an hour, I lay flat on my back with (as it turned out) thirteen pounds of baby between my spine and my full bladder, as the OB and the tech tried to count femurs and ulnas in a too-small space. Finally, they pronounced their decision: I was indeed having twins.

They were born six days later, one boy and one girl, perpetuating the gender tie. The first night we were all home together, saying bedtime prayers, my husband and I were stunned to hear Teddy add his usual petition: "And, God, please send us..."

"But, Teddy," we exclaimed, "your prayers were answered! Even though everyone kept saying there was only one baby, we really did have twins!"

He shook his head. "Yes, I know, and I like them just fine. But they're not the ones I asked for. They're not identical."

After ten more years, he's finally given up that prayer. I can't shake the hunch, though, that he's going to get those identical twins eventually... but they're going to be his children, not his siblings!

~Kalynne Pudner, Ph.D.

3

The Twins Have Landed

What was most significant about the lunar voyage was not that men set foot on the moon but that they set eye on the earth.
~Norman Cousins

On July 20, 1969, Apollo 11 landed on the moon, and the human race accomplished its single greatest technological achievement. Never before had a human being set foot on another celestial body, until that night when two spacemen stood on the moon and saw Earth in the heavens. Neil Armstrong's one small step and mankind's giant leap did not go unheralded by the eleven-year-old I was then. My fifth-grade studies in science had piqued my interest in America's space program, and I would not let drooping eyelids steal this historic moment. I stayed up way past my bedtime for this landmark event that I would someday describe to my kids and grandkids—that I had witnessed, as it occurred, the first moon landing and man's first walk on the moon.

Time travel thirty years out to July 20, 1999: Little did I know that in the wee hours of that morning, my own spaceboys, identical twins, would land on the face of Planet Earth.

Like most kids, I was fascinated by the idea of twins. Whenever Sis and I played "house," my imaginary brood always included one or two sets of twins. And when the two of us played the game of Life along with our brother, I loved landing on the spaces that allowed me to fill my car with blue and pink pegs. Nothing did that quicker than the twin-boy space.

Perhaps I was twin-struck because it did not seem possible that I would ever really have twins. There was nary a twin in my ancestral line.

After the home pregnancy test, I was off to my midwife. This was the same midwife who during my first pregnancy had compared a baby in the womb to an astronaut floating about in a spaceship. No gravity, just floating, bouncing off the walls. This time, she suspected two astro-babies and sent me for an ultrasound. And yes, there were two, but also a possible problem.

The docs thought the babies might be monoamniotic, floating around in the same amniotic sac (which causes twin-to-twin transfusion syndrome), with a risk of one or both babies being lost during pregnancy or at birth. Were my babies bouncing off their own walls or bouncing off each other in the same compartment of the space shuttle? Mission Control was reminded how dangerous childbirth can be even in these times of great technological advances. The next ultrasound would tell the story, and I was leaving it in the hands of our Heavenly Father.

Indeed, the next ultrasound showed the line, that most beautiful line that meant the babies were in their own sacs. Now we could tell family and friends, even the whole world, that I was pregnant with twins. We told the soon-to-be big sister first and let her tell the rest that we were "going to have babies."

The rest of the pregnancy was uneventful, except for monthly, then weekly ultrasounds along with stress tests. The boys continued to grow inside the command module. From the front, I looked huge; from the side, like a bus. Total strangers asked if I was expecting twins. Fun at first, but I soon tired of the questions and stares and took to staying home. My little spacemen were in tight quarters now, with no room to float or bounce. They still managed to kick me and flail their arms with sweeping motions that I could see crossing my grossly expanded belly. They were likely getting in a few punches between each other, too. Ouch!

My due date was about a month after my daughter's birthday, so I entertained the idea of having the babies at thirty-six weeks, on the same date I had delivered four years earlier. Then, all three children might share one huge birthday party each year. But at my daughter's party that year, family members took guesses on when I would deliver. Most picked days sooner rather than later. No one guessed I would go to the day before my due date.

With the countdown now two days before my due date, I went to the hospital Monday morning to have my weekly ultrasound and stress test. This exhausting routine was such a part of my life by now that I thought having two babies to care for couldn't be any more work. Ha!

From the ultrasound, the technicians estimated that the babies weighed about six pounds each. The stress test showed no contractions, and the doctors debated what to do with me. They scheduled me for Thursday if nothing had happened by then.

I don't remember what I had for dinner that night, except for the broccoli. A half-hour later, I had stomach pains. My husband Mike was a few blocks away at a church meeting, but I decided not to bother him. I called Mom instead and asked if she thought the broccoli was causing my stomach pains. (I was obviously in denial that I was full-term with twins.) In a quivering voice, Mom suggested I call the doctor and get to the hospital.

Mission Control decided to wait and see if the pain started feeling more like a contraction. My first labor had been long, and I didn't want to get to the hospital too soon. Within the hour, however, I had alerted Mike to come home, called my sister to pick up my daughter at a neighbor's, thrown my bag in the car, taken my daughter to the neighbor's with a quick explanation, and was beside Mike speeding to the hospital.

Labor was quick. Once I got past the denial, I delivered two babies in about one-tenth the time it took to have their sister. They were delivered naturally (no drugs, no epidural) about four hours after we arrived at the hospital, one boy, then twelve minutes later, his identical twin.

In the recovery room, a voice came over the intercom. "Baby Boy A weighs seven pounds, ten ounces." My jaw dropped as I hardly had time to process the thought that this must be the larger baby. "Baby Boy B is eight pounds," the voice from outer space continued. Mike and I stared unbelievingly at each other.

Recovery room? Ha! Ever since the boys exited Spaceship Mom, they have rocked our world. The family dynamic changed, and keeps changing as they and their sister have grown to be best buddies, fiercest rivals, and everything else brothers and sisters are to each other. Dad has found more joy in his career and getting out of the house in the morning, especially after a wakeful night with one or more cranky offspring. As for the space shuttle, let's just say that if anyone in the family needs a skin graft, I'm here for them.

"Houston, come in Houston: The twins have landed." Thud.

~Deborah A. Ein

Stephanie ©2008
Coming in for a landing
on Planet Earth!

Chicken Soup for the Soul

"What Do You Mean, Two Babies?"

Things are only impossible until they're not.
~Jean-Luc Picard, Star Trek: The Next Generation

"When are you due?" I asked the gal next to me in the doctor's waiting room.

"In two weeks," she responded, eyeing my tummy. "You, too?"

"Actually, I'm due on Labor Day."

She looked at me incredulously before shaking her head. "That can't be. It's only May. You must have miscalculated."

The doctor checked me over, and then sent me for X-rays. It was 1972, before the days of ultrasound.

"Come see!" Three young X-ray technicians hurried toward me.

"In this?" I muttered, tugging at my backless robe.

"No one will see anything. Hurry—come!" They led me to an alcove where large black films hung on the wall.

"You have two babies. There, see them?" They pointed to two little skeletons, one curled head down and the other spread across and above, making a "T."

I was stunned. Not a miscalculation, but a miracle! We were going to have two babies, after eleven years of trying. We thought there would be none, and now there were two.

I couldn't wait to tell my husband, Bill, but he was on a flight, so when I got home, I phoned my mother.

"How are you?" she asked.

"Fine. We're having two babies."

"How nice, dear. How's the weather?"

What was wrong with her? No reaction at all? We chatted a bit, and then hung up. I sat down, shaking my head in wonder and shock. Two infants. Two children. At once. And she didn't even acknowledge it.

The phone rang.

"Oh, my God!" My mother's Southern accent filled my ear when I answered. "What are you going to do?"

"I was hoping you'd tell me." And then I began to laugh, and Mother laughed with me.

Bill came home weary and began to unpack his pilot's bag and repack it for another trip the next day, while listening to the details of my doctor's appointment.

"... and I looked, and there were two babies!" I squealed.

"What?" He stared at me, his face filled with the most incredible grin I'd ever seen.

We realized we were in for the adventure of our lives.

Two weeks before Labor Day, my water broke at 1:00 A.M. Bill was home but due to leave early that morning. His children knew how to time their arrival.

"I've changed my mind," I told him. "I don't want to do this."

"Well, it's too late now." He put his arm around me. "Let's get going. Are you okay?"

I nodded and slowly moved to the car with a towel between my legs.

Mid-August was a busy time at our local hospital. There were no labor rooms available, so I spent the morning in the hall outside the doctors' crash pad. I wasn't really laboring. Having contractions, yes, but not painful ones. It was much different from what I'd expected. Lamaze really works.

By afternoon I was moved to a room. Groups of interns would come occasionally to watch my stomach suck in during huge contractions. By late afternoon, the doctors had decided to X-ray. Since my water had broken, it was vital that the babies be born soon despite my unusual labor.

"We have sibling rivalry in the womb," announced my doctor, looking at the film. "Baby #1 is head down but not making much progress so Baby #2 is sliding down feet first to get out of there. We're going to have to go in to get them."

"No! Not a Caesarean," I protested.

"We have no choice," he said as he hugged my shoulders. "It's been twelve hours, and you have two babies fighting to be born. We have to help them out of there."

"But I want to see. I've waited so long." I fought back tears.

Bill stood in his green scrubs and paper shoes with his *Twins and Supertwins* book clutched under his arm. "It'll be okay, honey. I'll be right here." But he wasn't allowed to stay. I was devastated. He was anxious for the babies to be born, and settled outside the door of the operating room.

"Can I have an epidural?" I questioned the anesthesiologist.

"I don't think it'll work," he said, eyeing my fifty-five-inch midsection.

"Please. I have to be awake," I begged.

"If you promise to let me know if you feel any pain at all."

"You think you won't know if I feel the knife?" I responded.

I did feel it. It felt like someone was drawing on my lower stomach with a pencil. No pain.

"What is that?" one of the doctors exclaimed.

Oh, no, what was wrong with my babies? "I don't know," another doctor answered. "Let's get the babies out of here, and then we'll go back and see."

I heard the most incredible sound in the world, the wail of our firstborn child.

"You have a beautiful girl," said the anesthesiologist.

"Heather," I replied. We had chosen two girls' names and two for boys, since we didn't know their gender.

A second strong cry.

"Another beauty," he said.

"Are you sure? It's supposed to be Michael."

"You can call her whatever you want, but she's a girl."

"Jennifer," I named her.

"Perfect," said the pediatrician, giving me a glimpse as he whisked our girls out to meet their father.

I remembered nothing after that until waking hours later in the recovery room. They had put me to sleep and removed a thick septum that ran from my cervix through my uterus.

"You couldn't get pregnant with this, and the babies never would have gotten through it to be born," the doctor told me in amazement. "We don't know how the twins managed to thrive in half the space. It's impossible..."

Well, God didn't know that. But it did explain why it took eleven years.

"Do you like them?" I asked Bill.

"Of course. They look just like you."

I looked at our beautiful little girls with heads full of black hair, big eyes with long eyelashes, weighing just under six pounds each. Healthy miracles. We knew we were blessed, and still are, thirty-six years later.

~Jean H. Stewart

5

A Sister's Miracle

A sister is a gift to the heart, a friend to the spirit,
a golden thread to the meaning of life.
~Isadora James

How often do you feel the hand of God reach down into your life and know with all certainty that he created a miracle? It's not very often you can see his artistry at work through our physical bodies, but it was clearly evident for my sister and me.

A few years ago, my husband and I were trying to get pregnant with baby number two. Our daughter, Isabella, was two and a half. We had been trying for a while to get pregnant, but every month we'd get a big fat "no." It was getting depressing.

At the time, my only sister, who is three years younger than me, was pregnant with identical twins. I was so jealous. I admit it. I wanted to have twins, too! After all, I was older than her, and I knew it would probably be my last pregnancy. I would have conversations with God about how my heart ached for twins. It was my closely held secret that I only shared with God.

The magic moment finally arrived! I got the solid double lines every woman knows is the clear message that a baby is on board. We were elated. All the while, in the back of my mind, I thought, "Could this be twins?"

At my first eight-week medical appointment, I brought my hopes to my doctor's attention. He listened to me tell the tale of how my sister was having identical twins. "Couldn't I be pregnant with twins, too?" I asked.

My doctor said, "No, Joanne. Identical twins are a fluke of nature or an act of God. Fraternal twins are hereditary. You have one baby in there. Now let's go get the sonogram done." Down the hall we marched.

I walked to the sonogram room a little discouraged. If you knew me, you'd know I don't give up on much until I have to. "Hope springs eternal" is my motto! I remember slowly getting undressed, taking my time and practically holding my breath in anticipation. The whole time, I kept thinking, "It's not over until it's over." It became my dressing room mantra. Honestly, I was afraid to leave the changing room! At least while I was in there, I could still hold onto the possibility of having twins. Once I left that room, the sonogram would begin, and the dream would possibly come to an end.

I got up on the examining table and didn't say a word. I felt like I'd jinx the moment. I was afraid to breathe. My husband Michael was by my side. I watched the woman doing the sonogram so closely, as if I could read her mind. I watched for changes in her expression—a small eyebrow lift or a tilt of the head that would show something was different. She must play a great hand at poker because there were no tell-tale signs on her face. Then I looked at the monitor. I blinked, and then I stared. I saw two little buds, curled up next to each other. Surely my eyes were deceiving me, considering I didn't know the first thing about reading a sonogram screen. I quickly blurted out, "Are there two?"

She replied, "Let me see if I have heartbeats."

Heartbeats? Did she just say heartbeats?

After the longest moment known to mankind, she exclaimed, "You are having twins!"

All the bottled-up anticipation began to spill down my face with the release of joyful tears. My husband began to cry, too. He grabbed my hand and held it close. It was as if, at that very moment, I could feel the grace of God reach down to me and say, "Here is your dream." I could feel it, I could sense it, and I felt like the luckiest girl on the planet.

I went on to have a very difficult pregnancy. I spent five months on complete bed rest. We were being monitored for twin-to-twin transfusion syndrome, a serious complication that can occur with identical twins. Each week we had sonograms to see if the babies had made it through another week. At twenty-three weeks, I had surgery to keep the babies safe inside. I also had gestational diabetes, which meant insulin injections twice a day. Without hesitation, it was all worth bringing these precious children into this world.

The day of their arrival was joyful beyond description. Our beautiful, tiny angels arrived and were placed in our anxiously awaiting arms. To feel them finally safe and close was such a relief. We named them Sophia Grace and Gabriella Faith because, with a little grace and faith, all things are possible.

The bond between twins is amazing. They were meant to share their life together. And the bond between two sisters' twins is a miracle. My sister's incredible boys and my delightful girls will share more than just being twins. They will share a friendship that will span a lifetime. Was it a fluke of nature or an act of God for two sisters to be naturally pregnant with identical twins at the exact same time? We all know which one it was.

~Joanne C. King

6

A Story of Forgiveness

To err is human; to forgive, divine.
~Alexander Pope

In April 1993, at a young and irresponsible age, I found out I was pregnant. With much prodding, I reluctantly and regretfully terminated the pregnancy. I struggled with what I had done and went through several years of feeling unbearably guilty. As a Catholic, I went to confession, but after a brief, tearful session, I figured the priest must not have heard me through my sobs because God couldn't possibly forgive me with a couple of Hail Marys and Our Fathers.

After dealing with several years of depression, I found myself on a different path of self-destructive behavior. I was motivated enough to go to college, but not for all of the right reasons. I did okay at school and attended class regularly, but I partied extensively and dabbled in drugs. Once again, I found myself pregnant. This pregnancy was the motivation I needed to get my act together. I moved home and finished the one class I needed to get an associate's degree, and I picked up additional classes at the local technical college.

In July 1999, I had a baby boy who gave me a wonderful and healthy reason to live. I enjoyed every part of being a mom. Because of him, my life turned around entirely. Although I did not remain with his dad, I knew I was doing the right thing in raising my baby.

After graduating from college with a couple of two-year degrees and then a bachelor's degree, I felt like I had my act together. Still, two dates continued to haunt me: April 26th, the day I'd terminated the first pregnancy, and November 22nd, the day the baby was due.

In July 2005, I got married to a wonderful man who was willing to accept me, my son and all of my baggage. We were fortunate to become pregnant that August, with a due date of May 23rd. We were ecstatic, and two ultrasounds at the beginning of the pregnancy revealed a healthy, growing baby. It wasn't until our routine ultrasound in late December that we found out we were having twin boys. They pushed up my due date to the week of April 26th.

I didn't want to have the babies on that day. I had always vowed that I would think of my unborn baby daily, to somehow repent for what I'd taken away from that child. I felt like I needed to leave April 26th as a day of mourning. It was sacred in my mind.

At a routine checkup on the morning of April 26th, my doctor found that I was five centimeters dilated. It was time to have my babies. As much as I was ready to meet my boys, I choked back tears and confided in her about the irony of the date. She held my hand and offered me different options, but I decided that God had His hand in this, and I needed to do what was intended. Although I am ashamed to admit it, despite the fact that my faith in God is true, I couldn't get it out of the back of my mind that this was His opportunity to take something away from me as I had done thirteen years ago.

Eleven hours later, I pushed out the first baby—a four-pound, eleven-ounce miracle. We knew the second baby was breech, and the plan was to turn him around and deliver him normally. After the expert medical staff turned him around and all was going as planned, he stuck his arm out in one last attempt to enjoy some space to himself. In their efforts to push his arm back in to deliver his head first, the cord got pinched between his arm and his head. With no vital signs on the delivery room monitors, my mind raced with the penance I must be paying now. Surely, the Hail Marys and Our Fathers had been enough. Surely, the guilt I'd carried with me for thirteen years had signified my repentance.

My second baby was born via emergency C-section, all five pounds, fifteen ounces of healthy baby boy. After a very brief stay in the NICU, the babies were released to our care. For weeks after I had the twins, amidst the feelings of being overwhelmed and ecstatic, I could not help but question why God had not allowed me to keep that day to mourn and remember every year. I still feared that something was going to happen to one of the twins or that they would be taken away from me, but they remained healthy, growing boys.

Nearly five months later, I was attending a class in preparation for the boys' baptism. As we were the only family baptizing our children in November, my husband stayed home with the three boys and I was the only parent there. The instructor was a very kind woman who told me about her own family of girls and how she used to take in infants as foster children. The thought of having to raise these infants and then turn around and give them to someone else left me both touched and heartbroken. Feeling emotional from her stories and the thought of baptizing my boys, I struggled to remain composed. She noticed my tears and asked if there was anything she could do. I sobbed out my entire story.

When I had finished, this woman smiled at me compassionately. With the most soothing voice, she explained to me that the boys were not brought into this world on April 26th as a coincidence. They were given to me that day as a gift to our family and as a symbol of forgiveness that I could not ignore. I know this woman was in that room with me for more than just teaching me about baptizing my boys. I think she was there to re-baptize *me*. The sense of peace and forgiveness this woman offered me redefined my faith in God. I was more at peace that day than I had been in thirteen years.

~S.R.

7

Water Babies

People are giving birth underwater now.
They say it's less traumatic for the baby because it's in water.
But certainly more traumatic for the other people in the pool.
~Elayne Boosler

Every time I recall the day our twins were born, I have to laugh—partly because it was such a joyous day, and partly because they came very near to being born in a lake! Here's how it happened.

After an X-ray at seven months in the doctor's office, we knew for sure we were going to have twins. But I had suspected that prospect for some time. We already had two girls—Erika, 5, and Sigrid, 3.

My pregnancies with them had been nothing like this. By four months along, I looked seven months pregnant. By eight months, my extra forty-five pounds let me balance a tooth powder can on top of the several watermelons I appeared to have swallowed.

I was so uncomfortable that I spent the last ten days, as often as possible, lying down. My husband's mother, Mio, had come to help out. False labor pains had already tricked me once into the hospital.

"Sorry," they said, "you're not ready yet. Go home."

This so embarrassed me that during the next week, trying to forget my recurring contractions, I looked around for any distraction I could manage. That's why, one warm Sunday, I was sitting on a rock with my feet cooling in Canandaigua Lake.

My husband Sieg stood some distance away, busy painting a

watercolor of the sparkling summer scene. Mio was somewhere up on the bank. The girls played happily in the water near me.

Suddenly, those contractions got much more businesslike.

"Go tell Daddy we need to go," I told Erika.

She waded over to deliver the message, but he'd reached a crucial point in his painting, and didn't notice her.

She came splashing back.

Another contraction hit. "Tell him!" I urged. I rose, waded awkwardly to shore, heaved myself into the back seat of the Jeep, and lay down.

Sieg appeared at the car window, his face concerned and furrowed with a question.

"Can you wait while I run the girls and Mio home?"

"Yes. Just get going!"

Halfway there, he glanced back at me in the mirror. "Can you hold out while I stop at the dairy? We're almost out of milk."

"Yes!" I said, gritting my teeth.

Sieg hustled a gallon, dropped off the family at the house, and finally raced to the hospital.

One hour later, six minutes apart, our fraternal twins were born by natural childbirth. Together, our boys weighed two ounces short of fourteen pounds.

Pregnancy had been a long and a huge stretch, but well worth it.

As I lay in my hospital bed recovering, welcoming the eager nursing of these two vigorous sons, I thought back to those last minutes on the rock in the lake. Surely, after this interesting start in life, my twins would learn to swim and love the outdoors. After all, they had almost been water babies!

~Lois Muehl

8

Chicken Soup for the Soul

Never Without Hope

Once you choose hope, anything's possible.
~Christopher Reeve

About six months before we married, I awoke in the middle of the night. I had been jarred awake by a vivid dream, so real that I was unsure whether I had been sleeping or awake. I reached for my glasses and turned on the light, but saw only the familiar contents of our bedroom, though the images of the dream were still fresh in my mind.

In the dream, two children came to me. The first was a handsome boy, light blond and strong. He had lovely hands with long fingers, a sweet face and a kind voice. He told me that his name was Joseph—"Joe" or "Josey" for short, but never "Joey" under any circumstances (about this he was adamant!). He told me that he had come for my husband, to soothe his soul and to "remove the sins of the father." In that dream state, he reached out to touch my face, and it felt so soft, loving and peaceful.

He turned away from me for a moment and told me that Hope was coming. In the distance, I could see a young girl approaching. She was lovely, with beautiful delicate features, darker than her brother, but just as angelic. She offered her hand to me and told me that she was Jenny's Hope, and that she had come so that my husband could start his new life with meaning. She played quietly while Joe spoke a bit more, and then told me in a whisper, "I don't know if I can stay." Before I could make sense of what she'd said, I saw her moving off, waving and blowing kisses.

Joe watched her go, and then turned to me and said, "You'll see. Don't worry." He waved goodbye and moved off as Hope had done just moments before. I woke then, with tears in my eyes. I was riveted by these images and ideas—that Thom and I would have not just one child together, but two! But even more heart-wrenching was the concept that these children would come to help my husband heal his wounds. At age five, Thom had suffered the loss of one of his greatest idols when his father was murdered. Later, in his adulthood, Thom had married Jenny, his guardian angel and first love. She died tragically of ovarian cancer, taking with her all of Thom's hopes and dreams for the future. He was devastated by her passing and struggled to keep his life together. It took him years to get back on his feet and to invest in life again. The children's messages were riveting and so clear. They were gifts for my husband that would come through me.

Six months after that beautiful dream, with our friends and family surrounding us in the garden, we married. We had made a decision to formalize our union, both to commemorate our love, but also because we had decided to try to conceive. Just hours before exchanging our vows, we learned that our efforts had paid off, and we were pregnant with twins. Nothing could have been sweeter than the sound of those two heartbeats thumping side by side. Following our wedding, we took time off to frolic in the sun in Mexico, and to take the time for ourselves that we would not have once our twins were born. We threw caution to the wind, stayed up late, and tried all the delicacies we were offered. We were in heaven.

It was only a few days following our return that I became violently ill. I grew weaker by the hour. Finally, my husband carried me into the doctor's office. Antibiotics and IV fluids were ordered, and we were told to call the obstetrician to schedule an ultrasound.

Days later, as I lay flat beneath the ultrasound wand, we watched the screen as our two babies came into view. Joe was emerging, already larger and full of life, while Hope seemed still. Joe's heart beat strong, but Hope's seemed to slow with every minute. We were told to return the following week for monitoring and left, worried and unsure.

The following week, we returned to the radiology department for another ultrasound. I lay back, eyes fixed on the screen, and again felt a rush of joy as Joe's movement elated me. Unfortunately, Hope's form lay motionless and appeared almost fuzzy. The tech turned off the screen and told us that Hope's heart had stopped beating, but that Joe appeared to be developing normally.

Time just seemed to stop. I wanted desperately to wake from this dream. "I don't know if I'll be able to stay..." I could hear Hope's words in the distant recesses of my brain. I wanted to scream, but nothing seemed to come out.

Week after week, we watched Hope fade away. In her place was her brother, stronger than ever and seeming to take over every inch of the cavity left behind with Hope's passing. By Week 40, we were told that he would be more than nine pounds at birth. And, shortly thereafter, Joe burst into the world at nine pounds, three ounces.

By the time Joe was a year old, the pediatricians were telling us that he was likely to grow to six feet, five inches or more in his adulthood. He was at the 95th percentile for height and weight, and seemed to do everything early. By the time he entered preschool, the teachers thought that our four-year-old was six! He could throw a baseball across the yard, hit both right- and left-handed, and recite songs and poems from heart. But we still hadn't told him about his twin. Would we? Should we? What would we ever say? But how could we not? What about all those people who'd lost their twin early in life, and then spent the rest of their lives feeling as if they were missing something? How in the world could we tell Joe about Hope without causing him pain and grief?

I prayed often. I meditated. I asked for guidance. I knew that we needed to tell Joe of his early loss, but in a way that he could appreciate what his sister had given to him—a place to grow, unhindered by anything or anyone else. She had given him the gift of life.

Then, one night, as I lay sleeping, I heard a sweet voice tell me, "You are never without Hope, Joe. Hope resides within you." The message was clear. Not only were these words that Joe could understand about the loss of his sister, but this was a message that we could all savor for the rest of our lives.

We are never without Hope.

~Sage de Beixedon Breslin, Ph.D.

9

Thank You, Trailblazer

Nothing but heaven itself is better than a friend who is really a friend.
~Plautus

We thought we were being so smart, the four of us women. We'd wait until we were in our thirties to have kids, when we were financially stable and satisfied that we'd traveled and partied enough to settle down. But we weren't done traveling.

The four of us were friends even before we traveled the road of infertility. Other friends sadly joined us along the way, but the four of us were the core as we received our ultimate life lesson.

The lesson was not just about the creation of life; it was about patience. The four of us control freaks had to learn how to deal with something out of our hands. We were so used to setting goals, planning, making things happen for ourselves.

So when each of us tried for about a year to get pregnant naturally—and failed—we turned to one another, to books, to the Web (as one husband called it, to crazyinfertilityladies.com), to a fertility painting (that voodoo work of art is another story), to gynecologists and, ultimately, to fertility specialists.

Stuff we had forgotten from biology classes early in our education suddenly mattered again. We learned more about our bodies than we ever thought necessary. We also learned to take our temperatures every morning, to chart our menstrual cycles, to use ovulation and pregnancy kits, to endure violating and often painful tests—and to face crushing disappointment month after month.

Our doctors seemed to double the journey, and we're not even talking twins yet. For every month we didn't get pregnant, our doctors made us take a month off to prep our bodies for the next attempt. Patience.

Our husbands were right there for the journey, of course. That included many somewhat embarrassing trips to drop off sperm. The men didn't have a physical problem; we did, and each problem was different, likely related to aging. One woman could get pregnant but couldn't keep a baby; another's fallopian tube was blocked on one side; I don't ovulate, among other issues; the fourth in our group may have been under too much stress.

So we took pills such as Clomid. That worked for one of the four. The rest of us resorted to injections of other drugs. (My dear husband tried to help with the shots, but it was easier to do myself.) And two of us, me included, ultimately opted for in vitro fertilization, or IVF.

After nearly two years and sixty-seven shots, plus too many pricks and draws for blood—and missed veins—to count, my infertility journey joyously ended.

I was ecstatic to find out I was pregnant. But I was terrified when, a week later, I found out that I would be having twins. I knew it was possible, given that I had two embryos transferred, but I hadn't even expected to get pregnant on my first IVF attempt. I wasn't prepared.

Yet I was. You see, my best friend, Jenn—one of us four women on the road of infertility—was our trailblazer. After her girl and boy were born eight weeks prematurely and came home several weeks later from the hospital, I took care of them one day a week while Jenn worked. I couldn't have imagined that I was preparing for my own twin motherhood.

I was the third of the four of us to deliver twins. We were lucky to have a built-in moms-to-moms support group. We never had to meet up with strangers to get tips on how to feed both babies at the same time, for product suggestions or for advice in transitioning the babies' schedule to the next phase. We understood one another's exhaustion.

But, most important, I don't know how I would've gotten through my journey without Jenn's path, especially because my mother had passed away five years earlier. Jenn guided me in countless ways—as a mom, friend, pseudo-doctor (including psychiatrist) and giver of baby stuff.

My lesson in patience still gets tested, of course, as I chase after my twenty-month-old girls running in opposite directions, and I'm wondering why they won't listen to me for their own safety. But I never could have imagined I'd feel as fulfilled as I do with my loving husband and our two vivacious daughters, as well as my best friend, Jenn. We are all blessed.

~Julie Armstrong

10

It's a Boy... Again?

Of all the animals, the boy is the most unmanageable.
~Plato

I must admit I was a little princess as a young girl. I played with dolls, jumped rope, loved make-up, and squealed at spiders. When my sister and I played "house" with our friends, my name was always Cher. I married Donny Osmond, and we had four perfect children. Of course, when I pulled that pillow out from under my pretend maternity dress, a little girl baby always emerged. I just expected to have girls! After all, I grew up with just one sister—no boys in the family. And my father—no offense, Dad—wasn't a particularly macho man. He didn't insist on watching the football game or drag my sister and me to any monster truck shows. In fact, he knew much more about cooking than kicking. As for me, I was lousy at sports! So I was certain that I'd have daughters when I became a mommy because I had no idea what to do with boys. I even saved my beloved Barbies, and my Chrissy doll that grew hair, to pass on to my future daughters.

Well, life is full of surprises, and my first pregnancy was certainly one of them. When they put my firstborn son in my arms, I was surprised yet thrilled. I was in my mid-twenties and hoped to have more children, so I figured my daughter would arrive with the next delivery. But when I got pregnant with my second child nearly three years later, the ultrasound technician drew an arrow pointing to a particular body part on my unborn child and typed, "It's a boy!" Hmmm, interesting. Okay, well, that wasn't exactly how I had planned it, but maybe it was better this way, I told myself. Two boys would be good company for each other. They could play with the same toys and wear the same clothes, just like my sister and I did growing up. The next one would be a girl....

Then life took another unexpected turn. Actually, many turns! I went through a divorce and nearly ten years of single parenting with my boys before I finally remarried. My new husband had no children of his own, and I was eager to meet my long-awaited daughter, so I decided to go for "round three."

We showed up at our first ultrasound appointment eager to check out our new family member-to-be. "What should we name her?" I asked, certain it would be a girl. My husband liked the name Hayley. "Hayley Heim?" I asked. Hmmm, I wasn't sure. Finally, the doctor came in and began the procedure. It seemed to take him an awfully long time to take the baby's measurements. I didn't remember it taking this long with my previous pregnancies, but it had been eleven years. I figured the technology had changed.

At last, the doctor turned the screen toward us, and we looked at him expectantly. It was still too early to know the baby's gender, but we expected at least a "Congratulations!" or a "Looks good!" Instead, we heard two words we never expected to hear in a million years: "It's twins!" I think my husband and I caught a few flies that day when our mouths flew open in shock. TWINS!

A few months later, after we had recovered from the news, I began to look forward to having twins. My brightest thought was that, surely, with two babies, at least one of them would be a girl, right? Wrong! Amazingly, I gave birth to two more boys! (And at seven pounds, thirteen ounces, and six pounds, nine ounces, they were ready to join the family football team!)

So now I am the mother of four wonderful boys. I must admit that a double dose of testosterone in one fell swoop has been quite a challenge! My twins have mastered wrestling, burping, and peeing while standing. (Their older brothers are an inspiration, of course.) And when I tried to present them with my beloved Barbies, they pulled off the heads and tried to cut off the dolls' hair. So, back they went in the box under my bed, getting older and dustier by the minute.

Now don't get me wrong... I adore my boys! I actually like snakes and building houses with Lincoln Logs. And I no longer blush when I pass the athletic cups at the sporting goods store. My childbearing days are over, but I'm not giving up hope yet for a girl. There's still a good chance that I'll be buying frilly pink clothes some day for a granddaughter. (I'm certain she'll be the most spoiled little girl ever.) Or, dare I hope, I might even get *twin* granddaughters! But, in the meantime, I'll embrace the color blue and know that I've been given the perfect family to love.

~Susan M. Heim

11

Chicken Soup for the Soul

The Ultrasound

All who would win joy must share it; happiness was born a twin.
~Lord Byron

"There's the heartbeat," the ultrasound tech says, pointing to a tiny blinking dot on the dark screen. "Everything looks fine."

I breathe a sigh of relief. It is the ninth week of my second pregnancy, and so far my body displays none of the signs that showed up the first time—signs that eventually led to the death of my son, Luke.

That was less than a year ago. I haven't finished grieving, but the landscape of my life seems so barren without the baby I should have had that I summon the courage to try again. As soon as I learn I am pregnant, I visit my high-risk specialist and am reassured by the sight of that blinking heartbeat. There is a baby in there and, so far, all is well. I sail through the second visit. By this one, the third, I am starting to relax a little.

And then the tech says, "Hold on a minute."

We are silent—the doctor, my husband Jory, and I—as the tech shifts the probe and stares at the screen. Then he and the doctor confer in low voices. Finally, the doctor turns to me.

"We're not sure what we're seeing here," he says. "There is something unusual on the screen, but it could be the ultrasound. We're going to move you into a room with a bigger machine."

Heart pounding, I cling to my husband's hand. "What might it be?" I ask the doctor in a shaky voice.

He looks a little like Santa Claus—white hair and beard, wire-rimmed glasses, and, even though it is March, a red and green tie.

"We're not sure," he answers kindly. "It could be the same problem you had last time, but let's not jump to conclusions. Why don't you stay here while we get the room set up?"

I wait, blinking back tears. It's impossible not to relive the downward spiral of my first pregnancy. First spotting, then cramping. Weekly checkups, multiple ultrasounds and, finally, a dark, depressing, three-week hospital stay that resulted in the severely premature birth of my son. Then his death. It was so wrong—and now it might be happening again.

Soon I am ushered to a room down the hall and hooked up to a machine with a better resolution. Jory and I hold sweaty hands while the tech again moves the probe and confers quietly with the doctor. Finally, they agree.

The doctor faces us. I grip Jory's hand and breathe deeply, steeling myself for bad news.

"Let me show you what's going on here." He points to a dark circle on the screen, in the center of which is a white smudge. "Here's the baby. You can see the heartbeat."

I nod.

Then he points to another, smaller circle, below and to the left of the first.

"And here," he says, "is the other baby."

"The other baby?" I repeat dumbly.

Looking more like Santa Claus than ever, he smiles. Then he says the words that change my life forever, bringing joy to my broken heart and rainbows of color to my empty landscape.

"You're having twins."

~Sara Matson

12

The Butterfly in Me

What the caterpillar calls the end of the world, the master calls a butterfly.
~Richard Bach

A year ago in January, I was riding the train home as usual when I remembered that a friend at work had given me her newspaper because it had an article she thought I'd enjoy. I honestly don't remember what the article was, but I was glad to have something to read for my hour-plus ride home from downtown. I hadn't read the paper in quite some time. I opened it up to the comics section. Immediately, my eyes were drawn to the Family Circus cartoon. It was a picture of the little girl character standing by her mother's lap. It read, "Mommy, do caterpillars know they become butterflies, or does God surprise them?" Wow! I thought. I read it again to myself. I felt I could write a whole dissertation on that question. I was so meant to see that.

Instantly, I knew I was in a metamorphosis stage myself. I'd just hired a spiritual life coach to focus on my life with greater intention, focus and meaning. Hiring that coach was a significant move on my part. Life had become very frustrating to me. I was miserable and yet felt close to turning a corner for good. I believed that having a life coach would get me back on track—the best possible investment for my overall well-being and happiness. He was a major splurge, but I knew it would pay off tenfold.

Days later, when I was perusing a catalog with the intention of finding a piece of jewelry my husband could get me for Valentine's

Day, I stumbled across a butterfly ring. It took my breath away. It was perfect, and it would be my Valentine's Day present. This was an extra special Valentine's Day because that week we were completing a second round of in-vitro fertilization (IVF). It was our second and last attempt. After eight years of trying for kids, including the discovery of a very serious thyroid condition resulting in thyroid cancer and multiple fertility treatments, I had decided I was putting all of my fertilized eggs in one basket. This was it. If it didn't work, my husband and I would have a fun life traveling, playing lots of golf, and enjoying ourselves. We would be happy either way. Kids would be like gravy, we always said. Deep down inside, I really wanted to be a mom, though. I so wanted to raise a child, positively influence that child's life, and learn from him or her.

Our first attempt at IVF the year before had been bleak. We were told that the four fertilized eggs we had didn't stand much of a chance, so it was no surprise when I didn't become pregnant. This time around, though, after working with my coach, I felt I was in a good place to give this IVF thing one more shot. The coaching work I'd been doing made my soul feel pregnant with new life and new perspectives. In previous months, I'd been shedding a lot of dead skin- layers upon layers of ill-serving beliefs. I was ripe, and I knew it wholeheartedly. Two weeks after Valentine's Day, I learned I was pregnant. I was about to become a butterfly! A true miracle had occurred.

At my first ultrasound at six weeks, we learned that the embryo had split in two—we would be parents of identical twins! Another miracle had occurred. Sophia (meaning wisdom) Skye and Grace Isabella joined this world in August of last year.

A year after that special Valentine's Day ring purchase, I found it sitting in my jewelry drawer. I had forgotten about that ring because I'd had to remove my rings from my swollen pregnant hands and tucked them away. My eyes lit up when I rediscovered that favorite butterfly ring.

I immediately popped it on my finger. We were a family of butterflies now! A family. How fortunate I was. I looked down at the ring on my hand again and gasped. The beautiful iridescent center stone of my butterfly ring was surrounded on either side by two peridot stones, the August birthstone. One for Sophie and one for Grace.

This one-time caterpillar was masterfully surprised once again.

~Betsy Jackman

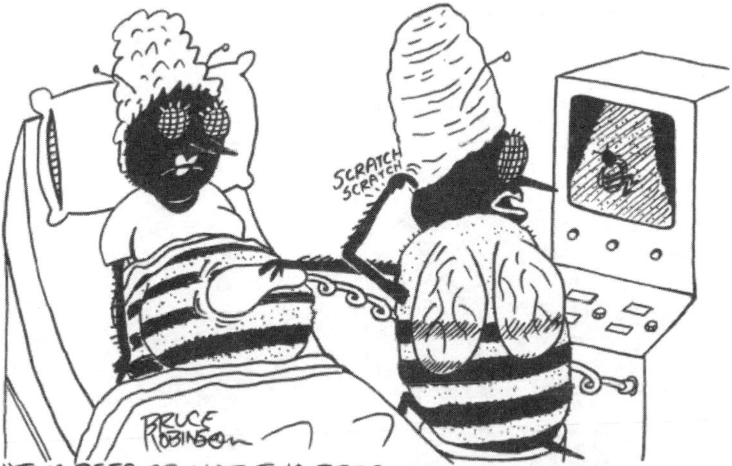

"TWO BEES OR NOT TWO BEES... THAT IS THE QUESTION."

Twins and More

Chapter 2

Sleep Deprivation

No matter how tired you are, take a deep breath, stop, and enjoy the moments.

~*Jodi A. Mindell, Ph.D.*, Sleep Deprived No More

13

A Dog, a Ham and Two Babies

You can always find a capable helping hand at the end of your own sleeve.
~Zig Ziglar

When my daughter gave birth to my wonderful identical twin granddaughters, Elizabeth and Virginia, her other daughters were five and not quite two years old. Even with lots of help in those first weeks, how could anyone manage such a brood—the mountains of diapers, oceans of formula, and that horror of new parenthood, sleep deprivation? Just keeping everyone fed and dry was a storm of nonstop activity! The babies looked just alike, so there was the added job of identity to keep up with. This was accomplished by painting one tiny toenail. But was Elizabeth the one with the hot-pink pedicure or was it Virginia? Between you and me, I wonder to this day if Elizabeth might be Virginia and vice versa. But back to my story.

My daughter has a lot of stellar qualities, of course, but one that stands out—and is definitely genetic, if I may say so—is her resourcefulness. A boatload of personal experience in this department and a hopeful spirit told me that this trait would be her salvation. Still, as she fretted over the tiny newborns, I worried about her—my first baby—and I prayed every day that my intuition was not misguided. As it turned out, the resourcefulness gene (which has seen me and no doubt countless numbers of my ancestors through all manner of domestic crises) was tested soon after my sweet daughter and her husband left my house to spend their first night alone in the baby outback.

As I slept fitfully next to my phone and car keys in case I got a hysterical call from either my daughter or her husband during the night, the aforementioned parents were being pushed to their very limits. Their neighbor, it turned out, had skipped town or suffered some terrible physical trauma, leaving his dog barking non-stop in his back yard. The incessant baying eventually woke my sleep-deprived older granddaughters. And then the babies. The one- or two-hour reprieve between feedings and diaper changes (and, in some cases, crib sheet and pajama changes) evaporated into the night. As you know, so tired and brain-dead are new mothers, that a pack of howling hyenas cannot stir them once they actually close their eyes, but the first whimper of the newborn has them flying into action. So the poor, spent parents fed and changed and rocked and patted as the bark-a-thon next door thwarted their every effort.

By some miracle, the following morning found them all bleary-eyed and ill-humored, but alive. An all-but-comatose husband staggered to his car, the promise of the relative nirvana of delinquent deadlines and ringing phones in his baby-less office giving him the strength to get to work. Mom was spelled by family and managed a nap. Someone fed the family from the bounty of casserole charity in the freezer, and they all passed out.

And then it started. The horrible hound, madder than ever at being neglected, began to bark. The babies, thrown off their precious schedule, began to cry. The older girls woke up. Consciousness—much less a solution to the problem—was a cruel joke as far as my son-in-law was concerned. He was dead to the squalling world around him. The poor mother was on her own and at her wits' end.

Luckily, this is when the resourcefulness gene went into high gear. Remembering the lovely spiral-cut, honey-baked ham I had donated to her freezer, my darling daughter wrestled the fifteen-pound delicacy from the fridge, lugged it out into the night, pulled a lawn chair up to the fence and hurled it over. The barking stopped. And it never started again. By the time the hound had chewed through the wrapping, eaten the ham, slept off the unexpected feast, and started in on the bone, his master returned. Thanks to a heart-to-heart talk between my son-in-law and the negligent neighbor, the dog has never been left to bark away the night again.

You might be wondering if I questioned my daughter as to why she couldn't have thrown a pack of hot dogs or even a pound of bacon to the offending mutt instead of my lovingly chosen and very expensive ham. Tempting though it was, I thought better of it. She did what she had to do. The ham served its primary, though not original, purpose. It helped her get through a difficult time. Besides, I really didn't want to know whether she had thrown that frozen missile *to* the dog or *at* the dog.

~Margaret P. Cunningham

"The neighbor twins kept me up all night."

14

In the Middle of the Night

I often think that the night is more alive and more richly colored than the day.
~Vincent Van Gogh

Long before my husband Michael and I became parents, some of my favorite moments between us had been when we would both be wide awake in the middle of the night. It always felt to me like we were the only two people in the world.

To me, there was always something special about the middle of the night. We could share our greatest secrets, have our biggest laughs or our best talks. It always seemed as though anything was possible for our future in the middle of the quiet night. There was always a sense of joy, peace, and love.

We went through a long journey to conceive and carry to full term our fraternal twin boys, Dominic and Zachary. They were born one minute apart, and in perfect health.

After their birth, I can remember the early months when my husband and I were half-awake with our newborn sons in the middle of the night. The Noah's Ark-themed nursery decorated with animals in two-by-two formation across the green and cream painted walls was the perfect place to dream of a whole new world of possibilities.

Each night, after changing diapers and warming bottles, we would each nestle into a rocking chair with one of our sons and begin to quiet the noises of hungry newborns. Once settled, only the sounds of rocking chairs slowly moving back and forth and babies gently drinking their bottles could be heard. It felt like we were the only four people in the world.

With reluctance, after they were asleep, we would gently lay them in their bassinets and be off again to our own bed. But amidst my exhaustion, in the middle of the night, I felt happy and content.

Things are a little different now as my twins turn three this year. It feels as though chaos is a typical part of our everyday lives, in one form or another. Spoons have been flushed down the toilet, and batteries have been hurled with glee at my dining room chandelier. Even bath time has become an event unto itself.

But on certain nights, when the boys, who can now get in and out of their own cribs, climb into our bed around 2:00 A.M., that same special feeling reappears. And after a few minutes of chattering, and rearranging of pillows and legs, my husband and both my boys fall back asleep.

I, however, will usually remain awake for some time, even though I know that I will be exhausted the next morning. In the middle of the night, I want to absorb these special moments that I know are fleeting, passing too quickly, by day and by year.

As I watch them sleep and listen to the sounds that are only heard in the middle of the night—the steady breathing of my sleeping family and the stillness of the air—I am happy and content.

The possibilities of our sons' future gently float through my mind as I eventually drift back to sleep. And in my exhaustion, there is joy; there is love; there is peace.

~Laurie M. Ford

15

Seeing Is Believing

There was never a child so lovely but his mother was glad to get him to sleep.
~Ralph Waldo Emerson

A few days after I brought my surprise twins home from the hospital, I was exhausted. My husband and I already had two boys. Overnight, our family had doubled in size to six. The wise advice to "sleep when the babies sleep" proved elusive when I was also chasing after a first-grader and a preschooler. By the end of the new babies' second week, I'd put the milk jug in the oven, brushed my teeth with hand cream and left my purse at the grocery checkout.

Friends and relatives dropped by with casseroles, but everyone I knew seemed terrified to take two newborns for even an hour. Life became an endless parade of feeding and changing, with my oldest son Nathan's math homework thrown in for good measure. Had I ever known the answer to nine take away three? As Nathan reminded, "That's easy, Mom. Just count how many in our family." After that, he asked his dad for help with arithmetic. I was a mom in desperate need of sleep.

Every day I plotted what I'd do if I found time. If only I could get the twins comfortable and down for a nap, I kept thinking, I'd do something important, like get dressed or wash my hair. But the kids always found my time before I did.

I finally broke down. I told my husband he could either entertain our two older boys for a few hours or else watch his wife have a meltdown. He wisely said, "I'll take them fishing!" I waved to the three of them as they drove off.

That afternoon, I sat on my bed and reveled in the quiet. The babies, looking cherubic in their bassinettes, both napped longer than usual. They each had the sweetest little rosebud-shaped mouths, the same wispy brown hair. My head touched my pillow, and I fell asleep, too.

I awoke with a start. At 5:00 P.M., my three fishermen were still gone. The babies weren't crying. I checked the twins, thinking that I shouldn't have let them sleep so long. I woke them—something no mom should ever do—and fed them, but the rest of the family still wasn't home.

On a whim, I decided to give my bundles of joy their first tub bath. I brought out the cute hooded towels I'd received as gifts and the miniature bottles of baby shampoo, lotion and powder. I used my elbow to test the bath water. One at a time, I bathed my newborns, and then swaddled each in a towel.

I dressed them in fresh diapers and laid them side by side on my bed. They kicked and cooed, two perfect children waving their newborn arms. But their hospital ID bands, which read "Baby A" and "Baby B," caught my eye. Wasn't it about time to snip those bands off? I grabbed a pair of scissors and went to work, thinking about how I'd scrapbook the bracelets in their baby book.

Suddenly, terror gripped me. Which baby was which? I stared down at my two-week-old twins and tried to think. I began to sob.

Just then, Nathan and Chris burst into the bedroom. "We're home!" Chris shouted. I nodded, still crying. My husband rushed to my side. "What's wrong?" He anxiously eyed the babies, still on the bed.

I sputtered and blubbered, but managed to blurt out what I'd done. "Now I'll never be able to tell them apart," I wailed.

My husband looked stunned for a moment, and then put his arms around me. "Take off their diapers," he whispered, grinning. I was so tired I'd forgotten that boy/girl twins aren't exactly alike.

~Linda S. Clare

16

Something Else Along the Way

The guys who fear becoming fathers don't understand that fathering is not something perfect men do, but something that perfects the man. The end product of child-raising is not the child but the parent.
~*Frank Pittman,* Man Enough

I sat across from my wife Jennifer at a tiny Mexican restaurant on a Saturday night. I rubbed my eyes, pressed my forehead and sighed.

"I just don't know if I can do this," I said exhaustedly, surprised at my honesty. "It's... harder than I thought. I figured, just assumed, I would be better at this."

Her eyes welled up a little. She tried to speak, then thought the better of it, knowing she'd likely say something bitter or mean. Or worse.

So we just sat there in silence. Tense. Painful. Silence.

She looked at me with something I'd rarely seen in her eyes. It was disappointment, I think. One of our first nights out in months had devolved into an emotional emptiness as I sat there realizing my own failures and fearing my wife thought the same thing.

We were about four months into life as the parents of prematurely born boy/girl twins. Sleep was nonexistent. So was conversation, except for the biting remarks about who'd changed more diapers, gotten up during the night more frequently or made formula last. I won't even mention the other stuff that wasn't going on.

The twins had been home for just two months, after three weeks in the NICU. And... can I admit this? At some point after they came home, I thought it was better—definitely quieter—when they were still in the hospital. At least then nurses could help out. Plus, Jenn and I could sit down and occasionally have a nice dinner, without both of us thinking silently how tired we were.

This fatherhood thing wasn't what I thought. I didn't feel like Ward Cleaver or Bill Cosby or anyone else from TV who effortlessly glided through it. And, frustratingly to me, I'd put "being a good dad" first on my list of things I wanted to do with my life. (Yes, I made one of those lists. In my defense, my wife made me do it.)

I felt like maybe I'd made a really big mistake and was in the process of letting my wife down along with these two creatures who'd abruptly dropped into our lives. (Abrupt is the right word when it happens at 5:00 A.M. on a Friday two months before you were expecting it.)

I was ready to throw up my arms and declare defeat.

Let me interrupt this story to say that I don't like to admit weakness. It's not that I am good at all that much, but the word "stubborn" would understate my personality. I drive myself and others (like Jenn) crazy with my borderline obsessive-compulsive behavior about dieting, exercise, work, politics, sports or whatever else I've decided is the focus of the week.

But this was different. You couldn't explain to those twisty little bundles of energy that life would be so much easier for all involved if they screamed less, cried less and slept more.

I tried to convince them, but they didn't listen, even to my most logical, well-rehearsed pleas. And I was finding myself frustrated, even a little angry, at how drastically my life had changed. I didn't like it or all that I was being forced to give up. I didn't like how horribly I was failing at this.

And there was this sudden ball, a knot really, of anxiety inside me, a persistent nervousness or worry that wouldn't go away. Even when

I did find a rare hour of sleep, I had these horrible dreams—ones where I couldn't find my son, Dylan, or where my daughter, Maryn, crawled to the basement stairs and fell.

Stop. Stop. Stop. Did I really volunteer for this?

My relationship with Jenn was testy or worse. We hardly slept in the same bed. For reasons unclear to me now, we decided that she should go to bed around 9:00 P.M. and get up around 3:00 A.M., while I slept from then until 9:00 A.M. and then rushed into work. And she was so much more emotional than I remembered, so much more patient than I was with the kids, which only made me feel guilty.

I didn't have the same patience or even the same connection with them. I kept waiting for this connection to click in. I figured it would just happen the moment I saw them. But it didn't. I say now with great guilt, but complete honesty, that for several months all I saw was an enormous burden. Two of them. And because Jenn always sees right through me, I knew she saw it, too.

It wasn't a fun or enjoyable period of time. Even the passing of three years hasn't smoothed it out so that I look back now with some wistful sentimentality and say, "Geez, that wasn't so bad."

Nope. It was miserable. It was brutal.

And it was exactly what I needed.

I can't recall exactly when, but it started to dawn on me that the reason I felt so selfish during this period is because I was selfish. And the reason I worried I wasn't as patient as my wife is because I wasn't. Not even close.

The anxiety I felt was the discomforting feeling of being exposed, feeling raw. For the first time in my life, I was so much more worried about someone else, their happiness and their every waking moment than I was about mine. I never worried about Jenn like that. Except for her monumental blunder in choosing a marriage partner, she'd always been level-headed, pragmatic and quite able to take care of herself.

But Maryn and Dylan were like a mirror, one that forced me to look at myself and ask what kind of person I wanted to be when

I grew up. Did I want to continue to revel in my own arrogance and aloofness? Did I want to continue life as a person who assumed the worst of others and rarely gave anyone the benefit of the doubt? Didn't I aspire to more?

It's easy, of course, to say you want to be someone your kids would be proud of. But doing it is far harder than any test, job or exercise I'd ever attempted.

As the weeks passed that fall, and our twins began to sleep through the night, began to react when we walked into the room or smile when they heard our voices, it was like a darkness had passed. Not just the darkness that comes with sleep deprivation, but rather the darkness that comes with feelings of pettiness and selfishness. And, finally, candidly, admitting that those dark, ugly traits are there inside you.

As years pass and the twins have grown, learned to crawl, walk, talk, eat, drink, smile, laugh and tell knock-knock jokes that make them laugh so hard they can't finish the joke, one thought often comes back to me: In struggling through those bleary-eyed weeks and months, and endeavoring to learn how to be a good dad—even when I wasn't sure what that was or how to do it—I got something else along the way.

Quite simply, I got a lesson in becoming a better person.

And for that, I will always be grateful to Maryn and Dylan.

Always.

~Jeffrey McCracken

17

The All-Night Twin Merry-Go-Round

Anyone who thinks the art of conversation is dead ought to tell a child to go to bed.
~Robert Gallagher

The night started out ordinarily enough. Jake and Tara, our six-year-old twins, were in their respective beds surrounded by books and stuffed animals. My husband, Pat, and I went to sleep upstairs. Pat, having recently explained to Jake that he would need to stop coming into our bed in the middle of the night, was looking forward to a restful night's sleep. In an effort to provide Jake the security he needed and Pat the uninterrupted sleep he wanted, we made Jake a makeshift bed at the foot of ours in case he needed it.

Sometime after midnight, Jake quietly touched me. "Mommy, I want to snuggle in there with you." Remembering his father's words, Jake's whispering voice pleaded, "Mom, I promise I won't take much room." Although I knew Pat would be far from pleased, I just couldn't send Jake away. I shifted gently to make room. My son soon fell asleep, curled up comfortably next to me. As I kissed his freckled face, the moon cast its light over Jake's contented smile as he drifted off to sleep. My husband snored rhythmically on my other side.

Then Mr. Motion (aka Jake) began. An arm flopped over my shoulder. A few moments later, legs jutted onto mine. Poking. Tossing. Turning. Kicking. "I need to get some sleep," Pat said emphatically.

"Please put him on the floor bed." I obliged. The motionless calm of night returned.

An hour later, the monitor carried Tara's voice into our room. "Mommy, Mommy, I need you." I carefully stumbled my way downstairs. "Mommy, my nose is all stuffed up. I can't really breathe very good." After retrieving her medicine from the bathroom, I gave it to her, spilling only a few of the bright red, sticky, dye-filled drops onto her pink bedspread. In a sad, congested voice, she pleaded, "Mom, will you please stay with me a little while?" Tara doesn't often get up at night, and I wanted to be there for her.

"Okay, Tara, Mommy's right here..."

She wanted me to climb over her and sleep on the side by the wall. That was the side on which all twenty or so of her stuffed animals slept. I quickly tossed them into a pile. A sudden "Ruff! Ruff! Ruff!" startled me. The battery-operated puppies barked as I lay on them. I smiled to myself as I thought of Pat's grumbling upstairs if the barking over the monitor woke him. I added the puppies to the pile of topsy-turvy animals and dolls. I then stroked Tara's hair and rubbed her back as I made a mental note to avoid the puppies when I crawled back over the pile on my return upstairs.

Ah, back to my own bed. I was determined to sleep. But to my surprise, I found Jake sleeping on my side of the bed. He looked so content that I couldn't remove him. Quietly and carefully, I squeezed back into bed between Pat and Jake. Shortly after I nodded off, it started. Poking. Tossing. Turning. Kicking. Pat begged impatiently, "Marian, please put him on the floor."

"Okay, okay." Jake returned to his bed on the floor.

I did manage to get some sleep before I heard Tara's voice again, "Mommy. Mommy." Maybe it was a dream. I fluffed up my pillow and closed my eyes. "Mommy, I had a bad dream. Mommy!" In a zombie state, I returned to tend to Tara. "Mom, please lay down with me a little bit. I had a bad dream, and I'm sooo scared."

"Of course, honey. It was only a dream, Tara. Mommy's here and everything's okay." We fell asleep in each other's arms. Later, I returned to my own bed only to find Jake once again occupying my space. I put him on the floor and climbed into bed.

"Mom, I just want to come in for one minute for a snuggle because I miss you so much," Jake pleaded. I was too tired to think. We were a trio again.

I turned over a short while later and noticed that Pat was gone. When he didn't return in a few minutes, I wondered if he was all right. Our bathroom was empty. No one was in the kids' bathroom. The kitchen was as we'd left it hours before. Tara slept peacefully alone. The house was quiet and night-filled.

I eventually found Pat. He was snoring in Jake's bed, tucked in amidst the *101 Dalmatians* sheets. His head was on Patch's face, and a myriad of stuffed animals surrounded him. I studied him with affection, surprised again by how much Jake resembled him.

Even in my sleepy state, I thought of how soon these nights of merry-go-round beds will soon be over. In their place, my twins will be grown. Jake will be a young man, looking even more like his father. Instead of nightmares, Tara will be dreaming of leaving for college. No doubt before I'm ready, our twins' rooms will be much too quiet and empty, with perhaps a sole stuffed animal and a few childhood mementos on dusty shelves. So it is especially on days when I'm exhausted after a night on this mom's merry-go-round that I remind myself that these very days—and nights—are, in fact, "the good old days," ever so precious and fleeting.

~Marian Gormley

18

Very Loved

There are two things in life for which we are never truly prepared: twins.
~Josh Billings

Have you ever had one of those days when you wish you could climb back into bed and pull the covers over your head? Hit rewind and start all over? (If only life had a remote control.) Recently, I did. Before I could open one eye, I felt a strange tug on my arm.

"Mommy," whispered my two-year old, "wake up!"

On the other arm, I felt a similar tug—a bit more energetic—but a tug for sure.

"Mooooommmy!" shouted my other two-year old. "Wake up!"

I must be dreaming, I thought.

"We want you to wake up! We are hungry!" the ranting continued.

Slowly, I awakened and realized I wasn't dreaming. There were actually two tenacious toddlers tugging on my pajamas. Twins. A boy and a girl.

Two years earlier, I begged the hospital staff to let me stay at the hospital, but insurance forced them to release me. A bit panicked, I minced, "What am I going to do with two babies? Look—two. I'm not ready for this. Twins and a four-year old? I have a four-year old waiting at home, remember?"

"Honey, you are going to be just fine. Women have been raising twins for centuries," they comforted me. "You are not the first woman to have twins."

After a huge pep rally and a bucket full of tears, I took a deep breath, gathered my two babies—one in each arm—loaded the minivan and prayed for courage.

"God," I prayed, "I'm a strong woman. I've handled a lot in my life, but this time, I think I'm in over my head. If you don't help me with these three children, I'm not going to make it. I remember hearing someone say that life doesn't give you more than you can handle. Okay, I guess I'm about to find out if that is true or not. Help me, God."

While driving home, I glanced at my husband. He glanced at me. Somehow, the silence spoke volumes. He placed his strong hand on my forearm and reassured me that everything was going to be okay.

"Easy for you to say," I mumbled. "You get to go off to work every day."

"Take life one day at a time," he half-smiled. "We can do this."

His words became my new reality. Living life one day at a time—one diaper at a time—seemed my only hope of survival. Days turned into months, and months turned into years, which resulted in hundreds of sleepless nights, mounds of dirty diapers, countless adventures and one exhausted mommy.

"Rob, I'm at the end of my rope. I can't take any more. Brooke and Grant have been running in different directions all day, and Candace won't quit asking me questions. If she asks me one more question...." I cried. "Is there any way you can come home early today? I need a break. A few minutes alone in the grocery store."

The minute he walked in the door, I walked out. Laden with guilt for shrinking under the pressures of motherhood, I drove away from our little home. Unable to cope, I began to cry. Weep, actually. Feelings of inadequacy, worthlessness and defeat overwhelmed me.

Suddenly, a car pulled out in front of me. Before I could honk my horn, my eyes zoomed in on the license plate. It seemed to glow.

"VRY LVED."

"Very loved," I whispered. "Isn't that interesting?"

As I said those two little words, "very loved," a hush came over my heart.

It was as if I heard a still, small voice say, "Yes, you are very loved. I am with you. You are not in this alone."

I drove on in silence.

A few minutes later, I noticed another license plate bearing the inscription "1 Petr 4 8" referring to the Bible passage in 1 Peter 4:8 (MSG).

Interesting. Could this be another message?

As I walked down the aisles of the grocery store, I calmed myself. There, amid boxes of cereal and bottles of juice, I remembered my prayer at the hospital, when I had asked God to help me.

Hurrying home, I unloaded the groceries, made dinner, tucked each child into bed with an extra-special dose of hugs and kisses, and went searching for my Bible—which was hiding beneath a mound of mail. Sinking into the couch, I took a very deep breath and began reading.

"Most of all, love each other as if your life depended on it. Love makes up for practically anything. Be quick to give a meal to the hungry, a bed to the homeless—cheerfully. Be generous with the different things God gave you, passing them around so all get in on it: if words, let it be God's words; if help, let it be God's hearty help. That way, God's bright presence will be evident in everything through Jesus, and he'll get all the credit as the One mighty in everything—encores to the end of time. Oh, yes!" (1 Peter 4:7-11, MSG).

The guilt and anxiety resting on my shoulders vanished. I felt ten pounds lighter. There, on two ordinary license plates and an ordinary street, God reminded me of his unconditional love. He reminded that I didn't have to do it all by myself. He would always be there to help me. For the first time in my life, although I felt completely out of control, I felt strangely at peace. I realized I didn't have to be perfect. I didn't have to do everything right. The only thing I had to do was love my husband and children like God loved me. Simple as that.

When I finally tucked myself into bed, I nestled close to my husband, and for the first time in a long time, I slept like a baby.

~Janell M. Rardon

"We really should ask the driver of that car for tips on coping with twins."

19

It's Not as Bad as You Think

Worry often gives a small thing a big shadow.
~Swedish Proverb

"Why do you always have to turn a good thing into a bad thing?" my husband asked in exasperation.

Danny and I had just crawled into our bed for the night after an emotionally charged day when I began to weep. Of course, he was elated by the news that we were expecting twin sons, but my joy was eclipsed by sheer terror. Why would God give me twins? Didn't I endure enough the first time around? Doesn't he know me well enough to know that I'm not able to do this? What little confidence I had built up during this second pregnancy was now washed away in the flood of memories from two years earlier.

If someone had asked me during the first year of my daughter's life whether or not I was depressed, I would have said, "No, I'm just tired." And it was true. I was tired, more tired than I'd ever been in my entire life. Danny was in chiropractic school at the time and working a part-time job to support us, so I shouldered all of the responsibility of the new baby. Addison was an extremely fussy baby who shared with us the one bedroom in our 850-square-foot condo.

We had no maternity insurance, no full income, and only a handful of new friends from our church as our support system.

Despite my severe exhaustion, I found myself unable to sleep more than three or four hours a night. And though I couldn't have articulated it then, being unable to console my baby not only frustrated me, but it made me feel like a failure as a mother. Under the strain of sleeplessness and constant stress, I become edgy and easily irritated, and I was quickly losing patience with my screaming child. My feelings of guilt progressed to feelings of shame. In my mind, I was no longer simply doing a bad job; I was a bad person.

Somehow, I survived that grueling year until Danny graduated school and we were able to move back to our hometown. I now had his help as well as the help of our extended family. My inconsolable infant slowly blossomed into a happy and affectionate toddler. Surrounded by support and a newfound joy in motherhood, my confidence began to increase, and I thought maybe I could do this again.

Shortly after our daughter's second birthday, we happily discovered that I was pregnant again. Then, at our five-month ultrasound, the technician pointed to a tiny pulsing image on the screen and said, "See? There's the heartbeat." Then he rolled the machine head four inches to the left and pointed to the screen again. "And there's another heartbeat." My initial joy quickly dissipated as fear whispered that I was unable to handle this parenting task. If you can't manage one baby, how on earth will you ever care for two? Guilt chided me for being ungrateful, and anger raged that I should hunt down and maim everyone who had promised me that the second time would be easier.

I spent the remainder of my pregnancy worrying, crying, and losing sleep over my impending doom. While I put on a brave face in public, tears would spring to my eyes if the subject came up at home. In addition to my fear of another bout of depression, I had more practical concerns. How would we pay for all the extra medical bills, not to mention the household expenses? What would this do to my health and my figure? What little, if any, time would be left for my daughter, my husband, or even me?

All too soon (and not soon enough), the boys arrived, and we were all home from the hospital. I waited for the nightmare to begin. Strangely enough, it never did. In many ways, the second time did turn out to be easier. I discovered that though multiples always bring their unique challenges, they also attract many helping hands. Family and friends rallied round in a way that I never would have imagined, bringing meals, cleaning my house, even staying overnight several nights a week so that I could get some sleep. Unlike my first experience, I was able to sleep when the opportunity arose, and the depression I'd been dreading never materialized. Somehow, we paid all of our medical bills, and we were given boxes upon boxes of hand-me-down clothes from a college acquaintance. I even reclaimed my figure (or most of it).

As much as I may hate to admit it, my husband was right—it wasn't as bad as I thought it would be. Our boys have been good babies, and Danny and I now joke that our daughter prepared us for having twins. All of our children make us laugh every day, sometimes so hard that we can't breathe and tears roll down our faces. The interaction between twins is amazing, and I hope and pray that their special bond is a lifelong one. Of course, there are those moments when I feel like I don't have enough arms, eyes, or even time; when I don't know where to start cleaning up a mess or which baby to chase down first. But this precious time flies by doubly fast with twins, and I am determined to absorb it all. Then, I can look around at my family amidst the chaos and think, not only is this not so bad, but it is really, really good.

~Stacie Roth Miller

20

InSeparable

Love is missing someone whenever you're apart,
but somehow feeling warm inside because you're close in heart.
~Kay Knudsen

In the middle of the night, I woke from a dead sleep. Had I dreamed someone was calling my name? On the other side of the bed, my husband snored softly. I felt another tap on my shoulder and heard a whispered, "Mom?" I rolled over. Timothy, my youngest son, stood next to the bed. "Mom, wake up." His voice wavered.

Eight-year-old twins, Tim and Alyssa, often came into our room at night, looking for reassurance. Most of the time, either my husband or I could offer a drink of water or a hug and a kiss before leading one or both of them back to the room they shared. I struggled to sit up in bed. What could be wrong?

I said, "Do you need a drink of water?"

Tim shook his head.

"Need the bathroom?"

Nope.

I pulled on my bathrobe and slippers and put my arm around my son. "What's the matter, honey?" I walked him out into the hall and to his bedroom door. Tim, wearing his favorite Superman jammies and clutching Sharky, his favorite stuffed animal, balked.

Suddenly, it hit me. This was the first night Tim and his twin sister slept in separate rooms. I held him close.

For weeks, my husband and I had prepared the twins for this night. Up to now, they'd slept in separate beds but shared a room. But people began to raise eyebrows. As my neighbor remarked, "Aren't they getting too old to room together?"

By modern standards, I guessed they were. We made plans for each to have a bedroom.

I remembered how shocked we'd all been when the twins were born. Even the doctor had been surprised. For a time, we'd bundled our two preemies sideways in a regular-sized crib because they slept better. They'd always had a close relationship. They hated being separated. And now they were sleeping apart for the first time.

At eight years old, you'd think they'd have been eager for their own space. No more bickering over whose turn it was to invite a friend to play. Alyssa wouldn't step on Tim's Legos strewn on the floor. Tim wouldn't be embarrassed by his sister's baby dolls propped in the corner. Best of all, they could each practice their violins in their own rooms at the same time—without making the cat howl in pain.

We'd sat them down and explained. "You can pick out paint for your walls," I said, "and decorate your own room. The rule is you ask permission to go into the other's room."

Alyssa had jumped up and down, her ash-blond ponytails bobbing. "Pink! I want pink!"

Tim, dark-haired and always serious, turned to his father. "Make mine camouflage."

They told everyone they saw about their new rooms. Over the next two weeks, each helped paint. My husband made name signs for each twin's door.

Finally, the day arrived. We dismantled the bunks into single beds and hauled one into the room next door. We were extra careful to make sure each room had exactly the same amount of existing and new furnishings. Alyssa carried a violin case and music stand into her bedroom, now painted Pepto-Bismol Pink. Tim settled for green walls and hung posters of fighter jets. Each agreed to the rule: Ask permission before you go into the other's room.

All evening, the twins arranged and rearranged their belongings.

They gave tours, leading me by the hand. "See? Sharky has his own spot," Tim declared, patting his pillow.

Next, Alyssa dragged me to her room, where baby dolls sat in a semicircle facing the music stand. "They're going to listen to my violin concert," she announced. The cat stayed out of sight.

"All right, you two," I said, tired from so much heavy lifting. "Jammie time."

By the time I tucked each into bed, heard prayers and last-minute requests for water, it was almost an hour past their usual bedtime. Not long after, I'd fallen into bed myself and slept deeply.

And now Tim was awake in the middle of the night.

In his new green room, I sat on the edge of Tim's bed and beckoned him to sit next to me. "Do you miss your sister?" I asked. He nodded, hugging Sharky. "I know it's tough," I said, "but you'll get used to it. We can leave the hall light on if you want."

Tim nodded again, but still hung his head.

Something else was wrong. I could feel it. I lifted his chin up and looked into his dark blue eyes. "What is it? You can tell me."

Tim took a deep breath. "I know we're supposed to ask to go in the other one's room," he said, "but Alyssa's got my violin, and I've got hers." He pointed to the violin case on the floor. "And I can't ask to go in her room cuz she's asleep."

I relaxed my shoulders and laughed. "It's all right, Tim," I said. "We'll straighten things out in the morning, okay?"

He looked up at me and, for the first time, smiled. I tucked him in and went back to bed.

The next morning, our fraternal but inseparable twins lay sleeping side-by-side on the carpet next to our bed, each hugging a violin case.

~Linda S. Clare

Chapter 3

Twins and More

Seeing Double

The frost never paints my windows twice alike.

~Lydia Maria Child

21

Mirror, Mirror

You can fool all the people some of the time,
and some of the people all the time,
but you cannot fool all the people all the time.
~Abraham Lincoln

It's indisputable: For twins, life really does imitate art—and vice versa. All I have to do is revisit my earliest memories for proof.

My identical brother, Kirk, and I grew up being constantly mistaken for each other. Classmates, friends, teachers, even relatives couldn't tell us apart. As a result, we were often unfairly punished ("Kirk, you're grounded for not mowing the yard!") or rewarded (i.e., an increase in my monthly allowance "for being such a good son... Kirk").

Talk about being blindsided! Imagine the uncertainty we faced 24/7, never sure what the day would bring... or what the other twin had done.

Eventually, we learned how to use the Mistaken Identity Syndrome (MIS) to our advantage. For example, we would play tricks on our friends and classmates, pretending to be the other twin—you know, just to play with their heads.

Why not? All the identical twins and/or cousins on TV were doing it. (I reference the double trouble plots of *Bewitched, Family Matters, I Dream of Jeannie, Saved by the Bell*, and *The Patty Duke Show*.) We simply enjoyed pulling off these innocent pranks as did our TV counterparts.

Nor were teachers immune to our impersonation shtick. On at least one occasion, when Kirk was sick, I covered for him by taking his tests. I ask you, who wouldn't help out his ailing brother by seeing to it that he passed his English exam?

Just for the record, we tried our little game out on Mom, but she always knew who was who. Guess the old axiom is true: Mother knows best.

Once we grew up, we even "covered" for each other at work. We didn't mean any harm; we simply started this as an experiment to see whether our bosses and co-workers could tell the difference.

They couldn't.

Again, this was a prime example of life imitating art, albeit TV sitcom plot points.

As we grew older, the MIS continued. I once had someone purposefully ram her grocery cart into mine thinking I was my brother. How embarrassing it was for her when she discovered the truth! Sure, I could've played to her innocent blunder, but that would've been cruel. After all, she seemed like such a nice person.

The MIS followed us throughout our professional careers, as well. As a bank manager, I meet with dozens of clients on a daily basis, while my brother supervises a staffing service for local employers. As a result, Kirk is constantly approached by people who want to discuss their various money accounts, while I am frequently thanked on the street for placing so-and-so with the area hospital administrative staff or as a department store customer service representative. As in the grocery store incident, we never allow these awkward moments to fester into bigger awkward moments... that just wouldn't seem professional.

We have our own identical twin code of ethics, after all.

However, the MIS took a truly ironic—and outright weirder—turn when Kirk and I found ourselves unable to tell each other apart.

Years ago, before we started our professional careers, my brother worked the graveyard shift at a box-making company while I slaved away as the grill cook in a nearby fast food restaurant. It was customary for my brother to come in to the restaurant after he finished his shift to order breakfast. One early morning, I was completing an order for a patron in the dining room while casually speaking to my manager. I looked across the grill and realized my brother was standing at the front counter. I waved to him, saying, "Good morning, Kirk!" My boss looked strangely at me and said, "What are you doing?" Not really thinking, I replied, "I'm just saying hi to my brother." I looked across the grill once more and gave another wave to my brother, hoping my boss would notice that my identical twin was standing there. At that moment, my manager and I broke into hysterics. I must have been half-asleep because I soon realized the person I was waving to was not my brother at all; it was me! I was waving to my reflection in a mirror.

Not long after this humorous event, my brother and I were traveling across country in a minivan with several friends. My brother is a lot vainer than I am; his hair must always be in place. Kirk was driving when he noticed in the rearview mirror that his hair was a bit messy. He lifted his right hand to brush his hair back into place and was disturbed when his hand did not appear in the mirror. Several times he repeated this action. Finally, he started laughing when he realized he was looking at me in the seat behind him.

Apparently, it is possible for twins to mix themselves up, too, falling victim to their own Mistaken Identity Syndrome. This isn't a plot point yet explored on TV situation comedies, but who knows, there may be a new bestselling Stephen King novel there!

Like I said, for this set of twins, life definitely continues to imitate art—in more than one medium.

~Kent W. Tarver

22

Cross-Country Race

A runner runs against himself, against the best that's in him.
~Bill Persons

"Hey, Brothers Tsvoya, wait up!" The twins heard a familiar voice call them in the hallway of Belgrade University one day in September 1950. This combined name for the twins was used because many could not tell them apart. Tsveya and Voya stopped and turned. "Hi, guys, what's going on?" Voya asked.

Three officers of the Student Association for the Architectural College of the School of Technology approached. "We need to talk to you," Boza, the president, said. "Let's go to the Student Association Offices."

Voya and Tsveya exchanged questioning glances as they followed Boza up the stairs to the third floor. These three men, older than the twins and former Partisan fighters, were Yugoslav communist party members. The twins were not.

The door to the sparsely furnished room was unlocked. A large picture of Tito hung on the wall. "Here, take a seat." Boza pulled a couple of wooden chairs around so the five men could face each other. Then he sat forward, hands on his knees, and began. Marko, who had lost a leg fighting the Nazis, sat on one side, and Milos, tallest of the three, on the other. Boza, a pilot during the war and still in the Reserves, wore his major uniform.

"Well, Tsvoya, you no doubt know about the school's annual intramural races next month."

"Yes. We saw the notice," Tsveya replied.

"Now this is our problem," Boza said. "The other colleges in the School of Technology—like mechanical, structural design, geology—they have a large male enrollment from which to select runners. Architecture, unfortunately, attracts many females. Now I have nothing against the fair sex, of course," he grinned. "But they're not usually athletes. So... we want you to represent our college."

"Us?" Voya said, looking startled. "Why us? We're not runners."

"No... but you're identical twins—the only twins in our entire school," Boza replied.

"Did you know the Architectural College never won one of these races?" Marko asked.

"Then you sure don't want either of us," Tsveya said.

"On the contrary," Boza replied. "You two are our secret weapon. We've figured it all out. One of you will start, and the other will finish."

"We can't do that," Tsveya and Voya countered in unison.

Boza raised a hand. "Hear our plan before you say no." He gestured as he spoke. "About halfway around the track, there's a four-foot-wide concrete pipe from an abandoned storm sewer. It's located behind a slope around a curve. The trick is for you, whoever starts first, to get far enough ahead of the other runners at the very start so you can slip into the pipe unseen. The other one will be hiding there, and he needs to slip out before the rest catch up. We'll put a plywood board over the end of the pipe so you're not visible."

"Sounds devious to me," Tsveya said. Voya nodded his head in agreement.

"Now, Tsvoya, this isn't the World Soccer Cup," Milos interrupted. "It's a friendly internal competition in a university. We just want to save face for our college this year."

"You can't say no, Brothers Tsvoya. We've already changed the date so it doesn't fall on your Sabbath," Marko added.

The twins sank back in their seats. Their fellow students knew of their strict observance of the Sabbath, and now these communist leaders had taken that into account.

"One tip. Watch out for the giraffe," Milos said. "That's Bogoljub in Mechanical Engineering. He's tall and has the longest legs and runs like the dickens."

"But what if we get caught?" Tsveya looked worried.

"No problem. We'll take full responsibility," Boza replied. "We'll tell them it was a joke. You guys are well-liked and popular. Nobody will take it seriously." He paused. "By the way, the two other runners from Architecture will be in on the plan."

"Well... I don't know." Voya looked at his brother.

"Good. Then it's a deal." Boza jumped up and shook their hands before the twins could respond.

The next day, Voya and Tsveya went to see the three-mile track. It was in a field of rolling grasslands below Kalemegdan Park. The event organizers had mowed a wide path all the way around to the finish line. It curved into a loop, with many other curves, and then returned to a place near the starting line. When the twins came to the concrete pipe, they found weeds grown up around it. As promised, a plywood board covered its opening.

"Why don't you start?" Voya suggested. "The runners won't go full throttle to begin. Everything depends on your getting a good enough lead."

The morning of the race arrived too soon. Every day of the preceding weeks, the twins had run the track and practiced sliding into and out of the pipe. Half an hour before the runners and spectators arrived, Voya took his place inside the pipe, pulled the board to him, waiting tensely in the damp, dank darkness.

Meanwhile at the start line, twenty-one runners, three from each of the colleges in the school, lined up. Tsveya, dressed in jersey number three like Voya, looked fidgety.

"Ready... set... go!" the referee shouted. Tsveya shot out like a lightning bolt.

"Look at Tsvoya. He'll never make it!" a bystander remarked from the sidelines.

"He'll lose steam before he's halfway," another observed.

Meanwhile, inside the pipe, Voya strained to listen. All at once, footsteps pounded on the grass, and Tsveya appeared at the opening. Voya jumped out and began to run. Tsveya had given him a lead of about fifty yards.

After covering about a mile, Voya suddenly heard heavy breathing, like a locomotive, behind him. Someone was running fast and threatening to overtake him. A quick glance over his shoulder told him it was the giraffe.

Voya picked up speed, pushing, straining. Footfalls pounded behind him, getting closer. Up ahead, Voya spied the finish line and heard the cheering crowd.

"The winner!" the referee shouted as Voya crossed the white line and nearly collapsed. Bravos echoed in his ears. Seconds later, the runner behind him came in.

"Congratulations!" Bogoljub gasped, extending his hand. "When you shot out at the start, I didn't think you'd make it." His tall, wiry form towered over Voya's five feet, nine inches, and his legs seemed twice as long.

"Thank you." Voya cringed. "Congratulations to you, too."

"You did it!" Boza and the others surrounded him, swallowing him up in bear hugs.

"Where's the other Tsvoya?" someone asked.

"Oh, somewhere around," Sava, the twins' friend, said, looking about.

As well-wishers gathered, Sava slipped away, carrying a change of clothing for Tsveya, who still waited in the drain pipe.

Flushed by the success of their plan, the student leaders caught the twins two days later. "We need to talk about the follow-up race, the race for the university championship," Boza said. "The track will be different, so we need to make plans."

"Oh, no," the twins replied.

"You wanted this once to save face for the college," Tsveya said.

"We did that, and we're done!" Voya added, and they walked away. "I don't ever want to run another race," he said to his brother.

Race or no race, the Brothers Tsvoya were already winners.

~Ann Vitorovich

23

Peek-a-Boo

The most wasted of all days is one without laughter.
~e.e. cummings

I was excited to travel for one week during my college break with my identical twin, Donna, and her husband. They traveled throughout the United States in the 1970s, evangelizing and holding special services. I had no idea what was in store for me.

We arrived early at a church in a small Indiana town for their next service. Everyone crowded around to meet the new evangelist and his wife. I was introduced as Donna's twin.

The novelty of seeing identical twins was evident. People were joking, laughing, and pointing at us. I was shy around new people, and this did not help ease my nervousness.

The evening service began, and everything progressed normally until the delivery of the sermon. My brother-in-law approached the pulpit to preach, and once again he introduced his wife and me. People were chuckling again about the twins. He said, "Yes, they are true identical twins. You can't even tell them apart in bed." Gasps and exclamations resounded from the mouths of the congregation, including mine! Dying of embarrassment, I wanted to slip out the door.

He quickly tried to explain his comment and proceeded to tell them about the last trip home at Christmas. Whenever Donna and I got back together, we always talked until the wee hours of the morning, catching up on everything.

On that particular night, I got sleepy first, and we continued our discussions in my bed. Well after midnight, Donna's husband came to the bedroom door and peeked in. Both of us were asleep with the blanket covering all but our noses, an old habit. He could not tell which one of us was his wife, so he let us sleep until morning.

By now, the congregation was howling with laughter. He had difficulty preaching that evening while the snickering and chuckling continued throughout his sermon.

Years later, Donna and I still enjoy a good laugh at this story.

~Dot Beams

24

DeTwinning the Twins

Nature made us individuals, as she did the flowers and the pebbles.
~Lydia Maria Child

When I was in my late fifties, I started dating Jack, a twin. In 2004, when I moved to Florida where Jack lived, I was anxious to meet his twin brother, Bud. The day arrived, and we drove to Bud's beautiful home on the Intracoastal Waterway across from the Gulf of Mexico, a few miles from the condos where Jack and I live.

Nervously, I got out of the car and walked up to the front door just as Bud opened it in greeting. I looked up and nearly had to jumpstart my heart. There before me was an identical replica of Jack. And, wouldn't you know it, that night, unbeknownst to either of them, they were dressed nearly alike in khaki shorts and a flowered print shirt, common attire in Florida. Even the colors were similar.

Bud's hair was the same as Jack's—thinning on top, an old-fashioned comb-over, and both dyed a sort of butterscotch color. Both men wore oversized, gold-rimmed glasses. Both had a big smile, were the same height, around 6'1", and both had a protruding belly—although Bud would argue that his was not as large as Jack's.

The twins introduced me to Kathy, Bud's wife, who was smiling at my confusion over how to tell the men apart. The four of us walked outside to their back patio where I plopped myself midway between Bud and Jack, who took seats at opposite ends of the oval patio table.

I felt like I was at a tennis match. My head bounced back and forth, back and forth, looking first at Jack, and then at Bud. I was determined to find a way to recognize the uniqueness of each of them for fear they would try to confuse me one day. I wondered what would happen if they made a devious plan to torment me by switching places to convince me that Bud was really Jack and vice versa.

As the two brothers sat there telling stories of their youth and how they'd even fooled a couple of their dates once in a while by switching partners without the girls knowing it, I became more and more determined to learn how to tell them apart.

Finally, after an hour of my head bouncing from one side to the other, desperately trying to find some detail that would tell them apart, I noticed a small, light brown mole, smaller than the size of a pencil eraser, on the right side of Jack's cheek just below his eye.

That's it! I thought excitedly. I kept the information to myself for fear that Bud would try to duplicate Jack's mole someday if the two pranksters tried to pull a fast one on me. But later, before we left, when they moved around the room and tried to confuse me, I laughed and spilled the beans.

But even that mole didn't always help, especially if we were in a dark restaurant or if the two men were walking toward me in a crowd.

In the months and years that followed, I encouraged Jack to make a few changes to his appearance—not because I didn't want him to look like his twin, but so he could look younger, especially since he's nine years older than I am. He got rid of the comb-over, starting getting his hair cut very short—almost a quarter-inch buzz in the summertime—and he stopped coloring it. When he got new prescription glasses, he bought more stylish, much smaller ones that didn't cover up half his cheeks.

These days, the twins, now in their seventies, don't look a thing alike. They still look very much like brothers, but not identical twins. And for awhile I didn't have any fears of being fooled by a couple of prankster twins who would think nothing of passing themselves off as the other brother to get a few laughs.

Then, one day, when my fifteen-year-old granddaughter, Hailey, was visiting me, she was sitting at Jack's computer when Bud stopped over for a visit. She could see Jack sitting at the dining room table facing her from the computer room. Bud's back was to her. She looked up at Jack when Jack said something of interest to her, but she was shocked to see that his lips were not moving even though he was talking.

She jumped out of her chair and walked to the dining room. "What's going on, Pappa Jack? Are you a ventriloquist? I know you were talking, but your lips weren't moving!"

The twin brothers started laughing. I moaned. At that moment I realized that although my man didn't look much like his twin anymore, they still sounded identical.

Now I'm just waiting for the day when the phone rings and the joke is really on me. I'll be spilling my heart out to Jack, but the words will be hitting Bud's ears.

Isn't there any way to do a voice makeover?

~Patricia Lorenz

25

Chicken Soup for the Soul

Mistaken Identity

She glances at the photo, and the pilot light of memory flickers in her eyes.
~Frank Deford

As a mom of identical twin girls, I am always on the lookout for those amazing twin moments—times when the special connection between the girls becomes apparent to the outside world.

I was sorting through a box of photos recently when four-year-old Naomi joined me. We enjoyed looking at the numerous baby photos of my oldest daughter, Sophia, and the twins. However, in many of the photos of the twins, I was unable to tell who was who, as I had not labeled them. But, much to my surprise, Naomi was able to point things out to me.

"That's Naomi, and that's Jillian," she said confidently as we looked at one that had me stumped. So I picked out another one in which the girls looked (to me) exactly the same. Again, Naomi pointed out herself and her sister without any hesitation.

We then sorted through the whole box this way, as I quickly scribbled an "N" or a "J" on each photo. "Wow!" I thought to myself. "She really knows the difference between herself and her sister. That must be part of the twin connection." Not only was I thrilled to witness this display of "twinness," but I was excited that I was able to finally label the photos. (Clearly, I was delirious in thinking I would ever get around to putting them into albums.) And Naomi seemed very proud of herself for being such a smart girl and helping Mommy.

As we continued to dig through the pile, we came upon a photo of a friend with her two dogs. Without missing a beat, Naomi pointed at the dogs and announced with great authority, "That's Naomi, and that's Jillian." She then methodically went through every other photo in the box, naming anyone and everyone Naomi and Jillian. Oh, well....

~Elaine A. Lederman

26

I Wish We Could Do It Again

Everyone is the age of their heart.
~Guatemalan Proverb

It all started when my father and I stumbled upon a television documentary. As we watched coverage of the twins' convention held annually in Twinsburg, Ohio, we arrived at the same conclusion: Somehow, some way, we had to get my grandmother and her twin to this event.

But thinking about something isn't quite the same as doing it. Gram and Bess were already in their late eighties, so traveling from Tennessee to Ohio wouldn't be easy or comfortable, even if we flew. Time passed. Gram and Bess continued to grow older. Oddly, Dad and I each held on to our dream. We rarely talked about it, but we both trusted we would someday get the twins to Twinsburg.

And then, by some strange twist of fate, it seemed to come to us. In the years since Dad and I had seen the documentary, I had graduated from college and relocated to Washington, D.C. I happened to be back in Memphis one August weekend for a friend's wedding. That Sunday morning, as my father and I sat in the kitchen reading the newspaper, he chuckled. "You're never going to believe this," he said. "There's a multiples convention at the Marriott today."

"Dad!" I shrieked. "We have to take them!"

He picked up the phone and called his mom. As expected,

Gram and Bess were sitting together watching television. My father explained the convention and told my grandmother that he and I wanted to take them to the event. Gram was resolute: she wasn't interested. I'm not even sure that she asked Bess for her opinion. My dad pressed for a minute, but couldn't persuade her.

After he hung up the phone, he looked at me. "Maybe you should call her. I bet you could talk her into it."

There was no way I was missing that convention, and there was no way I was going without Gram and Bess.

I dialed. She picked up.

"Gram, it will be so much fun," I pleaded. "We just have to go. You've never been to one of these. Please go. Please!!????"

Gram laughed. She sometimes did that when she was nervous. She paused, and then she explained to Bess that I really wanted them to go. I could hear Bess capitulate in the background. And then Gram said into the receiver, "Well, it's hard to tell someone as sweet as you no. We'll go."

"Great! We'll pick you up at 1:15."

When we arrived at the hotel, Dad and I parked Gram and Bess in some comfortable chairs while we registered them. As I looked around the lobby, I could easily identify the other attendees, primarily because they milled in pairs and were sporting matching outfits. Gram probably had no patience for the matching clothes. I'm guessing that she and Bess hadn't worn identical dresses for a good eighty-five years.

When we returned for "the girls" (as my father liked to call them), I could tell that Gram was increasingly ambivalent about everything. With every comment, she was uncharacteristically testy. My father just laughed her off as we headed into the ballroom, where we found at least thirty rows of chairs. Because twins and multiples were expected to sit in a reserved section up front, Dad and I helped Gram and Bess locate seats. After situating them in the first row, we claimed spots for ourselves at the rear of the room.

As I scanned the growing crowd, I realized what outsiders Dad and I were. It seemed that, everywhere we looked, we were seeing two, sometimes three, of each person. I felt like I had forgotten something, namely the twin that I didn't have! Gradually, though, we were joined by others in our same situation. In most cases, they were parents of twin children in attendance.

Shortly after two o'clock, the formal program began. It was really just an awards ceremony. There were awards for twins who had traveled farthest, the most multiples in one family, and the twins who were the cutest. The award that fascinated me most was for the twins who had aged most similarly. The competition was stiff: several middle-aged twins had maintained the same weights, hairstyles, and even facial structures.

Then came an announcement that had Dad and me on the edge of our seats.

"And now," the emcee announced, "we'd like to recognize the oldest female twins in attendance today." The ensuing pause seemed to last forever. "Please join me in congratulating identical ninety-three-year-olds Ann Cunningham Whitman and Bess Cunningham Lawing!" The crowd went wild.

Even though the other winners had gone onstage to accept their awards, Gram and Bess remained seated. I think this choice had more to do with Gram's slight embarrassment over the unexpected attention, and less to do with their inability to climb the stage stairs. Gram was using her first-row seat to her advantage.

In all of the ensuing excitement, I noticed something. "Dad, look! Do you see that news camera? It's right on Gram and Bess." Not only had the girls won an award, but they were going to be on TV!

Next, the oldest male twins were announced. They were only in their early eighties and were both bald as billiard balls. Upon winning, they immediately went over and congratulated Gram and Bess, who laughed but later confessed to being put off by their flirtatious ways.

After the awards ceremony, several twins congratulated Gram and Bess, who truly delighted in meeting everyone, particularly the children in attendance. By the time we headed home, Gram and Bess readily admitted that they had enjoyed themselves.

But the best was yet to come. That evening, the local news ran a story on the convention, featuring Gram and Bess. Within twenty-four hours, CNN Headline News picked up the piece. Soon, Gram and Bess were receiving calls from around the country, from both relatives and people who had grown up with their children. They heard from countless people who had once figured prominently in their lives. Gram and Bess could not have been more tickled.

Gram died three years later at age ninety-six, and Bess passed away more recently at 101. I have so many fond memories of them, but the best memory of all is the twin convention that almost wasn't.

~Kathleen Whitman Plucker

27

Making a Difference

Comparison, more than reality, makes men happy or wretched.
~Thomas Fuller

I dreaded my twin sister Rachel coming to my school. She was to serve as a judge for a "College Dreams" door decorating contest I was holding at the elementary school in which I am a counselor. A judge. No one had been judged more than the two of us. All our lives, we'd been stared at, gawked at, studied, mocked, compared, analyzed, chased down like celebrities avoiding the paparazzi, and treated like four-leaf-clovers. In high school, I'd written an article titled "I Know What It's Like to Be Famous." Drawing crowds when we worked at Montgomery Ward together, the inevitable always happened. Customers would begin to whisper, then rumble, until one brave soul would say: "Are you twins?" One of us would answer "yes," and the crowd would erupt in shouts, outdoing each other with "I knew it!" We'd force a grin across our faces and shoot a look across the register.

Our feet killed us after standing for hours in those dress code required shoes, so it wasn't easy to be nice day after day while answering a series of the same old questions we'd heard a gazillion times. "Can you feel her pain?" "Do you think the same thoughts?" "Can you finish each other's sentences?" "Who was born first (like that made a difference)?" I longed for originality, but had become a pro at answering repetitive interview questions. I guess we were good actresses because no one ever caught on how frustrating being a twin can be.

People wanted hugs, pictures, to chat, and could be downright hurtful sometimes. "She's the fat one." "She's the mean one." Or, "She's the wild one."

Our manager finally said, "We have to separate you two. You're causing a frenzy."

"Thank you," we said.

It's always awkward when someone you don't know comes up and talks to you like they've known you forever, when in reality you've never met. Once, I met one of my sister's coworkers in the elevator during jury duty. Having breakfast with her was fun, but strained. I didn't know what to talk about since I'd never seen her before, but she talked as though we were old friends. Another time, I got my sister into trouble when I sat next to a friend of hers and didn't say a word. Later, Rachel was confronted about how mean she was not to speak. When she explained that she had a twin, her friend burst into laughter.

Growing up, I tired of dressing in matching clothes. I wanted my own identity. By seventh grade, I protested that I wanted my own friends, to be completely separate from my sister, and to dress in my own style. My shop-a-holic mother protested: "Who will I choose for when I find a nice outfit?"

Now that we're older, I can appreciate having an instant companion my own age who goes through many of the same things I do. But I have never quite recovered from some of the torment of growing up a twin. Being stared at so much made me shy, and the last thing I wanted was to go to work and have to endure the same thing all over again. At this point in my career, I was beginning to wonder if I made a difference or if it was time to move on. But it was nice being known as an individual, with people getting to know me for me. Going shopping with my sister or out to eat with her always drew attention. Sometimes, we wanted to fade into the crowd with everyone else, but we never could.

So, now, what would happen when my sister came to my work? What would my coworkers and the students say? Would we have to entertain the same tired questions? Would they compare our mannerisms, our voices, our quirks while we uncomfortably stood there on display? I was already stressed enough, and it seemed that nothing was going right. Already, people had bailed on judging the contest. Out of desperation at the last minute, I had called up my sister. I knew that I could rely on her. "Of course, I will be a judge," she said. The day arrived, but at 12 o'clock, she hadn't. I called several times and got no answer.

Finally, I left a message on her voice mail and said, "If you make it, I'll be in the teacher's lounge having lunch." I figured she was running late and would arrive just in time to judge. In the lounge, we were also celebrating my boss's birthday, so there were lots of people. Mid-bite, the door opened. I heard all the gasps and looked up. In walked Rachel. I immediately held up a napkin to cover my face as I could feel all the eyes darting from her to me, her to me.

"Gosh, you two look exactly alike!" someone said. I could feel my face burning with embarrassment.

Without missing a beat, my twin said, "Hey, everybody. I was in the hallway, and a little kindergarten class went crazy, waving at me and hugging me. I thought, 'My goodness, these kids talk to strangers!' Then they started calling my name, and I said, 'No, that's not me. I'm her sister!' You should've seen their teacher's jaw drop! She said, 'You've got to be kidding me!'" Everyone in the lounge howled with laughter. My sister became instant friends with everyone as they joked and teased her about being my twin.

After lunch, we convened with the other judges, and I sent them off to look at each decorated door. After a while, I decided to check their progress. My sister was nowhere to be found. I spotted one of the judges and asked her if she'd seen my sister.

"Your sister is way behind. She keeps getting stopped by every class."

When I found her, she was surrounded by a swarm of children all chatting to her at once. At each door, the same thing happened.

When it was all over, my sister said, "My goodness, I've had a good day at your school. This was a blast!"

"Really?" I asked. "Sorry that you got stopped so much."

"I've never received so much positive attention in my life!" she said. "One thing I know for sure is that the students love you!"

"What makes you think that?" I asked.

"They all wanted to talk to me and show me their pictures and share with me what they're learning. They all thought I was you!" For the first time ever, I had fun being compared with my sister. For the rest of the day, I found myself laughing at some of the things the children said to us. I had been reaffirmed through my sister's eyes. I was making a difference.

~Tamara Mays

28

Are You the Twin I Like?

Truth will sooner come out of error than from confusion.
~Francis Bacon

My identical twins, Ashley and Christy, never tried to confuse boys about their identities on purpose, but sometimes it just happened naturally.

When they were starting middle school, Christy found out that a boy had a crush on her. She came home from school every day with news about the boy with the hopeless crush. He would say hello in the hallway or the lunchroom every day. And whenever he saw her, he always had a big smile on his face.

Then, one day, he passed her twice in the same hall—or so he thought. He was very confused until he learned that Christy had a twin sister! Our local schools have a school uniform policy, so the girls always had on the same clothing at school. This made identification for teachers and some friends a little difficult.

However, this did not put a dent in this boy's determination to get Christy's phone number. In fact, it became more of a mission, in spite of the difficulty in identifying Christy. From then on, whenever he would talk to one of the twins, he would say, "Hello, Christy... at least, I think you are Christy. Am I right?" Routinely, he would confirm which twin he was talking to before continuing the conversation. But as time went on, he got more confident that he could identify Christy, and he talked more freely.

Each day, we would hear a new story about the daily conversation, and it quickly became the hot topic of the day at our house. We were always treated to a comical tale, but soon we had the laugh that topped them all.

Ashley came home one day and told us that the boy who liked Christy had stopped her in the hallway to talk. He went on and on, but she just stood there and listened since she knew he thought he was speaking with Christy.

Finally, it dawned on him that perhaps he wasn't speaking to Christy after all! With a look of total horror on his face, he suddenly said, "Wait a minute, are you the one I like or not?"

~Karen H. Gros

"So, I was hoping I could get your number... at least I think you're the one whose number I want? Or, maybe, you could give me your sister's?"

29

Chicken Soup for the Soul

Weirdly in Sync

Be what you are.
This is the first step toward becoming better than you are.
~Julius Charles Hare

In the fall of 1955, my mother delivered identical twin girls. The only person more surprised than Mother was the doctor at the end of the table. Throughout Mother's pregnancy, only one heartbeat had been detected. And, in the normal world of obstetricians and pregnant women, one heartbeat equals one bundle of joy.

But not this time.

A few minutes after Dayle was delivered (seven to be exact), the doctor said, "Hold everything. We've got another one coming." Thus, my twin and I entered the world abnormally—and we've been a bit abnormal ever since.

Well, actually, "abnormal" isn't totally accurate. As kids, Dayle and I were just plain weird.

For starters, we ate weird things—like dirt. Where the dirt came from, or where the dirt had been, didn't much matter. To Mother's dismay, she often caught us sliding our hands beneath rugs and licking the spoils of our pursuit. Dirty shoes were fair game, as well, and our Mississippi mud pies were really Mississippi mud pies.

Another weird Blue Plate Special of ours was varnished wood.

Whenever the house became unusually quiet, Mother would find us standing side-by-side, chewing on a small varnished table.

No matter how many times she attempted to stop the chewing, it didn't stop.

Finally, after suffering major damage, the table was turned to reveal a non-chewed-on side. But not for long. Like two little beavers, homeless in the woods, we returned to the table and started gnawing again.

Our speech was weird, too. Decoding our vocabulary often took days.

After hearing us chatter about "tan-day-ya" for weeks on end, Mother marked it down as a mystery word in her proverbial book of "Weird Things the Twins Say." A few days later, while flipping through photo albums, a picture of Granddaddy appeared. "There Tan-day-ya!" we yelled, pointing at Granddaddy's picture on the page. Ah! Granddaddy. Tan-day-ya. Piece of cake.

Normally, Mother used the process of elimination for interpreting our babble, but it didn't always do the trick.

One day, I walked into the kitchen and said, "Momma, tuba." In her usual fashion, Mother commenced pointing around the room, but, alas, nothing was filling the bill.

After a lengthy exchange of "This?" "No." "This?" "No." "This?" Dayle walked in. In a tutorial tone of voice, she said, "Momma, ooh know what ooh put toopay on?" And with that bit of a clue, Mother figured out that I wanted to brush my teeth. Toopay on a tuba. Makes perfect sense to me.

But, undoubtedly, the weirdest thing about the Allen twins from Mississippi was the invisible bond that tied them together, dictating their behavior, like puppet and puppeteer.

Mother tells a funny story of us running in a department store one day. Like two actors reading from the same script, we both lost our footing and fell flat on our rears at the exact same spot of parallel aisles. Indeed, everything we did, we did in sync.

I remember going to the dentist when we were about six years old. While Dayle hollered bloody murder from the dentist's chair, I hollered bloody murder in the waiting room. Never mind that I was unharmed, alone with the magazines. Dayle's fears were my fears, and there was no escaping it.

Some say that little has changed since those early days of yore, and they have a point, I suppose: We're still weird in a wonderful kind of way.

We finish each other's sentences. We make up words as the occasion warrants. We laugh at nothing. We cry at anything. We play Scrabble till three in the morning, when normal people are in bed and fast asleep. Indeed, we're two peas in a pod, double trouble, God-created clones.

Imagining life without Dayle is impossible to do, and, in reality, it's a futile exercise anyhow. Even if I traveled to the far side of the moon, I could never be without her. As Dr. Landry discovered fifty-three years ago, our hearts beat as one. Forever and always, as long as I breathe, Dayle is here with me, breathing in sync.

~Gayle Allen Cox

30

The Band Test

The reputation of a thousand years may be determined by the conduct of one hour.

~Japanese Proverb

September arrived, and at last it was time for the band tryouts. Dot, my identical twin sister, had her heart set on a shiny black and silver clarinet. I dreamed of the brassy E-flat alto saxophone. We worked on Dad and Mom over the summer and convinced them that we wanted to try out for the band. Being a band member was so cool to an eighth-grader.

Thirty anxious and sweaty teenagers crammed into the band room to take the test. Some talked; others were quiet; a few giggled. Tensions were strung tight, like a pulled rubber band ready to pop. All those hot summer days of waiting were almost over.

A death hush spread over the room as Mr. Crow, the band director, entered. This man held our fate in his hands. He explained that the test would determine our musical aptitude and ability. He would play two notes on the piano. We were to decide if the second note was lower or higher than the first note by a half or a whole note. If you did not have any musical inclination, the test was difficult. However, the test seemed tailor-made for Dot and me. Mr. Crow didn't know that we already played piano and accordion. Our older brother, Bill, often joined us for an impromptu combo with his trumpet. We all enjoyed playing by ear instead of by note. It just came naturally to us. For the past four years, we spent many long hours in jam sessions.

Each of us graded our own paper. Dot and I missed two questions. Because we sat next to each other, Mr. Crow wanted to see us. We had missed the same questions and our answers matched, which raised a big red flag in his mind. It dawned on us that he thought we had cheated. He sure wasn't very familiar with identical twins! We were both mad and embarrassed. Mr. Crow asked us to return and retake the test after school. Since Dot and I wanted to prove him wrong, we agreed to return.

All through the day, I imagined a neon light blinking in my mind: "The preacher's twin daughters cheat." I could just see the rumors flying like BBs around the school. That was a very long, stressful day. Dot and I were determined to pass the test and reclaim our integrity.

When we returned for the test, Mr. Crow asked us to sit at opposite ends of the room. By being separated, he figured there was no way we could cheat. We were anxious and nervous while he graded our tests. The waiting seemed to string on forever. At last, Mr. Crow looked up, puzzled and amazed. A slow grin appeared on his face. He told us that, once again, we had the same scores and our answers matched. With a chuckle and enthusiasm, he welcomed us into the band.

Don't mess with identical twins... they win!

~Donna K. Hogue

Chapter 4

Twins and More

A Special Bond

The bond between twins is already an organic, established reality by the time the babies draw their first breath.

~*Patricia Maxwell Malmstrom and Janet Poland*
The Art of Parenting Twins

31

Being There for Each Other

Family means putting your arms around each other and being there.
~Barbara Bush

The scene was bittersweet as I dropped off my twins at preschool this morning. Taylor, my daughter, has always had issues with clothing. The fit of the shirt, dress, or shoe, the texture, or the size—all can send her into an emotional tizzy. After many frustrating years of morning battles to get ready, I now understand that she suffers from sensory processing disorder. It can be a common problem for multiples and in children with chronic ear infections. As the auditory system is being compromised by infections, the sensory system located right next to the auditory channels can also be affected. Children either become hypersensitive to a stimulus (meaning they have a greater struggle with it) or hyposensitive (which is a lack of a response to it). To make a long story short, there are just those days when Taylor struggles with what she has to wear.

The morning started out well. Our teeth were brushed, the clothes were on, and we were moving right on schedule. Well, today, the problem was the shoes. She didn't like the fit of her sneakers, and the tears began. As I began to lose patience, her twin brother, Griffin, went into her room and brought out her special blankets and handed them to her. In his subtle way of knowing, he was trying to comfort her.

The tears continued as we made our way into the schoolroom. She could not get her mind off the shoes as I tried my best to cajole her out of her mood. When we walked in, Griffin took her hand and led her into the room. The rest of the class was already seated on the rug for circle time as the setback had made us a little late. Griffin walked her over to the circle and found a place for both of them to sit. I explained the cause of tears to her teachers, but from the corner of my eye I watched a most beautiful picture play out. Taylor leaned her head on Griffin's shoulder, and he held her hand while she continued to sniffle. If I had a camera that would replay images from their lifetimes, I wish I had one at that moment.

A lot has been written about the twin bond and the truly unique connection that multiples share. But the true love and protection that Griffin offered his sister were awe-inspiring. In his five-year-old mind, he was only acting as her brother and caring for her, but it went so much deeper for me. Without being told, Griffin knew what to do for his sister. Her emotional well-being was more important than saying good morning to all his play friends. This isn't something we could have taught him; it was just a part of his being.

He and Taylor are connected through some deep and mysterious bond. They will always have this relationship, even when they grow older and move away. I thank God often for this wonderful experience of being allowed to raise twins and, more importantly, to witness every now and then a glimpse of the magical bond that links my twins.

~Karen Talcott

32

A Perfect Fit

Cure sometimes, treat often, comfort always.
~Hippocrates

In many ways, my twin boys are opposites. Benji, at the ripe old age of four, is a man of big emotions. When he's happy, his giddy enthusiasm is contagious. His eyes shine. His giggles bubble up from his very soul. No matter how tired I am, it's impossible not to return that toothy grin. However, when Benji's sad, he's like a character from a Shakespearean tragedy. He rails. He broods. And for days he'll talk about what made him sad, reliving it all in glorious Technicolor.

Jason takes a more middle-of-the-road approach. He has his extremes, but his highs and lows don't last as long as Benji's. Jason is more likely to talk things out. He's happy and smiley, but reserves deep-down belly laughs for special occasions.

From the moment they popped out into the world, Benji and Jason have had distinct personalities. One night, when the boys were six months old, I found out how lucky they are to be so different.

That evening, my husband Joe and I looked at each other, bleary-eyed. It was 3:40 A.M. Benji had been crying on and off for two hours.

At the beginning of the two hour marathon, we thought Benji's tears would be short-lived. In his sleep, Benji often got stuck in goofy positions, flailing around in his crib like a flipped turtle.

No big deal, we thought.

I hovered outside the bedroom Benji shared with Jason. I could hear Jason whimpering. Clearly, Joe and I weren't the only ones who had been awakened by Benji's squalls. I had to act quickly. Too much of a disturbance, and they'd both be up for good.

Conjuring up the stealth of a spy, I slipped into their room. After guiding Benji to the center of his mattress, I dashed out.

Smooth, I thought. Peace would soon reign.

Jason fell asleep almost immediately. Benji kept crying.

Joe and I conferred. Maybe Benji had wedged one of his arms between the crib slats, another talent of his. Again I dashed in, moved Benji to the safety of the crib's center, and dashed out.

Jason slept on. Benji wailed.

Panic found a foothold. I began to "catastrophize." What if we couldn't figure out what was wrong? He'd cry all night! I'd be a basket case in the morning. I couldn't afford the lost sleep—I'd never catch up. I'd snore through their college graduation ceremonies, all because of tonight!

Joe and I ran through other potential causes: wet? sick? hungry? Nope. He seemed fine, with the exception of the jet-engine-like wails that were surely keeping our condo neighbors awake.

Grasping for a cause, we finally settled on teething. We hadn't seen any new choppers coming in, but maybe one was lurking. I snatched Benji out of his crib. A dose of baby Tylenol led to ten minutes of silence.

Then the screams began anew.

Our meager shreds of parental confidence vanished like smoke in the wind. We lay in bed, planning our new futures as sleep-deprived zombies.

Then Jason woke up. How he had slept through an hour and a half of mayhem is anyone's guess.

As Benji paused to suck in a lungful of air, we heard Jason's voice: "Ba ba goo wa," he said.

All was quiet. Then Benji answered. "Ba wa wa ba ba."

The two of them began to chat.

"Ga nab a wa?" Jason asked.

"Na nab a ga," Benji replied.

For a few moments, their soft, sweet voices floated across the condo. I held my breath, straining to catch each sound.

Finally, silence.

And more silence.

Benji's crying had stopped. They had both gone back to sleep.

Joe and I began to giggle. What in the world had they said? It didn't matter. Benji slept the rest of the night.

And Joe and I began to realize something wonderful.

At the tender age of six months, the boys already had a bond. A bond that enabled them to comfort each other when their clueless parents were at a loss. A bond that thrived on differences. A bond that would last a lifetime.

~Sara F. Shacter

"Actually the twins are not hard to tell apart. When I put them down, the one that cries is Dennis."

33

Chicken Soup for the Soul

College Separation

Ever has it been that love knows not its own depth
until the hour of separation.
~Kahlil Gibran

The first time Jackie and I, identical twins, were separated for any substantial period of time was when we were thirteen years old. We both went to a sleep-away camp called Young Judaea in Amherst, New Hampshire. Jackie only stayed a month and then went to South Hampton with my parents, while I stayed at camp for the rest of the summer. It was our parents' intent to separate us for part of the summer to help us adjust to being separated in the future. It was a summer I would never forget, but I missed Jackie terribly after she left camp. Every day after lunch, I'd go behind my bunk where I could talk privately into the tape recorder, and recount for her everything I did, from water skiing around the lake twice without falling, to eating countless s'mores without getting sick.

And then the future arrived. Jackie and I were heading to two separate colleges, and the challenge was to get both of us to our respective schools on time and on the same day. My parents had planned the logistics for weeks, calling airports, car rental companies, Penn and Grand Central stations. Checking map after map, they outlined the routes. The decision was made to drive us.

Despite the hours of preparation, all I could do was cry. Dad made the situation laughable, though. He borrowed a friend's van. The thing was as old as a dinosaur and nearly as huge. However, the size of it could not have been more essential. It was filled with crates, clothes, a comforter, sheets, fluffy pillows, wooden hangers, music tapes, a typewriter, a clock radio and shoes, shoes and more shoes. And did I mention cowboy boots? What's more, Jackie had duplicates of everything I had, which meant the dinosaur was stuffed with a second set of crates, clothes, a comforter, sheets, fluffy pillows, wooden hangers, music tapes, a typewriter, a clock radio, shoes, shoes, shoes, and, of course, cowboy boots.

Once we reached my school in Hartford, Connecticut, we unloaded. Two hours later and dozens of climbs up four flights of stairs, my dorm room looked like I'd always lived there—bed made, pillows puffed, Champion sweatshirts stacked, sweaters and shirts coordinated. Even my cowboy boots were standing tall amid my line-up of shoes.

The dinosaur was ready to pull out, taking Jackie to school in Syracuse, New York. I was exhausted just thinking about my parents, Jackie and my younger sister, Michelle, doing the same hard labor again only a few hours later. (Luckily, as it turned out, Jackie had an elevator in her dorm building.)

I kissed and hugged my mom and dad. Jackie climbed in the back seat, plugged in her earphones and began listening to a new Fleetwood Mac tape I bought her. She was holding the tape player in one hand and a box of tissues in her other hand. I knew this parting was going to be hard so I would save it for last.

I reached for my sister Michelle. "How am I going to be single?" I whispered. Michelle, only a junior in high school at the time, had a very wise heart. She knew what I meant. How was I going to meet people without my twin sister next to me? I panicked. Why hadn't I chosen the same school as Jackie? Whatever possessed me to take on the biggest milestone in my life solo? What was I thinking? Without our twinness to inspire people's friendly curiosity about who was born first or if we ever dated the same guy, how would I ever make friends?

Michelle wrapped her arms around me. Her big blue eyes shining, she looked ready to reveal a deeply profound secret. "Walk up to a nice girl and say 'Hi!'" she said.

Before the scene could get too emotional, Dad put the dinosaur in drive and pulled away. I took it as a good sign. Jackie and I would never really say goodbye.

[AUTHOR'S NOTE: Ironically, many years later when my five-year-old son, Isaak, started his first day of kindergarten in a new town, I gave him the same profound advice Michelle had once given me. "Walk up to a nice boy and say, 'Hi!'" Thank you, Michelle.]

~Amy Davidson Lombardo with Jacqueline Davidson Kopito

34

Help One = Help All

If everyone is moving forward together, then success takes care of itself.
~Henry Ford

In 1960, our Cleveland paper, *The Plain Dealer*, featured an article on twins. Our West Technical High School senior class was selected for the article because we had ten sets of twins! My twin sister, Donna, and I graced the front page of the newspaper with our silhouette picture. We were called true mirror twins. The photo was followed by a lengthy article about all of the twins.

The article was read by all the teachers and students. Everyone yelled and cheered as we passed through the halls. The twins loved the attention.

All twenty of us got a big kick out of the notoriety. The ten sets of twins met after school shortly following the release of the article. We enjoyed talking to each other. Before the article, we knew each other only as acquaintances.

One of the twins mentioned, "Isn't it fun that all ten sets of twins will graduate together?"

But one of the fraternal twin girls replied, "I don't think my brother will be graduating with me. He is failing so far this year." You could tell she felt devastated that her best friend and twin would not be part of one of the most important events in their lives.

All of us jumped up and said, "We have to do something about it! What can we do?"

We brainstormed about what we could do to help her twin

brother. We discussed what classes he was taking and what subjects he was failing. Different twins raised their voice when it came to a subject he or she could help tutor. Amazingly, all of his failing subjects were covered by our small group. We were excited to do something to make this big event possible.

Days and months sailed by during our last year. The ten sets of twins met every week or two to discuss the progress of the one twin. Class scores were steadily improving; exams were increasingly passed. Things were encouraging, but the finals were yet to come.

During final exam time, the one twin had several twins cramming with him for all of his subjects. His head was spinning from all the help. If he could only remember all he had learned in the last several months... His head was exploding just trying to remember everything. He did not want to fail his twin.

Graduation morning finally arrived. The twins met backstage. All twenty of us were present.

More than five hundred names were slowly called out over the loudspeaker. When the formerly failing twin's name was called, all nineteen of us jumped up and yelled at the top of our lungs, "Hooray!" We were so proud of him. His and his twin's dreams were realized.

It did not take a village, but it took nineteen twins to help make a dream come true.

~Dot Beams

35

Sleeping Beauties

I'm all for going back to the old-fashioned thing of touching people.
~Leo Buscaglia

My beautiful daughters, Camryn and Emma, were born at twenty-eight weeks, weighing just two pounds, six ounces, and two pounds, seven ounces. After their birth, they were whisked away to the NICU where they spent the next six to nine weeks fighting for their lives.

I had heard that, in some cases, twins could better fight their medical issues if they were placed close to each other in the same Isolette, but this NICU did not allow it because all the machines, monitors and leads could potentially get tangled up. So, sadly, my girls were placed next to each other, but in separate Isolettes.

Emma struggled more than Camryn. She had a serious infection that caused her to hemolize her red blood cells. She was also anemic and had to endure a spinal tap. Both girls would stop breathing many times a day. But they were fighters, and after six weeks, Camryn was released to go home with an apnea/heart monitor. She had many apnea alarms over the next few weeks, but they were mostly false alarms, and her condition improved greatly once she was home.

Meanwhile, my husband and I traveled back and forth to the hospital several times a day to continue visiting Emma while Camryn remained at home. To our delight, Emma was finally released to go home after nine weeks, also on a monitor. But our joy at the news was also tempered with fear. Emma was still having many alarms each day, and she would often hold her breath and turn blue when she was given a bottle.

We arrived at home with Emma and decided to allow her to settle in by resting her in the Pack 'n' Play bassinet, which I had set up with inclines to hold the babies in an optimal position to prevent apnea and digestive problems. I still remember vividly the first time I placed Emma in the bassinet. At first, she became very upset and cried up a storm. Remembering the advice I had heard to place the girls close to each other, I decided to put Camryn next to Emma in the bassinet. Although it was designed for just one baby, the girls were still so tiny that they could lay across the bassinet side-by-side, with room to spare.

This was the first time in nine weeks that the girls were able to be so close together. They had touched once or twice in the NICU, but hadn't had the ability to feel each other's warmth since they had shared my womb. As we watched our precious babies' reunion, they each reached out their arm that was closest to the other and held hands. Then they immediately calmed and both fell into a peaceful sleep. I started snapping pictures through my tears because I just couldn't believe this phenomenon.

I had heard of twins being able to calm each other like this, but until you see it with your own eyes and realize the amazing power of this bond, you really cannot imagine it. After both girls came home and started sleeping together, the alarms decreased immensely, and very soon we were only seeing false alarms. Soon afterward, they were able to come off their monitors altogether.

Emma and Camryn are now almost two years old. They have no medical issues related to their prematurity, and they are thriving! They love each other immensely and are so sweet to one another. They bring each other toys, cups of milk, their favorite blankets, and their pacifiers. I can't wait until they are old enough to attempt to put into words for me what this incredible bond feels like.

~Stacey Tyser

36

If the Shoe Fits

Each day of our lives we make deposits in the memory banks of our children.
~Charles R. Swindoll

It was pouring rain when my six-year-old fraternal twin son, Michael, got out of bed early in the morning. Although it was a dreary and cold Saturday, and any normal, red-blooded kid would have looked out the window, shrugged his shoulders and headed to the television remote still clad in his pajamas, Michael quickly got dressed. "I'll be ready to go in a few minutes," he called to me.

You see, it was the weekend and his turn to have me all to himself. Last week, his co-twin, Joseph, had his "mommy-and-me time," which included a trip to the video game store where I patiently waited as he sampled all the gaming kiosks. Our afternoon of errands ended with his favorite lunch—big, juicy hamburgers and strawberry milkshakes.

I had started the practice when the boys were old enough to realize that they had never had any time alone with either parent. Unlike first-born, singleton children who get a year or two of uninterrupted time with Mom or Dad before the next kid comes along or even second-born singleton children who get alone time once their older siblings head off to school, multiples never get to experience the pleasure of a simple two-way conversation or even a solo trip to the store as someone—their co-twin—is always around. Like most twins, my boys learned early that they must take turns in just about every aspect of family life, especially when it comes to having Mom or Dad all to themselves. So even though it was cold, rainy and downright miserable, Michael certainly wasn't going to let a little bad weather cheat him out of his fair share. It was his turn. Case closed.

An hour later, we were sloshing through puddles as we headed to the downtown bookstore to peruse the aisles for the latest dinosaur books. We huddled together under a store awning while we watched a street performer strum his guitar. We stopped for hot chocolate and muffins, and Michael was gleeful, brimming with energy as he explained what a shame it was that dinosaurs didn't walk the earth any longer.

He was a trooper, too. He never complained as we ran headfirst into the deluge just so I could check out the sale rack in the clothing boutique next door. He did, however, finally inform me that his feet were getting soaking wet from the rain as we slogged from store to store. I looked down and, sure enough, his sneakers were oozing water, squeaking with every step he took. We laughed at the sight but pressed on as there were places to go and things to do. (Out of guilt, I did treat him to a frozen yogurt just an hour before heading home for lunch.)

By Monday morning, the rain still hadn't let up. "Hurry up, boys!" I called. "You're going to be late for school."

Michael opened the front door to retrieve his saturated soles from the front porch where—without my knowledge—he had placed them that Saturday afternoon to dry out. But dry they did not!

"Oh, no!" I cried. "They're still soaking wet!" I quickly scrambled to his closet in search of another pair of shoes. But then it hit me. He had no others. What kind of mother was I? But there was no time to critique my lack of fashion sense (or common sense, for that matter). "Get some paper towels," I called. "And the blow dryer, too."

As Michael blasted the hot air at his shoes and I used the paper towels to soak up the abundant moisture, we didn't even notice Joseph slowly emerging from his bedroom.

"Oh, my head," he moaned. "It hurts." He dragged his backpack to the front door and then slowly sat on the rug to lace up his sneakers for school. I looked up from my futile task to notice his face red with fever. One hand to his hot forehead confirmed what I already knew.

"Yup. You're sick all right," I said. "Looks like you're staying home today." Joseph just sat there, too weak to show any sign of enthusiasm for what lay ahead—six hours of uninterrupted mommy time (not to mention TV and lots of strawberry Jell-O).

I turned back to Michael. "These will have to do," I said, pointing to his sneakers. "They're still wet, but not as much."

"Uh, Mom?" Michael whispered. "Can I wear Joseph's shoes?" Brilliant idea! Why didn't I think of that? And without saying a word, Joseph slipped off his sneakers and handed them to his brother. "Thanks, Joe," Michael said with a satisfied smile. He quickly put them on and headed for the door. "I'm ready."

"Lucky thing I'm sick today," Joseph called out as he curled up on the couch.

"That is lucky!" Michael said.

I laughed. Funny how they always have each other's back.

~Christina Baglivi Tinglof

37

Chicken Soup for the Soul

A Nose for Food

It takes little talent to see what lies under one's nose.
~W. H. Auden

Of our twins, Derik has always been a more enthusiastic eater than Lars, something we noticed soon after they were born. The boys are four now, and to this day, Derik is our gourmet adventure boy, willing to try just about anything. Among his favorite foods are tacos, Indian biryani rice, and pesto on crackers. Lars, on the other hand, sticks pretty much to nuggets and apples, occasionally venturing as far afield as white bread toast or green beans.

Like many twins, the boys arrived prematurely (in our case, two months). We were blessed that, although small, they were both very healthy. Derik, the bruiser, was three pounds, six ounces, while Lars weighed in at a petite two pounds, fourteen ounces. In order to leave the Neonatal Intensive Care Unit (NICU) of our hospital, they had to accomplish three things: maintain their body temperature, gain weight, and be able to take a bottle or breast for twenty-four hours. The last was the most challenging, since preemies are weak initially and must be fed through a gavage tube (through the nose directly into the stomach) until they are strong enough to suck.

Lars was always more interested in his new environment than in eating. Once he was able to take a bottle, he would suck a few times, pull away and look around. Whoever was feeding him had to constantly refocus his attention. As one of his nurses told us, "For someone who can't hardly see past the end of his nose, he sure likes looking around!" After eating, he would lie awake, totally fascinated by the lights and sounds of the NICU. This invariably tired him out so much that he didn't have the strength to take a bottle at the next feeding.

Derik, however, stepped up to the feeding challenge, and within a week or so, he was taking the bottle like a pro. At mealtimes, he would quickly drain the bottle dry, stay awake for a few minutes and then crash into a deep sleep, gently snoring beside his brother. When it was time for the next feeding, he was awake and raring to go.

One morning while bringing the twins their breakfast bottles, the nurse on duty heard a strange sound coming from their crib. She grabbed the Polaroid camera they keep in the NICU for those spontaneous moments only babies can provide. Later that day when my husband and I stopped by to see the boys, the nurse proudly handed us the photo, which adorns our refrigerator to this day.

In it, a sleepy Lars stares with cross-eyed confusion at his brother. Derik, apparently deciding to chow down early, has somehow wiggled his head close to Lars' face and is latched onto his nose, sucking and tugging, our own little four-and-a-half-pound milking machine. When people ask us in what ways the boys are different from one another, we point to the picture. The caption reads, "Are you my breakfast?"

~Chela Wallace

38

One Big Day, Two Speeches, and Four Delicious Cakes

A graduation ceremony is an event where the commencement speaker tells thousands of students dressed in identical caps and gowns that "individuality" is the key to success.
~Robert Orben

My twin sister and I duked it out for valedictorian of our high school class. By the end of our junior year, we were tied to within a hundredth of a point on a one hundred point scale. Our guidance counselor said he hadn't seen anything like it before. We didn't even have identical scores in each of our separate classes. We just had different scores that somehow managed to add up to the identical overall score. So, senior year the pressure was on, and in the midst of college applications and athletics and band practices, we were still studying as much as we could. We shared most of our classes in common, but we had a couple that were different. At times, we'd cautiously question one another as to her performance in those classes and then duck our heads back into the books.

When spring rolled around and the scores had to be tabulated, my sister had overpowered me by a tenth of a point. Admittedly, if someone had told me junior year that my sister would win out in the end, I would have told that person that I'd have to hide my face in embarrassment and jealousy on graduation day. But when the time came and I was called up onto that stage in the spring awards ceremony that prefaced graduation day by a few weeks, something in me had grown, because being salutatorian was suddenly okay. It was even better than okay.

Because sometime during that year—maybe it was donating blood for the first time, or practicing with the junior varsity girls' basketball team, or taking a creative writing class in which a number could never be put on the excitement of writing each story—I learned there was a world beyond carefully calculated grade point averages. It took me a few years to understand that being second, and truly accepting and appreciating it, while giving my sister the praise she was due, was somehow a bigger accomplishment for me than getting first ever could have been. And my sister, determined, disciplined, and as astute as ever, was the person I would have most wanted to beat me out for first. My sister was gracious and never held her winning over my head, although she certainly had several opportunities to do so.

But we didn't really have much time to think about it all because graduation weekend was rolling around. As the top two in our class, we were both expected to give speeches. Known not only as among the most studious in our class, but also the quietest and shyest, the idea of the speeches and standing up in front of bleachers packed full of people terrified us. Knowing we were inordinately quiet, our class advisor gave us the option of letting someone else make the speech. Our class president was willing to step in.

But just as our mother insisted our kindergarten teachers push us on to first grade, even though our teachers had worries about our social abilities, our mother now insisted we were to fulfill the requirements of our class positions. It didn't seem to matter to her that we were graduating on our eighteenth birthday, which was certainly not the day on which we wanted to make our inaugural speeches. But neither of us wanted to let our mother or our community down, so we quietly and carefully crafted our speeches.

Standing up at the podium that afternoon, my hands were sweating so badly the ink on my speech was smearing. My voice was shaky.

I stumbled through parts of my speech. I stuttered at times. And I worried I wasn't putting on the showing that my community expected. But what got me through was knowing that my sister was going to make hers, too. Once again, we were in this together. It would be hard for her, as well, and yet she had also committed herself to it.

And after the whole thing was through—after the bleachers emptied out, and we were back at home and changed into comfortable shorts and T-shirts—we could joke about both of our speeches, could reenact particularly unsuave moments, and then laugh and forget it happened altogether. My speech was far from perfect, but I made it through.

We both made it through. And we both fulfilled our obligations as first and second in our class. In some ways, it was an even bigger victory than receiving the honors of valedictorian and salutatorian. While studying consumed a good amount of time and energy, it wasn't an overwhelming challenge for us—I even enjoyed a good percentage of it—but standing up at the podium in front of an ocean of people when we barely spoke in class was a victory of a magnitude we had never dared to dream of. I simply hoped that even if my classmates didn't catch half of my shaky words, they would remember that we had dared to stand up there and give those speeches, because we were all soon entering a world in which each of us would face fears of some kind or another.

Afterward, we ate in high style. Our mother may have convinced us to deliver those speeches (for which I thank her today), but we had convinced our mother that we needed four cakes. We each got one for our birthday, and we each got one for graduation. My mother had always viewed us as two unique individuals, and she had willingly agreed. My sister and I sampled each of the four cakes, relishing every bite. We eventually sunk into a sugar stupor in which we laughed so hard our stomachs hurt, we couldn't even begin to remember those speeches, and we were simply a pair of twins again, who nothing in the world could separate.

~Rachel Furey

39

A Cry in the Night

The miracle of twins transcends all boundaries, including age and death. Our oneness lives within each other for knowing you is knowing me.
~Samira Rao

In 1966, my parents set sail from England to emigrate to Toronto, Canada. All of their possessions and just $400 were packed into two suitcases. Starting over in a new country with six-month-old boy/girl twins, no place to stay, no job and an unsold house in Banbury, England, was a bold move to make, but not new to a man who had traveled as a young lad of seventeen from India to England in 1955. But, like every new immigrant, my father believed that Canada was where the future was brightest for him and his family. Once the immigration papers went through, my parents moved from their hotel into a two-bedroom apartment and bought two cribs for the nursery.

Our nursery was adjacent to my parents' bedroom. One frosty winter's night, my mother tucked us into our cribs, as was her routine. She put a sheet and then two thick woolen blankets on each of us. My father recalls the rest of the story.

"Usually, when I am sleeping, nothing can wake me up! Someone could rob our home, and I would sleep right through it. Many times, my wife would ask if I had heard the severe thunderstorms the previous night, and I would always look at her in surprise to hear that it had thundered.

"But one particular night around 1:00 or 2:00 in the morning, I heard a scream so piercing it was unlike anything I had ever heard. It was a scream that shattered my heart. The tone was as if someone was crying out to save his own life. I realized that it was coming from my son, Anil.

"Surprisingly, for someone who could sleep through the worst of thunderstorms, I was the first to wake up. I touched my wife's side to see if she had heard, and we both ran to Anil's crib. When we looked in, we were shocked to see that he was fast asleep! We looked at each other quizzically, and I said to my wife in amazement, 'He is sleeping!'

"Immediately, we looked over at Samira's crib, and we could not see her! I ran to turn on the light and found that the base that supports her crib mattress had flopped down on one end. Her head and upper body were angled down in a 45- to 60-degree position, with her legs upward. The blankets that were meant to keep her warm now swathed her entire head and body. Our daughter was suffocating!

"We quickly removed the woolen blankets from her face. Her eyes were still closed, and she was drenched in sweat and red as a tomato. It looked as if we had just given her a bath because she was completely soaked. Fortunately, she was still breathing. If her twin brother had not screamed, it would only have been a matter of time before she died.

"The amazing part of this story is that there was no noise to wake or startle our babies. Samira's crib was completely intact; only the base of the mattress was tipped downward. If the crib had totally collapsed, not only would the babies have awakened, but my wife, an extremely light sleeper, would have been alerted immediately. This silent killer would have had devastating results if it were not for the scream that came from Anil. So why did he scream? The only explanation we can come up with is that this was his inner connection to his twin to alert us that she was in danger.

"Also amazing is that Anil was sleeping when we went in. If he had been awake, our attention would have been centered on him and what made him scream so loud. It would have taken longer to get to Samira's crib, which could have had tragic consequences as every second counted toward her survival.

"That scream still rings in my ears forty-two years later. It is one of those things that one can never forget."

The new immigrants called the crib manufacturer to have the crib replaced, which they sent without hesitation. My parents realized only later just how serious the consequences could have been if Samira had died. Perhaps charges would have been leveled against them. Being new to the country and not knowing one person who could vouch for them as responsible parents, how could anyone believe that they were not involved in their daughter's death? Having twins had been an unexpected marvel for both of them, but the unspoken connection between the twins was the true miracle.

To this day, my twin brother and I share a unique connection of unspoken love. After many years of trying and several miscarriages, my husband and I adopted our little angel in 2003. Twenty-three months later, in July 2005, I was blessed to give birth to twins of my own. Anil took ten days off from work and traveled to Michigan, where I now live, to be at my side. He held and welcomed my son into the world... and then he held and kissed my daughter goodbye. She lived just long enough to be sure that her brother was safe and healthy, and then she went back home.

My brother wrote a poem to me not long after Sandhya's passing. (Her name means "sunset" and "name of God.")

Dear Sister,

This is a special prayer for Sandhya: I pray that she will be shielded in a blanket of white light as her spirit will be entering the next life. I pray that her soul will be at peace, and that she will be baby Raj's special guardian angel, always looking over him in his time of need. I pray that she will be remembered and never forgotten, and that her memory will be always with our family. Sandhya entered our world briefly and left quietly like the setting sun. The time of sunset is the time of Sandhya.

God Bless, With Love, Anil

A year later on July 26, 2006, at the exact time Sandhya was born, my husband, her twin Raj and I released her ashes into Lake Michigan, where she was finally set free. At Anil's wedding on August 11, 2006, he played "Time of Sunset," a song he dedicated, composed and wrote for his niece, Sandhya.

~Samira Rao

40

Chicken Soup for the Soul

The Past Sixty Years

A sibling may be the keeper of one's identity,
the only person with the keys to one's unfettered, more fundamental self.
~Marian Sandmaier

As I heard our grandfather clock chime twice, I suddenly realized that it was two in the morning. My twin brother, Ed, and I had been talking steadily for more than six hours. I was delighted that he had decided to spend a weekend with my wife and me since it had been almost three years since I had last seen him. That occasion had been very sad for it was his wife's funeral. She had been killed instantly in an automobile accident. But this visit proved to be much happier.

As we talked, I slowly realized how much we really had in common. You would have thought that after sixty-some years of being twin brothers, we would have known almost everything there was to know of each other. Unfortunately, the past twenty years had been spent eleven hundred miles and short phone calls apart. Now, we had the opportunity to really compare our lives.

While we both shared the Weaver receding hairlines and features with our dad and our other two brothers, Ed was always smaller in stature. I had always been a little taller and heavier than Ed, but now I outweighed him by about thirty pounds. This seemed amazing, as I had earlier watched him devour four pieces of Kentucky Fried Chicken (his favorite food), a big mound of mashed potatoes and gravy, and a dish of cole slaw. All I could surmise was that he must burn the calories off quicker than me.

I remember that our dear mother loved to take pictures of her twin boys dressed alike. She took great joy in showing them off at the twins' club that she belonged to and to anyone who would take the time to look at them. We, on the other hand, hated to be dressed the same. And even more than that, we hated to be referred to as "The Twinnies."

To add to the already great burden of being a twin, we were forced to share a room for twelve years. Consequently, we chose to make separate social contacts and were never really close. Ed's bubbly personality and constant line of chatter endeared him to everyone. Throughout all our school years, he seemed to top me at everything, even though I had been born a few minutes before him and weighed a couple of ounces more. Ed always said that I had received a stronger heart and lungs. Maybe so, but they never enabled me to top him.

Because his name was Ed and mine was Ray, his name would always be called before mine at roll call and graduation exercises. His name was listed before mine in the phone book. His picture was before mine in the school yearbook.

In high school, everyone liked Ed. He charmed everyone with jokes and goofy stories, even if he had to make them up. There was never a dark side to Ed, and everyone loved him.

As the two of us sat sharing popcorn and drinking soda at this late hour, we kept interrupting each other. We compared the questions that everyone asked us about being a twin. "Do you both look alike?" "Which one is smarter?" "Did your folks ever get you mixed up?"

This last question made Ed recall the time that he had broken mother's favorite lamp. She was furious, and I got blamed for it. "And," I replied, "it cost me a month's allowance!"

Yes, Ed seemed to have topped me at everything for the past sixty years. He joined the army before me, married before me and bought a house before I did. When I reminded him that I finally topped him by producing the first girl in the Weaver clan in thirty years, he just smiled and stated, "But you forget that I had two girls."

Finally, Ed told me how busy he had been for the past twenty years telling everyone about me. You see, I finally did something first: I moved to Florida, while Ed stayed in our hometown of Toledo, Ohio.

As we both started to yawn, Ed jumped to his feet, exclaiming, "I forgot that I brought a present along for you and Ellie." He went to his room and returned with a large white box. "I want you to see what I do four days a week now that my Nancy is gone."

I opened the box and was surprised to see that it contained a white heart-shaped pillow with red lettering on it that said, "From my heart to yours."

"Nancy and I started to make these for heart transplant patients before she died, and I have continued making them. It gives me great comfort and joy to take them to the transplant patients in the hospitals. I thought that maybe you would know someone who would like this one."

I thanked him as I thought that the reason that everyone liked Ed was because he had such a good heart.

Finally, as we decided to call it a night, Ed announced that he would be leaving in the morning after breakfast. His daughter and her family were picking him up to take him to Disney World. Ed's treat, of course.

As I climbed into bed, my wife awoke, looked at the clock and said, "Gosh, Ray, it's almost three o'clock in the morning. What on earth have you and Ed been talking about?"

"Just the past sixty years, that's all."

~Raymond P. Weaver

"I feel like I'm always competing with my twin brother for attention."

41

Reflections of a Shared Life

One's sister is part of one's essential self,
an eternal presence of one's heart and soul and memory.
~Susan Cahill

My life has been a dance of duality, choreographed by the physical and emotional bond shared with my identical twin sister. She has been the cornerstone of my self-esteem, a champion of my confidence, my life's foundation.

While maintaining our individuality, we continue to delight people with our mirror-image resemblance and harmonic mannerisms. Like words joined by a hyphen, we can stand alone, but are enhanced by each other's presence. Our verbal shorthand and telling glances are integral to our unique communication. We can converse in half-sentences that resemble a well-rehearsed repartee in stereophonic sound. Often, there is no need to speak any words at all; we can feel each other's thoughts. Together we generate a palpable energy that radiates and is absorbed by those around us.

We share countless personality traits, as would be expected with our identical genes. Yet we do have a number of differences that add sparkle to our lives. She's the diplomat; tact is not my strength. I am in awe of her ability to maintain composure in the face of situational absurdity, calmly stating, "Help me understand..." to resolve an issue. I, however, when confronted with an irrational incident, struggle to contain the fire burning in my eyes. My sister prefers gold jewelry;

I favor silver. Her ice cream choice is vanilla; mine is chocolate. I became a mother early in my life; she did not.

I had my son at twenty-three and my daughter three years later. I placed my obstetrical nursing career on hold and stayed at home. In 1971, that was Standard Operating Procedure. My sister was an essential part of their lives, a super-aunt showering my children with affection and gifts. I longed to return the favor, wanting desperately to enjoy loving a child without the daily responsibilities. But she was a dedicated businesswoman years before that became routine. I settled into a life jam-packed with play groups, carpools and PTA, and she continued, year after year, to thrive in the corporate environment.

Months after our thirty-sixth birthday, she called me to nonchalantly announce that she might have a surprise for me. My sister and I are never blasé about anything. Casual isn't our thing. My twin radar screen was activated. I could feel it was something monumental. I whispered, "Are you pregnant?" "Maybe," she said. After eighteen years of marriage and a successful career, she had decided to take the plunge into the unknown depths of motherhood. My sister usually slept past noon on Saturdays and Sundays, and she still wasn't quite sure that there was truth to the rumor that mornings existed on weekends.

"Can you pick up a pregnancy test on the way over here?" she asked.

"Are you kidding? I'll be right there." I bolted out of my house and took three deep breaths before I drove there. I bought one of the "new" at-home pregnancy test kits and drove the four miles to her house in a state of exhilaration. Of course, this was the dark ages of pregnancy tests, when they required thirty minutes of patience before revealing the future. (Today, more than twenty-four years later, the tests are incredibly easy and results are virtually instantaneous.)

We diligently followed the instructions, a huge departure from our usual carefree demeanor. She gingerly placed the sample on the table. Now we were to wait for the formation of a donut-shaped ring that would make me an aunt and, incidentally, make my sister a mother-to-be.

We sat anxiously waiting for the minutes to pass. She flipped through a magazine, barely glancing at the pages. My eyes were riveted to the clock's second hand as it crawled past each number. "Come on," I said silently, trying not to peek at the test every few minutes. Throughout our lives, we have been together for all important as well as various trivial events. On a one-to-ten scale, this was an eleven.

The instructions warned us not to shake the sample. So we sat, barely breathing. I began to get morning sickness while we waited. We both shot an exasperated look at her refrigerator, which picked those few minutes to begin a persistent vibration. "Shhh," we said simultaneously, and smiled. We often say the same thing at the same time.

To fill the minutes, I began to create a mental checklist of all the changes that would be necessary in a house that was anything but baby-proofed. Breaking the tension with a chuckle, I said, "Floor plants have to go. They are poisonous. A playpen will go there. The highchair will fit perfectly here, and the spare room needs redecoration as a nursery. You need locks on the cabinets, safety plugs in the sockets and gates to block the staircase."

She grinned. "We don't even know if I'm pregnant, and we've begun renovating the house...?"

"I know," I said with certainty. "I can feel it." And a few minutes later, the ring formed and confirmed her pregnancy.

"Congratulations, Auntie! You'd better dust off your Dr. Seuss books." We hugged and giggled like excited children.

"Okay," I said as I transformed into my drill-sergeant obstetric nurse mode, "no smoking, drinking or caffeine... drink some milk... call the doctor ... you need prenatal vitamins."

She had an amniocentesis due to her "advanced age," and I was a wreck by the time the results came in. As a distraction, she bet me that the baby was a girl. "No, it's a boy. I'm sure of it." Winner buys lunch, we decided. When the results came in, she notified me that my "healthy" nephew would like to take me to lunch. I cried.

I was exhausted throughout her entire pregnancy. As an obstetrical nurse, I had a major case of the "what-if-this-happens." But she breezed through it. She continued working and had no nausea, leg cramps, or fatigue—not even one stretch mark. We laughed about that difference between us.

When her labor began, the doctor, a personal friend, allowed me to observe the birth, as a sister, not as a nurse. After an hour, the fetal monitor indicated that the baby was in distress, and the doctor decided to perform a Caesarean section. As I had assisted in so many of these procedures, I thought that I could remain calm while watching this one.

I wish I could say that the nurse in me triumphed over the anxious sister. But no, my legs turned to gelatin. My brother-in-law literally held me up during the entire delivery of their perfect and incredibly beautiful baby boy.

Our song of synchronicity has continued throughout the years since my nephew's birth. We have shared the joys, difficulties and triumphs of our lives. My children have presented me with three beautiful granddaughters whom my sister adores. We share them. They are fascinated by our similarities and delighted when we dress alike. My sister and I are now eagerly anticipating her son's wedding in several weeks.

I look forward to sharing with her whatever future joys that will bring.

~Lee Rothberg

Chapter 5

Twins and More

Twin Trials

The gem cannot be polished without friction nor man without trials.

~Confucius

42

Twins Stay Twins

Shared joy is a double joy; shared sorrow is half a sorrow.
~Swedish Proverb

As identical twins, Ana and I share everything—the same fingerprints, moles in the same places, the same missing teeth. Once, we even had the same dream. We call each other the same name, "M'a," a made-up merged word for "my Ana" and "my Isa." One more thing we share is the same genetic lung disease, cystic fibrosis (CF). Since our zygote split, we have kept each other alive by raging mightily against CF. United by the need to breathe, we have relied on each other for hours of daily chest physical therapy, pounding on our backs since we were twelve to loosen the secretions in our lungs. Each clap I gave her really meant "I love you," and each clap she gave me meant "I heal you." Though we fought frequently because of our treatments, we recognized that we were a team of two that would win the game of CF. Despite routine hospitalizations, together we thrived in school and careers. Though we wanted independent lives, CF was an insidious thread that tangled our lives together into a tight knot.

Ana and I also share a lifetime of fear that we'll lose one another. As CF progressed, we took turns being critically ill. In 2000, I watched Ana struggle with end-stage cystic fibrosis. I witnessed her amazing double-lung transplant and her drive to start living again. In 2004, my lungs failed, and Ana watched a miracle unfold when donor lungs became available at the eleventh hour. I was resurrected.

Before our transplants, all we asked for was to breathe. After our lung transplants, Ana and I tasted the chocolate of life for the first time and were addicted. We ran and swam in the Transplant Games, hiked Yosemite's Half Dome, and camped in the snow. We did everything that healthy, active young women do. With each adventure came profound gratitude plus the awareness that this could end, since lung transplants are the least successful organ transplants.

Six years after her transplant, Ana became short of breath while training for a marathon. She was diagnosed with chronic rejection of her lungs, and despite aggressive immune-suppression, Ana lost half her lung capacity within two months. The drastic loss shocked Ana's psyche.

I remember Ana's exact words after her latest treatments for chronic rejection failed. "M'a, I've fulfilled all my goals," Ana said, dejected. "I've had a career, won medals, bought a home, traveled the world. I've done everything I've wanted to do. I think I'm done." She sounded breathless on the phone.

Lying in bed next to my husband, Andrew, I became breathless, too. I couldn't believe these words were coming from the mouth of Ana, the stronger twin, the Energizer Bunny, the one with whom I couldn't catch up, swimming, running, even working. We both lived the same number of years, yet she had lived so much harder.

A wave of desperation overcame me, and I broke down. "What about me? Don't you want to live for me?"

Andrew reached over to caress me as my tears soaked the pillow. Thank God I had him, who completed my trinity. At least if I lost Ana, I'd have him.

I forced hope onto Ana.

"Don't you want to find your true love? There's marriage, unimaginable goals in the future... What about the book?" Our book, *The Power of Two*, had just been accepted for publication, and we had to see it come out—together.

In the ensuing months, the rejection continued its relentless, downward course. In February, Ana hiked breathlessly to the top of a local ridge, as I ran to the top. By early April, she struggled to walk the milder hills as I pushed her up the steeper parts. In late April, she had to wear supplemental oxygen just to walk three flat miles. By May, she breathed heavily walking around the block. In June, she struggled to just walk down her driveway. Seven months after her rejection started, Ana was wheelchair-bound.

Thankfully, right before she required supplemental oxygen, Ana found the man who completed her trinity. Her dream-like boyfriend, who saw her for who she was and not her destroyed lungs, was the kind God sends to remind us of higher forms of humanity. Her boyfriend, plus increasing anxiety about end-stage lung disease, whipped Ana into full-blown fight mode, and she agreed to be listed for a second transplant.

I did errands for Ana. Once I bought groceries for Ana, and a clerk asked, "You're feeling better today, eh? Last week you needed that oxygen." Ana apologized for being a burden, and I'd reply, as she would have, by saying, "I love M'a. It's mutch!" (That's twin-speak for "mutual.")

In early June, Ana called me, breathless, tearful, saying, "M'a! I can't do it!" She was having a full-blown panic attack because her oxygen tank wouldn't fill. "I don't have time to be sick! I have things to do, goals to fulfill!" She was supposed to volunteer for the California Transplant Donor Network in a half-hour, and she was so breathless that she wanted me to go instead. Yet she didn't want to be alone at home, so she came with me anyway. On the drive there, I begged her to stop everything and focus on herself. Ana's thin frame shook with deep heaving, sucking in air. Still, her long dark brown hair was pulled back neatly, and she wore professional clothes. She emanated a beauty and elegance. We volunteered together cheerfully, giggling at our own folly, as I pushed Ana around in her wheelchair. In the end, the Energizer Bunny prevailed.

In mid-July, Ana received the call that donor lungs were available. Once again, we felt sorrow for the donor family and prayed in gratitude for their generous blessing. Yet we rejoiced cautiously, recognizing the dangers of an experimental second lung transplant. Before Ana entered the operating room, we embraced. "I am with you and you with me, always," I said, just as I had before her first transplant, and she did before mine. And they wheeled her away.

Ana's recovery has been miraculous. Once more, we are hopeful yet fearful of rejection. Ana talks to her lungs, trying to befriend the ghost that is breathing for her. Like she did for me, my fitness level serves as motivation for her to stay active. Six months after her lung transplant, Ana hiked six miles.

I am so thankful Ana chose to fight for me, for love, for life. I glance at the colorful prayer flags hanging on my wall, made by loved ones while I was in surgery for my transplant. My mother wrote on her pink flag, "Twins stay twins." We laughed afterward about that odd statement. And now, after the third Stenzel transplant, the woman who gave birth to us was right. What gratitude I have to God, doctors and organ donors that I still have my twin! Our book has been published, and we have promoted it together. It is our shared story, which continues.

~Isabel Stenzel Byrnes

43

A Twin Nudge

Death leaves a heartache no one can heal;
love leaves a memory no one can steal.
~From a headstone in Ireland

"Janice, we'll never understand why Frankie had to die, but we know God wanted you to live. Frankie will always be by your side. You'll never be alone."

Those three short sentences, spoken by my wise parents in the aftermath of a DeWitt, New York, polio epidemic that ravaged our family and community, have made all the difference.

•••

Born one minute apart, we were a rambunctious twosome, enthralled with our twinship. We were the products of the post-World War II era, growing up in a suburb where parents delighted in a renewed promise of peace and good fortune for their offspring. Like children throughout America, Frankie and I were full of Halloween anticipation that autumn—of ghosts, goblins, princesses, and treat bags overflowing with candy.

Frankie had had a little cold for a few days—nothing serious, but Mom wanted to make sure that he would not contaminate other children in our first-grade classroom. On the afternoon of October 30th, Frankie's breathing became labored. My parents rushed him to City Hospital in Syracuse where he was given a spinal tap and promptly placed in an iron lung. By the next morning, the worst had been confirmed: Frankie had bulbar polio, rendering him unable to breathe or swallow without mechanical assistance.

My parents were told that a new treatment, injections of a blood component called gamma globulin, might lessen my case as it was almost certain that I had been infected. I was brought to the hospital and was given multiple shots of the blood serum—a serum that was considered "liquid gold" in the days before the polio vaccine.

Sixty-one hours after admission to the hospital, at 10:25 P.M., Frankie died. It was November 1, 1953 (All Saints' Day in my family's religious tradition). Sadly, my parents' anguish continued as I was admitted to the same hospital, with a diagnosis of paralytic polio, on the night of Frankie's burial. Later that week, my mother suffered a miscarriage. For several days, my parents didn't know if I would survive the raging fever that always accompanies the acute phase of the disease. In the end, eight children in our first grade classroom of twenty-four were diagnosed with polio. Eventually, the virus claimed the lives of two other DeWitt children. Our story was not unique—it was repeated each day, all over the globe, before the polio vaccine was introduced.

I was the lucky twin—the one who benefited from intensive physical therapy. But I was also the twin who benefited from Frankie's speedy diagnosis and the aggressive intervention of the medical staff. If I had fallen ill before Frankie, our twin fates may have been reversed—an overwhelming thought for a little girl who loved her brother with all her heart.

Fortunately, my parents saved their surviving twin from a lifetime of horrific guilt because of those few words, "... God wanted you to live. Frankie will always be by your side. You'll never be alone."

•••

I eventually made a complete recovery, becoming a proficient dancer and ice skater. I even tried my hand at cheerleading in high school. My life became focused in the aftermath of that cruel 1953 fall. I received a master's in rehabilitation counseling from the University of Pittsburgh—Jonas Salk's university. You see, I knew all too well what it was like to suffer physical pain and illness. I knew all too well the "grief work" that children can be forced to endure. Yes, God had let me live for a reason.

I was likewise certain that Frankie stayed by my side in a very real sense—in a way that perhaps only twins who have lost their birth partner can comprehend. There has never been a day that I have not felt Frankie's love, guiding me, protecting me, and occasionally giving me a serious nudge.

Like most people in the developed world, I was under the misconception that polio had been eradicated worldwide. It was not until 2003, when I received a copy of the *Rotarian* magazine from my college friend and grad school roommate Michele Moore Ridge, that I learned that polio still held its evil grip on several developing countries. Michele had attached a short note to that magazine: "Jan, now you have to tell your story."

For many years, friends and family had encouraged me to write. I had always resisted. I believed that our story was a personal one, certainly not one of interest to anyone who did not know the Flood twins. But my dear friend's note forced me to reevaluate my life's path. Yes, God had let me live. Was there something Frankie needed me to do with this story of ours? Maybe Frankie had a new job for me in this new millennium.

•••

That was five years ago. Nearly every day since, I have spent my life researching, writing, and speaking about the importance of polio eradication. You see, it is now believed that if polio is not soon eradicated, we will lose our last best chance to rid the world of this cruel killer and crippler that prefers only the young of our planet.

In the winter of 1954, as I was beginning my life's journey without Frankie, I found it necessary to conjure up a wonderful vision of heaven, Frankie's eternal home. My parents had reassured me that

God had called Frankie home for a very special reason. In my child-like scheme of things, I envisioned that Frankie's job was to greet other children who had died from polio.

If there is any truth to my childhood vision of the afterlife, I am saddened that Frankie still greets children who have lost their battle. I am emboldened by the belief that the little boy I have missed every day of my life since November 1st so long ago, is determined to see that his sister does her part to rid the world of polio. I am a private citizen without a celebrity platform, but I can write and speak, calling attention to a disease that can be so easily prevented.

Through my friend, Michele, I received a special "twin nudge" that has empowered me every day since! Thanks, Frankie, for keeping me on track. I love you.

~Janice Flood Nichols

44

The Fighter

I have fought the good fight, I have finished the race, I have kept the faith.
~2 Timothy 4:7

Early in my childhood, I was diagnosed with both sickle cell anemia and a kidney disease. I was unable to take gym classes or defend myself in fights. Because of this, I always believed that my twin sister was the stronger of the two of us.

Arlise would never back down from a fight with anyone, and often would come to my rescue if she thought that someone was bothering me. If she so much as heard that I might be in a fight, she would come running down the school hallway ready to do battle. My fights were Arlise's fights. She became my protector.

For our Junior High School Talent Show, we decided that we would sing a Gladys Knight and the Pips tune, "Got Myself a Good Man." We had practiced with two of our best girlfriends and were dressed in our silk shirts with the French cuffs and our pinstriped bell-bottom pants.

When we took the stage, the crowd started popping their fingers to the beat. Arlise began to move her hips and feet and sing the words to the song.

While we were working hard at our routine, one of the belts on her pants fell to the ground. And, if that wasn't bad enough, one of the buttons on the blouse of our girlfriend with an oversized chest popped right off!

Someone yelled loudly from the crowd, "Go ahead, baby, and strip for us!" The laughter from the crowd was enough to set my sister right into putting on her boxing gloves. The fight was on!

Arlise yelled through her microphone, "If any of you think that you can do this any better, why don't you come up here and do it now!" The whole school took on the challenge. The main culprit was a bully who wasn't afraid of anybody. She took the challenge to lead the entire school to either get us to fight or to run.

Arlise wasn't about to run. That meant we all had to fight, and fight we did. It didn't take Arlise long to finish the job of winning that fight, and she gained the respect of that girl, along with all of her "homegirls."

Years passed, and one day after we'd graduated from high school, Arlise came running into the house. She allowed the door to slam and abruptly informed my parents that she was not going to wash another dish. Even though we were eighteen, we still had to obey our parents' rules. That was the day I knew I was going to lose my best friend. She was leaving home, and my heart was broken.

My sister moved in with her boyfriend. After they were married, she discovered that she still had to wash dishes—for her husband and her employer! She worked as a barmaid while she went to school to study nursing. I felt truly as though my right arm was gone when she left home. But life goes on, and we kept in close touch.

I also worked as a barmaid while going to school to become an Occupational Therapist Assistant. One day, Arlise and I found ourselves working in the same building. She paged me to come to her floor. My sister showed me some small, dark moles on her skin, which indicated that she was going into kidney failure.

Later, we cried together as we sat in the doctor's office. We had lost our younger brother at the age of nineteen from this same disease. Eventually, after counseling with the doctors, Arlise was able to return to work and drive until she began to have cramps in her legs, which prevented her from walking. Blood clots in her legs caused constant and excruciating pain. The sister who always took care of others now had to give up her independence. She was unable to care for herself, and it was a fight getting her to leave her home.

One day, my husband called me into our bedroom and placed his strong arms around me as I laid my head on his chest. He knew that I was unable to get Arlise to leave her home. He said, "Do you mind if I talk to Sis and ask her to come to stay with us?" I cried and laughed at the same time. At the age of forty-four, Arlise was confined to a wheelchair, but my husband's reasoning won her over. I am so grateful to this man of God.

We moved some of her clothes and other personal items into one of our bedrooms even though we had a full house during this time. Our two teenage sons were big eaters, and our grown daughter had just moved back home from Atlanta, Georgia, with our baby granddaughter. We also had a small dog and two cats. I felt as if we were the Brady Bunch plus two.

My twin's condition began to worsen. She wasn't a good candidate for a kidney transplant because she was an unstable diabetic. One day when she left our home for her dialysis, I sensed that something was wrong. I had a headache all day long.

Arlise arrived at the hospital and immediately went into cardiac arrest, which caused her death. Never has a day gone by when I don't think of my twin—the one who was always the stronger of the two of us.

While going through her things after her death, we found a letter that Arlise had written to us. It said, "Please do not weep for me. I want my funeral to be all yellow, with yellow roses and beautiful music." And that's just what we did. We didn't cry at her funeral, but we thanked God for her life.

I didn't know then that I was later going to need all of her fighting spirit to sustain me. I now have two painful medical conditions that cause me chronic pain each and every day. But I endure when I think of her favorite song. When she was in agony, she would always sing, "I Won't Complain."

I thank God for the legacy of faith and strength left by my twin sister, Arlise. Her will to live and fight lives on in me, no matter how much pain I am in. I watched her suffer through dialysis, many blood transfusions, and much pain. And I vow to sing the song she sang right up until the end. She was one heck of a fighter.

~Denice Porchia

45

Skipping the Witch

True love stories never have endings.
~Richard Bach

Skylar and Kerry lie sprawled across my bed in their pajamas, engrossed in the movie *Enchanted*, the latest obsession in their three-year-old world. With the evening sunlight of June still filtering through the windows, the twins aren't interested in sleep. "It's eight on the clock, girls. Almost bedtime." They don't move. The ceiling fan twirls above us, fanning our hair and filling the room with a fresh-from-the-bath aroma of baby shampoo. I sit cross-legged with my laptop in front of me, being grilled by the Quicken WillMaker program I just installed. Question number three: Married or Single? I'm stumped.

An animated Susan Sarandon begins snarling on the screen, and Skylar buries her face in the pillow. "Skip the witch, Mommy! I don't like the witch." I lunge for the remote on the nightstand and fast-forward through the scene.

"Okay, she's gone." Remote in hand, I'm a fairy godmother with the power to banish witches, trolls and monsters. I create a world where all is well. Skylar peeks through her fingers to make sure it's safe. With her widow's peak hairline and intense gaze, she has the look of a baby Jack Nicholson.

"Are witches real, Mommy?" Yes, I want to answer, you'll meet some in high school.

"No, sweetie. It's just pretend." She rests her chin in her palms and settles back into the movie.

Like all my childhood friends, I grew up on the same kind of fairy tales, learning early that I would meet my true love and live happily ever after. No future included the possibility of being puzzled when asked "Married or Single?" or raising twin girls alone. I was brought up in the era of Movies of the Week, so I knew that given two hours and enough tenacity, an ordinary woman could overcome any obstacle and find her happy ending. I had the peace of knowing that if my mom needed to crawl through an avalanche or cure a rare disease to save me, she would. And I was sure that I could do the same for someone I loved.

I place the remote back on the nightstand, between the tub of wet wipes and the portrait of me and my husband laughing at our wedding. The twins call the picture "Cinderella-mommy." I'm in my poofy dress, a head shorter than him. My husband's blue eyes—Skylar's eyes—are watching something to the left. "Look this way," I think to the picture. "Look at me." For five years after that day, all I wanted was to make him happy. The four years after that, my goal was simply to keep him alive. In the end, it turned out I couldn't cure cancer, no matter how much I loved him.

"Can I push the button?" Kerry asks, leaning over the computer.

"Sure, bug. Come here."

She crawls into my lap, and I guide her index finger, pressing the buttons to turn off the computer. "Look, you did it!" Kerry smiles and turns her attention back to the TV, her just-washed hair cool and damp against my cheek.

I want our girls to grow up feeling safe, as I did, not with a cynical mother who was powerless to save their father. Kerry reaches back and twirls my hair in her fingers, as she's done since she was a baby. She pulls too hard, and a strand snaps like a rubber band. I wince, but I don't move. When will she realize that if I couldn't save Daddy, I can't possibly protect her and her sister? I can make a witch disappear from a movie, but I can't conquer all the dragons that will come our way.

On the dresser, the twins' clothes are laid out for tomorrow's big Father's Day party at preschool. Just lately, the girls have been catching on that our household is different. The "family board" in class is full of pictures of smiling daddies who are actually alive and spend time with their children. The twins see their friend Jordan's father bring him to school and kiss him goodbye. At first, I thought I'd keep the girls home from the Father's Day event—hit fast-forward and start fresh on Monday. But there was no way to skip the weeks of father-focused crafts and rehearsals all leading up to the big day. Instead, I improvised and called my husband's best friends to fill in. Uncles Moyn, Chris, Ken and Kevin will be there, cameras in hand. It's not the fairy tale, but it's the best Mommy can provide.

On screen, the princess and her one-true-love kiss. The twins jump up and down, holding hands and yelling "Yay! Yay!" as the computer bounces onto my toes.

"Okay, girls, but what does Cinderella do before she marries the Prince?" They squeal our rehearsed response in unison.

"She goes to college!" I tackle them into a heap of giggling toddlers.

"Come lay down with me. Tomorrow's a big day." We watch the movie, the twins on either side of me, all of us cuddled together like puppies. Kerry drifts to sleep, fingers wrapped in my hair. Skylar curls her hand around mine.

"You know what?" I whisper into Skylar's ear. "You'll be surprised. There isn't only one happy ending."

"I don't like the dragon, Mommy." I fast-forward, erasing everything sad that happens before the final song.

~Mia Daveline

46

The Rescuing Hug

Sometimes even to live is an act of courage.
~Lucius Annaeus Seneca, Letters to Lucilius

On December 21, 2007, my twin sister was told she had cancer. My sister and I have always had a great coping mechanism through laughter, but this one was tough. To make matters worse, this wasn't a cancer one could discuss over the Thanksgiving table. The mere mention would make our friends squirm. She had first-stage anal cancer. She had had no symptoms. It was discovered by luck through a colonoscopy.

She told me the news on Christmas Eve. I was lucky to have my son, daughter and friends around me because the thought of losing my sister was insurmountable. I knew I wasn't ready to become a twinless twin.

She said I couldn't visit her until I had a colonoscopy, too. The mere thought sent me running for cover. I cancelled two doctor's appointments, but I finally did it. As awful as it was, it gave me great relief in knowing I was cancer-free. This procedure saved my sister. It was a small price to pay so I could be by her side and know I was fine.

She started an aggressive six-week treatment of radiation and chemotherapy in late January. She had a shunt put in her chest for the chemo pump and went every day for radiation. I saw my sister's body get burned from the radiation, and I saw her bend over in pain as they burned this disease from her body. If this didn't work, there was no alternative treatment except for a colostomy. It was a very humbling experience.

On Friday, April 4, 2008, we were stunned and thrilled to hear that my sister was cancer-free. We had been geared up to hear that she had further to go. But even though her treatment is now complete, I don't think we will ever get back to "normal" again. I am thankful for my sister now more than ever. The thought of not having the person I was born with was hard for me. But what she went through was even harder. I don't know if I could have endured what my sister did. I am so proud of her courage.

We both have framed a newspaper article called "The Rescuing Hug." The article tells the story of a set of infant twins and how one was not expected to live. It goes on to tell how the hospital nurse went against the rules and put the babies together in one incubator. When the twins were together, the healthier twin put her arm around the other in an embrace. The smaller baby stabilized. My sister and I live in different states, but I was there to hug her during her treatment. The article ends with a simple statement: "Let us not forget to embrace those whom we love."

~Susan Lack

47

Always There

Having a sister is like having a best friend you can't get rid of. You know whatever you do, they'll still be there.
~Amy Li

Rachel and I were identical twins, but we didn't grow up the same as most twins. Although we were identical, we were different. Very different. I suppose when we were younger, we were more alike, but when Rachel was two she got scarlet fever. It left her partially deaf and wholly different from me. She was labeled "handicapped" and shipped off to a "special" school with "special" kids, who were actually handicapped.

Meanwhile, I was left at home alone to go to a normal school, to be a normal kid. But to Rachel, it must have looked like I was "special." I got to live with Mom and Dad, and have all their attention. As far as Rachel could see, I was an only child—a "perfect" child.

Life was never easy for my twin. After the fever, Rachel's health was poor. Besides being partially deaf, she now had epilepsy, suffering seizure after seizure in a "special" school with "special" people, away from her family and home, away from love.

Growing up, I tried to help my twin, to be there for her, but it was hard. She always turned away from me, especially as an older teen when she finally moved back home to stay.

I tried to warn her against the guy she was dating—the guy she "stole" from me. I think she only set her sights on him to have something I wanted, since I'd had everything she desired when we were growing up. But this guy was not good. Certainly not good enough for my sister. But the more I tried to convince Rachel of this, the more she clung to him.

"We're getting married," she announced one day. "So, don't worry about it," she spat. "You can go back to being an only child." It hurt that she said that and felt that way.

Two months later, she married him. Right away, I could see he was hurting her—maybe not physically, but definitely mentally. Still, she stayed with him. Together, they moved to the other side of the country. Soon after, they had two children, and she finally seemed happy, really happy. Being a mom, she had little people to love—people who loved her back. And she got her nursing degree—more people to love.

Although her life with her husband was rocky and painful, it seemed she was doing well, so I loosened the worry-reins on my sister a little and gave a sigh of relief. That is, until I got a call from my dad telling me Rachel was in the hospital due to an overdose. When I flew to the hospital, I learned her husband had left Rachel months ago, but my twin had refused to tell me.

"I just didn't want you to know," she sobbed.

I took her in my arms and told her she could tell me anything. I would always, always, always be there for her. And I felt she believed me. I hoped so anyway.

I stayed at her house for as long as I could, watching out for my delicate twin and caring for her children. When I left, I worried I would never see her again. But it seemed silly. She'd had a moment of weakness, but she was back on her feet, back to living for her children.

"Call me if you need anything—anything," I said.

And she promised that she would.

A few months later, she called to ask me to watch her children while she had surgery on her small intestine.

"It's just minor surgery," she had said apologetically. "I wouldn't bother you, but you're kind of all I've got."

"Rachel, of course I'll come," I said. "I'm glad you called."

And I was glad, so glad. Glad she called, glad I could help.

The surgery was a success, but she had a heart attack during the night and died alone in the hospital.

Once again, I had failed her. All our lives, I had tried to be there for my twin. But she had died alone. I feared she died thinking that no one was ever there for her.

I was filled with deep despair... until the day her lawyer handed me a note that Rachel had written to me. She explained why she had made me the guardian of her two beautiful children: "Because you were always, always there for me—always."

~Michele Nichols

48

Miracle on the Mexico Border

All God's angels come to us disguised.
~James Russell Lowell

My twin sister and I were standing on opposite sides of the Father Kino statue in Nogales, Arizona, reading the inscriptions, when I heard a piercing scream. I hurried quickly to the other side and saw my twin lying on the ground. Her hand was grasping her heel, trying to cover a spurting stream of blood. "Call 911!" she cried out.

As I dialed the number on my cell phone, hundreds of thoughts flooded my mind. We are identical twins. We look alike, talk and think alike, even finish each other's sentences. We love being together. This was supposed to be a fun day of sightseeing and shopping. We had driven from my home in Northern California to Southern Arizona, where my twin was a volunteer for a senior ministry of her church. After several days of household chores as she moved into a rented townhouse, we were being tourists. We drove over the narrow country roads up to the mountains and then down the wide paved highway into Nogales. Since we were first-time visitors, we automatically exited at the blue Visitor Information sign. As we pulled into the driveway, we were disappointed that the Information Center was closed. Then we saw the statue across the driveway and uphill in a grassy surrounding. Since we were already there, we thought we would see the statue.

It seemed like an eternity, although it had been just seconds since my sister was injured. I couldn't reach the Arizona emergency system with either of our out-of-state cell phones. My twin was in pain and becoming frantic. "Never mind 911," she said. "Get me to a hospital. I am bleeding to death." What hospital and where?

I noticed a woman and two children sitting a short distance away in the grassy park. Maybe she could help. I'm a senior with rheumatoid arthritis. My standard pace is a slow walk, but I ran there with unexplained energy and agility. "Do you speak English?" I asked. She shook her head as she clutched her children closely. Fifty years previously, as a freshman in high school, I took one year of Spanish. I tried to remember some of the words. "Español?" I said. She nodded. I said, "Policía; hospital." She began to give directions in Spanish. Miraculously, I understood them as though she were speaking in English. I ran downhill to our car and grabbed some paper towels. I drove up close to the statue. My sister was hurt too badly to walk, and I couldn't lift her. How could I get her into the car?

Suddenly, a small red car with two occupants pulled into the Visitor Center driveway. The man appeared to be Spanish. He was heavyset with black hair and a mustache. The woman was blond and spoke softly. They spoke English! Yes, they would help me. The gentleman asked my sister's permission to lift her into the car. As soon as she was safely in the back seat and her foot wrapped in towels, I looked up to thank them. They had disappeared!

I drove toward the hospital, following the directions provided by the young Spanish woman. Suddenly, a sign announcing the Mexico border loomed into my vision. Had I misunderstood the directions? A quick stop at a small convenience store and a brief chat with an English-speaking clerk confirmed that the hospital was nearby.

The emergency room was filled to capacity. After what seemed to be a very long wait, a soft-spoken, sandy-haired doctor appeared. A few hours later, we were on the road back to the townhouse. Healing was painful and slow. A rusty sprinkler head hidden in the grass at the statue had severed an artery and come within a quarter-inch of severing the tendon in her heel. In just a few hours, on a beautiful day, life for us twins changed dramatically.

Who were the Spanish-speaking woman and the couple in the red car? Whether earthly or angelic, the Carr Twins thank you.

~Vi Parsons

49

Chicken Soup for the Soul

Twin Tryouts

The sudden disappointment of a hope leaves a scar which the ultimate fulfillment of that hope never entirely removes.

~Thomas Hardy

"Well, how did it...?" froze on my lips as I saw the devastated look on Sara's face.

Tara smiled wanly as she pulled open the screen door. Sara immediately rushed to the bathroom to blow her nose.

I mouthed, "What happened?" at Tara.

"I made it, Mom," whispered Tara, "but Sara didn't score high enough."

I couldn't believe it, and obviously neither could they. As Sara reappeared, Tara made the excuse of "a lot of homework" and rushed upstairs. I knew she was hurting for her sister. The happiness of her own success was ebbing away with this devastating news. Never had it occurred to her that she would be donning the green-and-gold uniform without Sara to share the marching band experience. Tara was confused, and so was I! What could I say to comfort my child when her dreams had crashed?

"You can try again next year. Think of all the things you'll learn while you watch Tara and all your friends this year."

"It's no big deal. You're good at lots of other things, and just think of all the extra time you'll have for your books."

"Perhaps it's a blessing in disguise. For once you won't just be 'TaraSarawhatever' and will finally have your own identity."

Or I could demand that "Beaker" (as all the kids called the new red-headed Band Director behind his back) take my matched pair of musicians, or else the lioness would be unleashed!

As I hugged Sara, she sobbed, "I don't know what happened. I did the best I could. Why wasn't it good enough? Why wasn't I good enough? Why is Tara always better than me?"

"Uhhhhhmmm," I stammered, and Sara dissolved into a puddle right there at the kitchen table.

Without my badgering, the girls had practiced their music daily for the past three years. For the final two weeks before marching band tryouts, their twittering scales had rung out, seemingly *ad infinitum*. They had been heel-toe marching around the backyard for hours on end, ramrod straight, chests out and hands glued to their hips.

"Sara, did you drop your flute, trip or something?" I asked.

"No! I did everything perfectly. I really, really did. Beaker even thinks Jodi is better than me," she sobbed.

I winced. Sara had always been seated at the top of the flute section and Jodi at the bottom—always.

She looked up as I passed the tissue box. "Why is Tara always better than me?"

"But you're good at so many things, Sara," I said trying to soothe her. "Look at your grades."

"But Tara's are better."

"Your music then."

"But Tara was picked for All-Regionals, and she got the solo in the last concert. Name one thing I'm better at than Tara, one—just one!"

I gasped in desperation as I came up with a big, fat zero. It was true. Tara always scored just a few aggravating points higher on tests. She was the one to win ribbons in competitions, be it writing, art, or swimming.

"See?" snapped Sara. She released my arm and flew upstairs to sob in her pillow.

Why was I making such a total hash of things today? I had read a lot about rearing twins, attended monthly Twin Club meetings and listened attentively to speakers at Convention. Twin "experts" in the 70s strongly advised treating twins as separate individuals, stating classrooms should be different, as should their clothing.

At age four-and-a-half, Tara, in a red dress, and Sara, in a blue dress, started kindergarten in an open classroom system but in separate classrooms. They adapted well, knowing that with just a little effort they could still see each other around the central column on the other side of the room. However, by the end of third grade, their teachers told us they would like them to enter fourth grade together. Tara was in a more challenging class, and to keep them separated would be a disservice to Sara. We happily agreed. Continuing to follow the recommendations of the "experts," we gave the girls options of differing hobbies and experiences, but they really enjoyed the same things. In different classes, they did make separate friends, but often the child would insist that both girls come over to play. Tara and Sara didn't really seem to want to be singletons; they genuinely wanted to be a matched set!

Sara's sobs echoed down the staircase as I bolted next door to beg my neighbor for insight. Charlotte had known the girls since we moved onto the hill when they were three. Surely she would have an objective view.

"Sara is more personable. She's got better social skills," Charlotte quickly said.

Unfortunately, that wasn't much more than I had to go on. Normally, I'm a quiet, easygoing person, but there was a lioness deep inside me, and she was growling now.

The last time the lioness had snarled was when Tara and Sara had both been tapped to be tested for the Gifted Child Program in the third grade. Tara, testing well, was accepted. Sara had become physically ill during the test, so tested poorly. My husband and I were in quite a quandary. We could growl and demand that Sara be retested or just wait until next year. After much deliberation, we decided to wait. Our rationale was that this would be a life lesson. Just because you want something doesn't mean you're going to get it, but if it is that important and you try really hard, it will happen.

To this day, I don't know if my husband and I made the correct decision. In retrospect, it did not hurt her psyche, and Sara has a strong personality today.

However, as a teenager, this was not the time for a follow-up life lesson. This was an ego-crushing blow that went too deep to be ignored. She needed equal time to shine, as I knew she could and should. "Beaker" was in the lioness's sights, and she was preparing to leap.

I could hear the phone ringing as I crossed back under the trees to our house. Tara answered it as I entered the kitchen.

"She made it! She made it!" resonated through the house.

"What?" I shouted from the kitchen.

"What?" echoed Sara as she tore open her bedroom door.

"Beaker apparently can't do math!" Tara blurted out as she galloped down the stairs, closely followed by her sister.

The lioness purred.

I grabbed my cubs in a tight group hug. "I knew it. I just knew it! You two are each great on your own, but together... look out, Beaker!"

Twenty years have passed since that climatic day. Both girls enjoyed singleton identities at their respective colleges and moved on to differing careers. However, as they did as small children, they sometimes switch to each other's path, weaving their lives into a rich fabric shared in a close twinship. My twins are different, yet very similar, and that's the way we know and love them.

~Rosemary Francis

50

Chicken Soup for the Soul

Blessings from a Hurricane

I am not afraid of storms for I am learning how to sail my ship.
~Louisa May Alcott

The year 2005 will forever be embedded in my heart and mind as a year of tragedy and triumph for me. On June 2nd, I joyfully suspected that I was pregnant, and I completed a home pregnancy test before work. Once I read the positive results, I was so blown away that I contacted a friend on her cell phone who was en route to work and asked her to come over to my home right away to confirm the very thing I knew I was seeing. Upon looking at the test, she said, "Yes, you are pregnant!"

Miraculously, I got an appointment to see my doctor that same day, and he confirmed that I was indeed four weeks pregnant. Somehow, I managed to keep my news to myself for the rest of the day, but when my husband walked in the door after work, I handed him a gift bag. He proceeded to empty the contents—a baby bottle and some baby spoons—and was speechless at first, but when the meaning of these gifts hit him, he instantly began to cry tears of joy. We then called our families to give them the happy news.

Then, the unthinkable happened... on June 29th. I thought that something was wrong with the baby, so I went alone to my doctor's office for an emergency ultrasound. I remember hearing my doctor question his nurse, "Do you see what I see?" But, mysteriously, his nurse was smiling. My doctor then turned to me and said, "You are not just having one baby. You are having two."

"Twins? Doctor, you are lying."

"No, you are having twins."

"Doc, I am about to faint."

"Well, faint while you are lying down!" he laughed.

What a way to begin parenthood.

I arrived home with the ultrasound photo of our two-ounce babies and couldn't wait to share the news with my husband. When I showed the picture to him, he looked at it in shock, but did manage to utter the word, "How?"

My pregnancy progressed beautifully until August 27th when the threat that Hurricane Katrina would hit my hometown of New Orleans became a reality. I was forced to evacuate my home and temporarily move to Baton Rouge, a town I knew nothing about. And as if that wasn't enough, I had to leave my husband behind because his job required him to stay. After I evacuated with my in-laws, I was certain that the hurricane would dissipate rather quickly so that I could return home. However, that was not the case. Once the hurricane passed, I finally came in contact with my husband, who informed me that his employer had evacuated him and his co-workers to Mobile, Alabama. Furthermore, he told me, the levees had broken, and our home was flooded along with a majority of the New Orleans area. All we had worked for, all of our belongings, all we had started to collect toward parenthood was gone. My husband told me he would join me in Baton Rouge in a couple of days, and we would figure out then what was best for us and our unborn children.

I never went to see my ruined home in person; I only saw the pictures my husband took once he made it into our dirty and mold-infested house. I felt helpless and devastated, and couldn't say goodbye to the memories that remained. Then reality hit: I would have to adjust to a new "normal," which would mean being uprooted from the safe haven we had started to build for ourselves and our children. Despite the tragedy, my husband and I were determined to forge ahead in order to build a new life for our babies.

Eventually, I found a new doctor in my adopted city to care for me and my unborn twins, and my husband and I participated in classes to prepare us for their birth. Unfortunately, though I tried to alleviate as much stress as I possibly could, my babies were delivered prematurely during the thirty-fourth week of pregnancy. They weighed only three pounds, seven ounces, and three pounds, fifteen ounces, but they were quite beautiful and healthy. They remained in the hospital for a bit of time in order to gain some weight.

Since the storm, we have moved five times (twice in Baton Rouge and three times back in the New Orleans metro area). At the same time, we have had the enormous task of dealing with insurance companies, contractors, roofers, plumbers, electricians and more in trying to put the pieces of our lives back together.

For the first year and five months of their lives, the twins became acquainted with apartment living and outgrew it rather quickly. But they were content as they didn't know anything about the day that changed their parents' plans forever.

Today, two years after the horrible storm that uprooted our family and turned our lives upside-down, I am back in my rebuilt home and loving parenthood. The twins are healthy and strong toddlers, still oblivious to the unusual beginning to their lives.

~Lynel Washington

51

Separate Ways

A sister is a gift to the heart, a friend to the spirit, a golden thread to the meaning of life.
~Isadora James

Betsy and I were always close in a way that I like to imagine is unique to identical twins. We don't have a secret language or a telepathic connection, but we grew up together, inch for inch. Our toddlerish mischief was always for two. In first grade, there was a magic show at our school, and the magician chose me as his audience volunteer. When I arrived on the stage, I whispered in his ear that I wanted my sister to come, too, so he pulled her up beside me. Later, my teacher punished me, but I was never sorry. We belonged together.

As we grew, we could feel forces pulling us in different directions. She went to a private high school; I went to public. We were together at home in the evenings and in our ballet class, where we giggled when the teacher's back was turned, but our lives had started to branch. Nobody knew me as one of "The Twins" anymore. We studied different subjects in school. The two of us began to make an effective team against our parents when we played Trivial Pursuit.

The true challenge came when we both began to think about college. As we visited schools, we realized that we would most likely be living under different roofs in the years to come. Our choices of potential schools overlapped, but we each had to make our own decision. We mailed off our applications and waited. Then Betsy made an announcement: She would choose a school, but defer admission for a year. She wanted to travel the world before settling down for four more years of classes. It sounded like fun. I was tempted to follow her lead, but I had been looking forward to college since seventh grade. I was going.

When the letters came, I chose immediately: I would go to Vassar. Betsy chose Oberlin and began to research travel programs. By high-school graduation, she had signed up for a group expedition to India. She would stay a few weeks with a family and then spend a month backpacking in the Himalayas. That summer, while I shopped for a computer and new sheets for my dorm room, she bought hiking boots and a backpack. I bought notebooks; she bought iodine tablets. I e-mailed my new roommate, and Betsy went to the doctor to get all the necessary shots.

My adventure started first. Betsy came to Vassar to help me settle in. I hugged her close when she left. I would see my parents soon, but when I came home for my fall break, Betsy would be gone. We had never been apart for longer than two weeks, and then we'd been able to talk on the phone. She left, and I thought, "This is it. Now we are separate." She'd be on her way in less than two weeks. I would get postcards and maybe an occasional e-mail. She called from the airport to say goodbye. I understood that it wasn't the morbid goodbye of someone not sure she'd return, but the goodbye of someone knowing that she would come back a changed woman.

She returned in one piece, but thinner and with longer hair. She nurtured a new passion for yoga and Buddhism, and was overwhelmed by the selection at the supermarkets. She had pictures and exciting stories. I wondered if she had made the better choice. She had a bit of contempt for me, I thought, with my nose in a book, unaware of what else was out there. But I had learned things that she hadn't—not just about James Joyce or how to use statistical tests, but about how to get along with people.

Another year passed, and things began to seem even more different. She went to Oberlin for her freshman year as I began my second year at Vassar. By some people's count, I was ahead. I was thriving, whereas Betsy was nervous and wanted to come home. She had managed India, but this was different.

Her misgivings proved founded. She did well in school, but things didn't feel right. She needed time to recover before attempting another semester. I stayed at Vassar while she spent a few months at home working in a nursery. I learned about the human brain and English poetry, and she learned about plants and managing her paychecks. I came home that summer ready to go back as a junior, and Betsy was deciding how to finish her freshman year. I wondered if the gap that was growing between us would ever be closed. I wasn't worried about the years that would separate our graduations, but rather about the worlds in which we lived. Had we begun to grow so far apart that I would never again feel the urge to break the rules and bring her close to me?

That summer, she worked during the days and took a night class. I'd been invited to join my cousins on a trip to Maine's Mount Katahdin. I agreed to take the trip as soon as I was invited, but quickly learned that it was a bigger undertaking than I had realized. Instead of the day hike I'd envisioned, we would camp on the mountain for two nights and would need gear: backpacks, clothing, dried food and heavy boots. I was not prepared.

Betsy came to my rescue, hauling out the equipment she had taken to India. The backpack was the perfect size for me. Her boots were already broken in for feet just like mine. She brought out clothes and her sleeping bag and offered them all to me. She had everything I needed.

As I packed, Betsy struggled with a paper for her English class; she knew what she wanted to say, but it wasn't coming together. She knocked gently on my door.

"Can you help me?" she asked. This was just what I'd been training for during the past two years. She listened and agreed with most of my suggestions. A few more hours, and the paper was all set. Betsy looked over at all her gear packed up for my trip and agreed that I, too, was ready.

A few days later, when she had submitted her paper and I was standing at the summit of the tallest mountain in Maine, I imagined that, for the first time in years, we were both thinking the same thing: What would I do without you?

~Amy P. Knight

Chapter 6

Twins and More

It's Triplets!

The great advantage of living in a large family is that early lesson of life's essential unfairness.

—Nancy Mitford

52

Against All Odds

I know God will not give me anything I can't handle.
I just wish that He didn't trust me so much.
~Mother Teresa

The whole family called on Aunt Clara in times of crisis. This time, when the summons came, she arrived prepared to lend moral support to the family and assist the doctor with what he expected would be a difficult home birth. Florence, my petite grandmother, had gained so much weight during her pregnancy that the doctor was concerned. When the long hard labor was over, Aunt Clara rushed out to break the news to my grandfather, pacing nervously in the parlor.

"Henry, what would you say if I told you that you had a baby daughter?"

Smiling broadly, he replied, "Wonderful, just wonderful!"

"Henry, what would you say if I told you that you had two baby daughters?"

Still struggling to smile while wiping a thin sheen of perspiration from his forehead, he replied, "Why, that's better yet!"

"Henry, what would you say if I told you that you had three baby daughters?"

His face ashen now, he stammered, "Why I… I'd say you were a liar!"

But it was no lie. On November 17, 1915, my grandmother gave birth to three healthy baby girls. Estanna, born first, had red hair and weighed in at seven pounds. Identical twins, Clara and Alice, both blond and blue-eyed, weighed four and four-and-a-half pounds respectively. From then on, they were known as Estanna and the twins. Perhaps due to her advantage as largest and eldest of the three, Estanna quickly established herself as "The Boss."

Two years before the birth of the triplets, Henry and Florence had lost a son at birth, not an unusual occurrence in 1913. At the beginning of the twentieth century, infancy and childhood were such fragile times that 100 to 165 out of every thousand children died before their first birthday. In addition, before the discovery of antibiotics or immunizations, serious childhood illnesses such as whooping cough, diphtheria, measles, and smallpox snuffed out the lives of many children who had managed to survive that first crucial year.

In 1915, triplets were rare. So the birth and survival of those three little girls in the tiny hamlet of Locke, New York, caused a sensation. Curiosity seekers arrived in droves to see the babies. To make life a little easier for herself, my resourceful grandmother displayed the triplets in their bassinets in front of the bay window in the living room. People swarmed onto her front porch to catch a glimpse of the new celebrities.

Characteristically conservative and cautious, Henry dealt with the shock of his suddenly expanded family by carefully weighing his options and considering how he could support them on a bookkeeper's salary. He immediately started a search and located a more lucrative position in a nearby city. He planned to move the family there as soon as he was settled, but had to temporarily leave Florence and the babies, only seeing them on weekends when he traveled home by train.

Somehow, after a full day of caring for the babies, my grandmother found the physical strength and the will to write my grandfather at night after the babies were asleep. Here is an excerpt from one of her letters, written in pencil on faded, yellow paper.

As the babes are all abed and asleep, I will take a few minutes and write to you, dear. I was ashamed to make such a "baby" of myself last night, but somehow realized this week the responsibility resting upon me when you are away. I know you are just as lonely or more so than I... Well, we washed today. We had eight lines outdoors full, besides the porch full and had to take down a few to hang up the last... We have entertained all the afternoon and there has been one steady stream of callers.

She ends by naming ten people who called that one afternoon and then, "Now, how is that? So goes Sunday and Monday—so goes the week!"

Although there were primitive washing machines on the market in 1915, it is doubtful my grandmother owned one. She almost certainly had to heat the wash water on a wood-burning stove and do the wash by hand. She then hung the laundry for the family and diapers for the three babies out to dry. In the winter, she would need to hang it throughout the house or on the porch.

No wash-and-wear fabrics then. No disposable diapers. Small hand-stitched cotton dresses for her three girls had to be ironed with large heavy flatirons heated on the stove. Not until 1929 would jars of strained baby foods become available. Any food preparation for the babies was done at home from foods grown in the backyard garden. No public-spirited corporations provided help for families with multiple births in those days.

After my grandfather settled into his new job, the family moved to the city, and celebrity followed the triplets. Alice remembers that everywhere they went, people lined them up in birth order to get a better look at them. Photographers vied with one another for the privilege of taking their pictures. One photographer passed out free pictures of the triplets at the county fair.

Eventually, Florence's parents sold their farm and moved to the city to help with the growing demands of toddlers. Her mother lent a hand with the endless chores and provided an extra lap to cuddle in for a bedtime story.

When the girls were teenagers, the Great Depression hit the

family hard, and my grandfather and great-grandfather, each contributing to the family income at the time, both lost their jobs. Grandma, in characteristic fashion, lost no time in self-pity, but found a job in the hospital laundry to help them through those difficult days.

In spite of growing up in the public eye, the triplets matured into self-reliant, productive adults. True to her independent personality, Estanna was the first to leave home. She and Clara, my mother, both married and had large families. Alice, however, followed a different path. She remained single, studied for the ministry and was ordained as a pastor long before it was a commonly accepted practice for a woman. Now eighty-nine years old, feisty and witty (she is said to have told her college friends that the reason she adjusted so well to college life was because she had two "wombmates" before she was born), and a favorite aunt to three generations of children, she is the sole survivor of the threesome.

Reading my grandmother's faded letters highlighted the drama of a story I had taken for granted. I hadn't given much thought to what life must have been like for her, struggling with three tiny babies, without any of the labor-saving devices we take for granted. I do know the extended family was a source of irreplaceable support for her while raising her girls. However, that the triplets beat the odds and grew to responsible adulthood, and that the family held together during those hard depression years, demonstrated for me my grandmother's uncommon strength, love and quiet determination.

But this gentle, self-effacing woman thought she had never done a single extraordinary thing in her life.

~Sally Kamerling

53

Cookie Cutters Are for Cookies

Most of us are like snowflakes trying to be like each other, yet knowing full well that no two snowflakes are ever identical.
~William E. Elliott

"He is such an easy baby because his mother was happy during her pregnancy."

"He was a fussy baby because his mother was tense when she was pregnant."

"She's such a shy child because her older brother is so overbearing."

Have you ever heard similar attempts to explain a child's personality? Environmental circumstances, such as birth order and parenting styles, certainly play a role in affecting behavior. But my triplets, although raised in the same environment, were born with very different personalities. Although we can do a lot to shape our children, we also need to recognize that they come to us not merely to be "molded," but to be "unfolded"—to bring out the best in each child's unique personality.

My two boys and a girl were born within minutes of each other. In the early years of their lives, they shared a bedroom, wore each others' clothes, ate the same food, came into contact with the same people, listened to the same stories and music, and breathed the same air. Because they happened to be part of a four-year medical study of premature babies, evaluations revealed they were also very similar in their physical and cognitive development.

Yet their personality differences delight and sometimes amaze us! While I strive to be consistent and fair, they each have different wants and needs that I take into consideration. I've learned that a "cookie-cutter" approach to raising kids doesn't work, and it isn't fair to my children to try to fit them into the same mold.

For instance, when my kids were four years old, they decorated gingerbread man cookies at Christmas time. Three pairs of little hands were washed. Three little aprons were tied around three excited "bakers." I divided the cookies equally and placed dishes of colored frosting, gumdrops, candy sprinkles, and M&Ms on the table, then gave them each three gingerbread men to decorate.

Fun-loving Bryce immediately began slathering frosting with wild abandon, cramming as many candies on his cookies as possible. This bothered Sarah Jean, who likes things more controlled. She began wailing, "Mommy, make him stop! He's using all the candy up. Stop him!" I quickly intervened, dividing the candies equally.

Meanwhile, thoughtful Blake hadn't yet begun his decorating.

"Blakey, how are you going to decorate your cookies?" I asked.

"I don't know yet," he said. Analytical by nature, he needed time to think about it.

"Blake," I said, "you can decorate them any way you want to. There's no right or wrong way to decorate cookies."

"Will you help me get the face right?" he asked.

"Honey, you can do it. There's no right or wrong way to decorate a cookie."

"But I want it right!" he insisted. So I guided his hand with mine, and we carefully made the eyes, nose, mouth, and hair.

"Now you decorate the body." And he did, with a single yellow M&M "button," perfectly centered on his gingerbread man.

"Don't you want to put anything more on your cookie?" I asked.

"No," he said. "I want to wipe my hands now so I can go play Legos."

"What about your other two cookies? Don't you want to decorate them?"

"Nope," he answered happily. "I like this one!" And off he scampered to his "work" of building with his Legos. After all, he had created his perfect cookie; to make any more would simply be redundant.

"I'll take his candy," Bryce immediately volunteered.

"No, Mommy!" Sarah Jean squawked. "Divide them!"

Three peas in a pod? Hardly.

My children have shown me that every child is a unique individual, a miracle that can't be duplicated. Each has been given a separate body, personality, and soul, divinely chosen. Each is a holy miracle of God.

~Cheryl Kirking

54

Peace on Earth

The best of all gifts around any Christmas tree:
the presence of a happy family all wrapped up in each other.
~Burton Hillis

"Peace on earth, good will to men" sang out from the stereo. I usually love Christmas carols, but peace on earth had absolutely nothing to do with me this Christmas. I hadn't felt any peace since August when I had heard the doctor say excitedly to me, "Donna, it's triplets!" My mouth had dropped open as I gazed at him with unbelieving eyes.

They were due in October, and suddenly we were catapulted into a frenzy, having only two months to get ready for three babies instead of the one we had thought was coming. We already had two children. Melissa was three-and-a-half and David was two. They had begun to understand, as much as very young children can, that soon a baby was supposed to emerge from Mommy's watermelon tummy and they would be a big sister and a big brother. How do you even begin to prepare them for three helpless infants? We went into panic mode.

"We need two more cribs, Randy. How will we ever fit three cribs into this ten-foot-by-ten-foot room?"

"Do you realize how many diapers we are going to need?"

"Can you breastfeed triplets?"

"Will we ever sleep again?"

October arrived along with three very healthy babies, two boys and a girl. Our lives became a whirlwind of activity, with feeding, bathing, feeding, diapering, feeding, consoling, feeding, crying (it was usually me doing the crying), feeding, tending, feeding, feeding and feeding. "I can get through the next minute without screaming," I would often tell myself as I heard one of the babies start to cry again. Somehow the days passed until it was December and time to think about getting ready for Christmas.

We had some wonderful Christmas traditions, our favorite being a family get-together on Christmas Eve with my parents and my sister and her family. How could I ever prepare for a family party with five children under the age of four? "Please put the tree up in the living room for me," I begged my husband as I sat each baby in a swing and one toddler temporarily on each end of a couch, as far away from each other as possible.

I'd get a few decorations on the tree before having to pluck a crying baby out of the swing. "Melissa, please don't throw the ornaments," I begged as I used my free hand to grab the back of David's shirt to keep him from climbing into the just-emptied baby swing. I wondered if a decorated tree was going to be impossible as I stood looking at the total confusion in the room. After a few moments of contemplation, I called to my husband. "Randy, set up the playpen. I've got a great idea!"

It looked quite strange to see a Christmas tree in a playpen, but it looked beautiful from outside. No one could tell just by driving by that our decorations were quite unusual. I don't remember where we hung the stockings. I gave up completely the idea of baking Christmas cookies. We didn't hang any lights outside, and I can't imagine how we ever got any presents purchased, let alone wrapped. The presents did fit nicely in the playpen, too, out of the reach of busy little hands.

I saw my family drive up on Christmas Eve and stuffed a few toys under the couch. It was pretty much chaos throughout the house as my sister's little girl joined our two little ones. "Santa's coming, Santa's coming," they chanted while running in circles around the room. One of the babies kept crying. I couldn't imagine what was wrong until I suddenly realized that I had fed his brother twice, and he had missed out on his dinner. Where was the peace that you hope for at Christmastime? I didn't think I would ever feel peace again.

We ate dinner, and as my mom got the kitchen cleaned up, we tried to corral the kids. "It's time to tell the Christmas story. Please quiet down! And stand still," I begged as I tried to use old towels to dress Melissa and David up as Mary and Joseph and my niece as a shepherd girl. I'm not sure which baby boy was the infant Jesus, but the other made a great sheep dressed in his snowsuit, and Melanie made a beautiful angel, dressed in her blessing dress. "Shhhh," I hushed the kids as Grandpa began to read from the Bible.

And then a miracle happened. The babies completely quieted down, and the older children turned all their attention to the quiet words and listened with rapt concentration to the beautiful story of the baby Jesus being born. As I looked around at all of the adults in the room, there were tears on everyone's cheeks. The spirit of Christ was in the room, and the peace I had wondered about earlier had arrived.

Most of that Christmas is still a blur, but I will always remember with great clarity the overwhelming calm I felt as I listened to the Christmas story that night and watched my beautiful children experience the feeling of the spirit of Christ in their hearts. I knew then that peace on earth was possible, for it was in my home that night.

~Donna Milligan Meadows

55

Potty-Training Times Three

Sisters is probably the most competitive relationship within the family, but once the sisters are grown, it becomes the strongest relationship.
~Margaret Mead

Armed with an apron, gloves and my trusty mop, I headed for the bathroom to potty train my two-and-a-half-year-old triplet girls. It started as it usually does: coaxing, encouraging, clapping hands, washing and scrubbing. Any progress at all was rewarded with a sticker on the hand. Slowly, but surely, Potty Training 101 was moving forward.

I was trying hard to be patient, but they were wearing me thin. I looked everywhere for help and advice. Several books on potty training did not cover training multiple children at the same time. The Internet, the local library, friends and other parents produced nothing.

Unprepared for the day, my worst nightmare arrived. There I was, coaxing and encouraging my three girls to go onto their individual potties, and then, suddenly, almost in synch, they all went on the floor. This was the last straw for me, since it had happened only eight times earlier that morning. Feeling discouraged, tired, in need of a pep talk and maybe a stiff drink, the doorbell rang. I had no idea that the pep talk and refreshing drink would come in the form of my neighborhood cable man.

Opening the door, covered in poo and smelling like pee, I was a scary sight.

"What's wrong?" the young man asked. He had come to fix a cable wire my dog had chewed up days earlier.

He looked calm as I tearfully shared my bathroom disasters of the morning.

He simply said, "Have you tried teaching them one at a time?"

"One at a time." The words resonated in my head over and over and were soothing to my ears. Finally, something made sense. And to think it came from the cable man!

"Actually, no," I admitted with shame.

From day one, I had done everything with the triplets together: naps, feedings, playtime, etc. It just always made sense to save time. It was easier, or so I thought. The thought of potty training one child at a time hadn't occurred to me.

Mr. Cable Man suggested this would create a sense of competition, and then perhaps the others would soon follow.

I had tried everything else. I had filled the girls up with lots of fluids to cue their bodies for training. I had bought them pretty panties as incentives and gave them each individual potties. I had even performed a little potty song and dance to make things fun. And, of course, there was always a trusty sticker on the hand for each try.

All great ideas, but none of them worked. Something was still missing. With nothing to lose, I decided to foster competition and begin with one-on-one training. Laila showed the most initiative, so I began with her.

The very next morning, after our routine of cereal with lots of milk, juice, watching our "Potty Time" video and having some playtime, the magical hour arrived. For us, that was usually 45 to 60 minutes after breakfast.

Taking Laila by the hand, I led her to the bathroom, and told my other two girls, Bailey and Kamali, "Mommy will be right back. Laila's going to the potty." They didn't show any interest at all. Laila was successful and received her reward—Mommy's special song and dance, and a bright, smiling sticker on her hand.

When my other girls saw the sticker, they wanted one, too, but I explained the stickers were for potty results only. This got the ball rolling, and before I knew it, a race was on.

Gradually, my other girls grew interested in what was going on with Laila and me. When their curiosity got the better of them, they came into the bathroom to investigate. First, they followed us each time Laila and I went to the bathroom. And then they each began sitting on their own potties. Pretty soon, the desired result was reached, and all three received a potty dance from me as well as stickers.

The cable man was right. What my girls needed was a sense of competition, a goal. For her sisters, Laila's success offered a visual difference of where they were and where they could be. Who knew that help would come from a newly married, young father of one, wearing a cable company uniform? But it did.

The technique of role modeling and competition happens naturally in pre-school settings or with older siblings around. For moms with toddlers close in age or for an at-home mom like me with triplets to train, it was a tremendously helpful tip and, at the very least, sanity-saving.

Laila led the way, and a few short weeks later, all three were potty trained. Stickers definitely helped. We still have accidents here and there, but I'm proud (and relieved) to say that I have retired my apron and mop.

~Patricia Hoff

"I'll bet potty training was a three-ring circus."

56

Re-Thinking Children

Making the decision to have a child is momentous.
It is to decide forever to have your heart go walking around
outside your body.
~Elizabeth Stone

I'll be honest... you would have hated the person I was six months ago. I was *that* woman. I chatted on my cell phone as I dashed through the supermarket, rolling my eyes and wondering why the little girl with the pigtails and pink puffy dress couldn't move any faster. I even avoided the under-six set at church.

Even *I* hated me.

The plain truth was that I didn't want to have kids. I wanted a high-powered career as a New York City magazine editor instead of a high-powered position as president of the PTA.

I wanted to be roused every Saturday by the morning sun sweeping through the nearby window and the smell of freshly brewed coffee, instead of being jolted awake by shrieks from the next room or the smell of a not-so-fresh diaper.

That's how I viewed motherhood. Not a very flattering portrait, was it?

All the sippy cup, Dr. Seuss, bubble bath fun?

Well, I'd just leave that to the Mommy Bunch.

I considered myself a Career Woman.

It wasn't that I grew up with horrible motherly role models. My childhood was quite the contrary, in fact. My mother threw herself into motherhood, raising my younger sister and me. Because our mother was a stay-at-home mom, the three of us spent our days rummaging through large piles of children's books at the library or sitting on the banks of the nearby lagoon feeding the ducks.

If anything, you'd think I'd want to be my mom, Part II. But one lap around my bedroom would reveal I'm nowhere close to filling her large shoes.

My bookshelves are lined with writing books, various anthologies and the *AP Stylebook*; my mother's shelves were lined with family health books and framed family photos. I keep cold cans of Coke in the fridge; she always had fresh juice boxes on hand, the plastic wrapper already removed from the straw, of course.

That all changed when I met Grayson, Matthew, and Christian.

After years of trying to conceive, my mother's coworker, Jessica, and her husband, Chad, gave birth to their three bundles of joy. I visited them in the NICU, all curled up under a blanket and the overhead heat lamp. For some reason, I felt an instant connection with each of them.

We continued to visit them every few months, first as content eight-month-olds, then as clap-happy ten-month-olds who could sit up.

Then one fall day in October, with orange and yellow leaves swirling in the front yard, my mom and I found ourselves on their doorstep.

There was Grayson, face and hands making homemade window clings on the front window. Jessica opened the door with one hand as she steadied Matthew on her hip with the other. Christian held tightly to her knee and buried his head in her jeans.

"Oh, I'm so sorry about the mess," chirped Jessica as we entered the living room.

Picture books dangled from the edge of the coffee table, a toy car had found its way smack dab in front of the fireplace, and small bags of Halloween treats lay strewn across the brown carpeting.

I'll admit I felt a bit out of place, almost as if I'd stepped into a room in which I didn't quite belong. A private club.

As I sat down a bit nervously, Grayson came over to the couch and proceeded to offer me his pacifier, not once, but twice. I declined, naturally, picked up the picture book that lay next to me, and the two of us sat down for a little reading and relaxing.

"What's that? A yummy pie," I said as he pointed to a colorful picture.

"Oh, that's a tri-angle," I said, neatly sounding out each syllable of the word.

Was I really using baby talk?

Over the next two hours, we (yes, me and three eighteen-month-olds) shared laughs, more books, strawberry Pez dispensed from a Jasmine dispenser (a big hit), and even shook and swiveled our hips to Shakira tunes.

As we were leaving, the fun continued with meal time.

I noticed that Jessica bore no resemblance whatsoever to the "typical" mother of triplets that I'd envisioned. Her hair was neatly combed. She didn't walk around the house carrying a million lists and a pencil tucked behind her ear. She even spoke in a calm and soothing tone. At all times.

And she never lost that spark in her eyes, that constant glow that comes from being a mother.

That's when it hit me: She was there, fully present and engaged, with her boys.

I may have entered that house a cynical, independent woman who had resigned herself to a life of spinsterhood, but I left a woman who, for the first time, could actually see herself with a baby in her right arm instead of a cell phone clasped to her ear.

I looked back to see all three boys throw their hands in the air and wave goodbye, a skill they'd just learned and proudly displayed.

I waved back.

"Thanks so much for coming," Jessica said as she walked us out. "Come again soon."

Thanks to Grayson, Matthew and Christian, I knew I would.

~Melissa Blake

57

Chicken Soup for the Soul

Triple the Joy

Love and pregnancy and riding on a camel cannot be hid.
~Arabic Proverb

"Wait... what's this? Let me see this again... There are three heartbeats..." the doctor reports in a confused tone.

"Three? What does that mean?" I ask, not comprehending his words.

"It means you have three fetuses... triplets," the doctor replies, his face scrunched up at the ultrasound machine.

"Check again," the nurse calls from behind him.

"I already did. There are definitely three heartbeats," the doctor says with finality.

Obviously, I hadn't totally comprehended the situation by the time I left the office. "I was prepared to love one. Now I'll just triple my love!" I said as I headed out the door.

I drove right to my husband's office. This was supposed to be a routine ultrasound, a follow-up after a positive blood test I had taken a few weeks before. Triplets? Was the doctor serious? I arrived at my husband's office and put the small black-and-white blurry copy of the ultrasound on his desk. He gazed at the doctor's notations of A, B, and C. He caught on quicker than I did and said, "Triplets?" He was out of his seat and hugging me before I could even respond. I will never forget his face. It displayed sheer joy and excitement. I, however, was quite worried and in a state of shock.

About three months earlier, I had undergone an induced labor after my baby's heart stopped beating in the second trimester. It was the most devastating time in my life. I was depressed and easily brought to tears most days. We had just found out from an autopsy and genetic analysis that the baby had Down syndrome. I was frightened at what could happen to these three babies.

Late one night while I lay in bed, my husband started to read to me from a book on multiple pregnancies. He got very animated and said, "You are not eating enough. It says here that by Week 24 you need to gain thirty-six pounds. Listen, this research shows..." I could hardly hear what he said after "you need to gain more weight." I listened to him read from the book and realized that what he was sharing was rooted in scientific research. All of a sudden, I started to cry. I was so upset that I was not doing what I was supposed to be doing for my three babies. Twenty-five weeks was coming up soon. Call it hormones, late-night fatigue or general guilt, but I could not stop crying. Seeing how upset I was, my husband put his arm around me and said, "Don't cry, honey, just eat!"

That book became my new bible, and I was its biggest disciple. I spoke to the author, who just happened to have moved to a teaching hospital in my town! She outlined a diet for me that was high in protein and fat, and absent of sweets, except ice cream. I was excited and eager to follow her guidelines. My diet changed dramatically. Snacks for me now included sausage sandwiches, strips of bacon, and handfuls of meatballs! My good friends sympathized with me and made meat in any form they could—meat pies, meatloaf, meat sauce. Finding a new recipe in which meat could be prepared was a challenge for the best of cooks! I was feeling so much better. With each bite I took, I knew I was feeding my babies and helping them grow big and strong.

My images of babies hooked up to feeding tubes in the NICU began to vanish. I was determined not to have tiny babies. The thought of leaving the hospital—and leaving my babies behind as so many parents of multiples do—was more than I could handle. I had read too many stories about babies' long stays in the NICU and incredibly small birth weights. This was not in my game plan. These babies were coming home with me, healthy and hearty.

While I was eating high-fat foods every few hours, people at work would say, "Any excuse to eat!" and start laughing at me. If a pizza was being ordered, an extra one was ordered for me and would arrive at my office unsolicited.

At a routine ultrasound around the fourth month, the perinatologist found a marker for Down syndrome on Baby B. "This can't be happening," I cried. The doctor rambled on about all the options, but all I could hear was "Down syndrome." I was sick with worry. Not again, I thought. Can lightning really strike the same person twice? Sure, I knew the "odds" from reading, but I just did not think this was possible. My husband and I went home, depressed and shell-shocked. We talked to a lot of people about the situation. In the end, we both believed that Baby B was going to be healthy; these results were just a misreading.

At exactly thirty-four weeks, my doctor and I decided to schedule a birthday for the babies. On the big day, as I lay on the operating table waiting for my three bundles of joy, I was hopeful but still so nervous. There was roll call in the operating room, and it seemed like a hundred people were there, along with lots of equipment. It was scary, but also so exciting. All these people were there to help my babies get into the world! The anesthesiologist was at my head. I had met him only a few minutes earlier when he gave me my epidural. I thought he was friendly, nice and relaxed—an easygoing guy, just what I needed.

When Baby A was delivered, I heard him say, "Wow, that's a big baby!" He sounded so surprised, and it made me feel good. I knew he had seen a lot of babies and was a good judge of size. Then the next baby came out. Again he said, "Another big one!" Finally, as the third baby was delivered (and she was not eager to leave her coveted spot), I heard him rise from his seat, as if at a baseball game, and shout, "Another big one!" There was a lot of commotion and movement, and it seemed like an eternity until one of my babies was brought up to my face. They all looked good to me, but it happened so quickly that I could not really see what was going on.

Next, I was stitched up, and the OR slowly became a ghost town. Finally, I was taken to a recovery room, while my husband went with the nurses and babies. When he came to my side after what seemed like an eternity (but was really only ten minutes), he came in with a piece of paper. His face was elated! He read the babies' weights as if reading off the winning lottery numbers—Baby A: 6 pounds, 6 ounces; Baby B: 6 pounds, 11 ounces; Baby C: 5 pounds, 7 ounces. Every baby was healthy and perfect!

As I lay in my bed, I smiled and cried with joy. My dream had come true: We were all going home together!

~Maureen Kenny Winick, Ph.D.

58

The Triplet Who Was Raised by Wolves

Friends and family can set us right and help guide us back to the light.
~Sera Christann

I grew up as an only child without any siblings, but a few months into my freshman year of college, I became a pseudo-multiple. I was jokingly renamed "the triplet who was raised by wolves."

Coming into my freshman year, I was looking forward to the college experience because I had academic and athletic goals to pursue. I moved into the dorms the Saturday before classes began, but I never expected to meet people right off the bat who would impact the rest of my life. The charismatic identical twins, Dave and Adam, were friendly and engaged in what I had to say from the very first night. I was very impressed with them from that point on, but I didn't realize how special these characters were to the rest of the world until a few nights later.

During a freshman orientation party at the student union, I was sitting with a bunch of people from my high school. Adam saw me sitting at the table, and he offered a pleasant greeting and a few witty comments. Then he went on his way. As the conversation at the table progressed, I let the group know that Adam had an identical twin brother named Dave.

One of the girls from my high school enthusiastically asked for clarification. "Wait! There's two of him?" That was the first time I ever saw someone react to the boys like that, but I've seen it replicated time and time again.

At first, I did not fully open up to the boys, but I watched with amazement from afar at the way they joked around with one another and found a way to have fun with life's simplest tasks. My feelings were probably similar to how an adopted child feels when he or she is thrust into a new family situation.

It took about three months for our bond to truly grow, but that was my fault. My insecurity from high school reared its head in the early days of college. Even though the boys were nothing but friendly to me, I always assumed I was flying close to the sun, and my wings would melt. Adam and Dave would grow tired of me and want nothing to do with me.

I was acting like a little brother who assumed that his big brother would give him a beating if he did or said one thing out of place. However, brothers can surprise you and show you nothing but love. The boys slowly invited me into the world that they had been creating for the past eighteen years.

A great example of this is how I would position myself partially in the hallway and partially in the boys' room when I would come by their room to say hello. After several weeks, Dave caught on to my technique and the implied insecurity that went along with it, and he would enthusiastically invite me to come deeper into the room. Just like a newfound brother, I became the recipient of unexpected love in an unexpected way.

As my relationship with Dave and Adam grew, I received a 360-degree view of what it is like to have siblings. From the practical joke of hiding unwanted objects in my room, to a roughhousing game called pink bellies, I loved it all and ate it up. We even came up with an elaborate story that we thought would be a hit among naïve bar patrons. The story involved a plane crash, a stranded toddler and a jungle with a loving pack of wolves. Adam, Dave and Chris grew up as triplets, not realizing until they were older that Chris was adopted. Even though we talked about telling our Tarzan spinoff to some unknowing stranger many times, we never went through with it.

Many people commented to Dave and Adam that they thought the boys were mean to me. These people assumed I was made of glass because I use a wheelchair to get around, but these critics didn't understand the gift I was being given. During my late teens, I gained something that I didn't even realize I was missing: brotherly love.

If you have a sibling who is lacking in some way, the true gift is to treat him just like everybody else because you need to prepare him for the vast world that awaits him. That is exactly what Adam and Dave did when they embraced me as a brother. They did a great job of showing me the brotherly ropes. They made me tougher, which also allowed me to widen my view of the world.

For several years now, I have joked with Dave and Adam that they are womb mates. I understand that multiples have a bond that is nearly impossible to replicate, but my bond with the boys is still something I will be thankful for every day for the rest of my life.

Now, years later, the beautiful thing about my relationship with Dave and Adam is that even though many of our hobbies are different, we don't work together, and I don't even live within 500 miles of them, our bond is still as strong as ever. Just like family.

~Chris Rathje

59

Hi Ho, Hi Ho, It's off to Work I Go

The supreme accomplishment is to blur the line between work and play.
~Arnold Toynbee

It was 11:00 on a Monday morning. As I walked through the kitchen, I heard a car door slam. This surely could not have been my husband, who had only left for work a few hours ago. He had been hard at work at his new job of four months. I was home, trying to decide if I should go back to work, while our new triplet babies slept peacefully.

Months earlier, we had returned from living in Africa as missionaries. We resigned sadly after eight years living there when I found out I was pregnant with triplets. The medical demands of a high-risk pregnancy and an injured back led us to reluctantly decide to come back to our native New York.

Starting over would prove to be difficult. It would mean coming back to an unfamiliar, competitive workforce, having to adjust to the change in climate, saying goodbye to friends who had become family, and leaving a country we had called home.

Just then, the door opened. It was my husband, standing in the doorway, looking grim.

"Hi, honey," I said. "What are you doing home so early? I thought I had heard a car door."

"I got laid off," was the response.

"What?"

"I got laid off."

I sat there, dumbfounded. He then proceeded to tell me the whole story leading up to him losing his job—a job we waited so long for him to get.

This could not be right. He had been looking for a job for eight, long, anxious months. He was a hard worker, and we needed the money. We knew when we returned to the United States that it would mean him, not me, working. After all, who in their right mind would take the risk of hiring a pregnant woman who was carrying triplets? My husband knew it all depended on him.

It would mean an uphill battle. The unemployment rate in New York was very high. New York was expensive, and the triplets doubled our family size. We also had a three-year-old daughter.

After searching high and low for a job, we were thrilled at the thought of my husband getting a permanent position at a nationwide, well-known company. Who knew this thrill would be short-lived?

Laid off? The words resonated through my head again and again. At that moment, everything stopped. My husband was the breadwinner, making good money, and had six of us to support. This wasn't supposed to happen. We were supposed to live happily ever after, or so I thought. What were we going to do now?

Just then, something in me snapped. What were we going to do now? I was going to work and work hard. This plane was not going down. Not on my watch. What was wrong with me pitching in and helping out a little to bring in some much-needed income? I could work around the girls' feeding schedule. Besides, I had just received my real estate license and was deciding whether or not I should work. For me, real estate offered a flexible schedule, and this could be the opportunity for which I was waiting.

After discussing this with my husband, I decided to get focused and get to work. He was all for it. Besides, we needed the income and had nothing to lose. He could watch the kids and look for work while I was out. Everything began to come together. I gained the confidence I needed to begin my quest to make a living as a nursing mother of four.

Being goal-oriented, I made a decision to sell as much real estate as I could. I would have to work around the triplets' feeding schedule. My plan of making endless phone calls, handing out flyers and searching the Internet for properties began.

My day began with breastfeeding the triplets at 5:00 A.M., getting ready for work by 6:30, getting our older daughter ready for preschool, dropping her off, breastfeeding the triplets again and then heading out the door for work. My husband and parents watched the triplets while I worked. They were only three months old and were feeding every four hours. When I left for work, I knew I only had four hours to get back home so I could feed them again.

At work, every moment counted. I would get in, hit the phone, greet clients, have appointments, and eat at my desk. All this, while trying to get as much done as possible.

My much younger, single, childless co-workers often came into work late, strolling in, chatting at the water cooler and checking their e-mail for hours. They thought it strange that I was there, a new mother and all. Several of them disagreed with my decision to be there. Four children under the age of four! Many of them would ask me what I was doing there. Sometimes, I would ask myself the same question. Their looks of disapproval always greeted me at the door. At times, their comments would eat away at me. What was I doing there? Shouldn't I be home with my girls? Was I missing out on something by being at work? But in my heart I knew this was my only option for work, and a good chance for making the income my family so desperately needed.

A few short weeks later, my hard work paid off. The following three months were my most financially successful ever. I sold four properties in four weeks. My co-workers were astonished, my manager was proud, and I was, again, dumbfounded—but this time at me, not my husband. I guess where there's a will, there is a way. And, sometimes, a woman must make her own way.

When my manager gave me my first check, there were so many zeros I couldn't count them because my eyes were full of tears. I had never seen a check of that amount next to my name. I photocopied the check to save the moment.

That amount would be increased over the next few months as I made more money in that time frame than the average American made in a year. My greatest accomplishment was being awarded the "Salesperson of the Month" award for bringing in the most money in sales of any other salesperson—including my younger, single counterparts as they watched in amazement. My husband was most proud.

Two months later, I had made enough money for us to buy a small house on Long Island, something I never thought I'd have. On our first night living in our new home, after tucking my girls into bed, the first thing I hung up on my wall was, you guessed it, my Salesperson of the Month award.

~Patricia Hoff

60

Chicken Soup for the Soul

Triple Trouble

Each patient ought to feel somewhat the better after the physician's visit, irrespective of the nature of the illness.
~Warfield Theobald Longcope

It was the end of a busy morning. I had ministered to children with mundane colds and serious bacterial infections, including a toddler I had to admit to the hospital with bacterial meningitis. I was looking forward to a lunchtime respite where I could just sit down and close my eyes for a half-hour. I shut off my office light, put my feet on the desk, and leaned back in the chair. It couldn't have been more than thirty seconds when the intercom came to life. "Dr. W, Mrs. Jamison just came in with Scott, one of the triplets. He has a nasty cut on his forehead. What would you like to do?"

What I wanted to do was rest, but I realized this wasn't meant to be. "Why don't you put him in one of the examining rooms? I'll be out in a minute."

I went to the bathroom and splashed cold water on my face before going to see Scott. When I entered the room, I stared at him. His brown freckled face was spattered with red blood. A bandage covered most of his forehead. I removed it and applied pressure to the two-inch, horizontal laceration. "What happened?" I asked.

"He ran into a metal basketball pole," his mother, Janis, answered.

"That's using your head, Scott," I said. "Just kidding. Maybe you can find better ways to use it."

"Is it bad, Dr. W?" he said.

"You'll need a few stitches, but you'll be as good as new."

"Will it hurt?"

"It won't hurt me, and you only a little." He returned my smile. "I'll have to give you a little pinch with a small needle in the cut to numb the area. Then you won't feel anything."

As I injected and sewed, I kept up a running banter to distract him. As his family was originally from Texas, he was a rabid Houston Astros fan.

"My Marlins are going to sweep this weekend series," I told him. "The Astros don't have a chance."

"Won't happen, Dr. W."

"We'll see."

When I finished, I gave Janis instructions for care of the wound. She wiped a tear from her eye and thanked me. I was glad she had brought Scott in and her husband hadn't. Many fathers profess machismo, but pass out when they watch me sew up their child. I never had a mother do this. Cry, yes, but pass out, never.

"Bring him back in a week, and we'll take out the stitches. This is just one of the rites of passage that boys go through. Since the cut is horizontal with the grain, scarring will be minimal."

On the way out, I high-fived Scott. "Let me know how the Houston series turns out."

He smiled. "I'll let you know right now. The Astros will take three."

He left the office with his mother's arm wrapped around his shoulder. I wanted to go back to my office to finish my respite, but by then the waiting room had filled, signaling the start of my afternoon hours.

The following week, Scott returned to the office to have the stitches removed. The wound had healed well. I put the stitches in a fresh piece of gauze and handed it to him. "Put this under your pillow and see what the stitch fairy brings you."

"I'm too old for that kind of bull, Dr. W."

I smiled. "Then put them in your scrapbook. And do me a favor: don't fight with basketball poles anymore. They'll always win."

He smiled. "By the way, Dr. W, I told you the Astros would take three."

I shrugged. "Just lucky. We'll get them next time."

That afternoon was particularly busy. All my examining rooms were full, and the waiting room was packed. As I finished in one room, the intercom buzzed. "Dr. W, Mrs. Jamison's back with Steven, another one of the triplets. He hit the same basketball pole and has a cut on his forehead."

"Send them back to room four," I said. "I'll be with them in a minute."

When I looked at Steven, it was déjà vu. He had the same brown freckled face speckled with red blood, and the same size horizontal laceration. "Hey, I know you and your brothers are close, but you didn't have to copy this."

Janis had a look on her face telling me she had become used to these shenanigans. This time, she had no tears. "You know the drill," I said to her. "Same as last time." Then I explained to Steven what would transpire.

"I know all about it, Dr. W. Scott told me. He also told me to give you the needles about the Marlins and Astros."

Steven was more stoical than Scott, perhaps because he had already lived it vicariously through his brother. I wondered if he viewed it as a badge of honor or a rite of passage as I had, or if he just couldn't let his brother get one up on him.

When I finished, I gave them the same instructions to care for the wound, and told them to come back in a week to have the stitches removed.

On the way out, Steven elevated his hand and we high-fived. "Thanks, Dr. W."

I guess he could be so glib because now his brother Scott would have nothing to laud over him. I wondered about the third triplet, Shane.

One week later, Steven and Janis returned. I removed the stitches, revealing a well-healed wound. I went through the same shtick about the stitch fairy and a scrapbook, with an identical response from Steven.

As they were leaving, I looked at Janis. "Maybe we should just make an appointment for Shane this afternoon."

We both smiled. "Don't even think it," she said.

I nodded, and wondered if my smart-aleck quip would be just that, or if it would have some basis in reality.

That afternoon wasn't busy. I was grateful that I had time to give each patient the attention they deserved, and that I didn't have to make short shrift of some of the visits in order to reasonably adhere to my schedule.

Again, as I was leaving an exam room, the intercom blared. "Dr. W, Mrs. Jamison's here with Shane."

"A cut?" I asked.

"No, he's holding his left arm. He banged it into the same basketball pole."

"Send them back to my office, please."

When I walked into the room, Janis glowered at me. "You jinxed us." Then she smiled.

I returned her smile. "Let's have a look."

I felt all over, and when I touched one spot on the lower arm, he winced. "Ow, that hurts."

"You don't seem too upset," I said. "Couldn't let your brothers go one up on you, could you?"

He shrugged and then smiled, all the while holding his arm.

"Let's get an X-ray to see if it's broken."

The film revealed a hairline crack. I splinted the arm and made arrangements for Shane to see an orthopedist to have a cast placed. "It will only cover up to the elbow and will heal fine," I said.

Shane smiled, but it was interrupted intermittently with a grimace. "Will I be able to keep the cast?"

I nodded.

"I'll need a big scrapbook to put it in. Will you sign it for me?"

"You bet."

As they left the office, I thought about the Spearmint gum commercial, where twins sing out about "double your pleasure, double your fun." It seemed that, with these eight-year-old hellions, it was "triple your trouble, triple your tribulations."

~Paul Winick, M.D.

Stephanie ©2008
"Show off!"

Chapter 7

Twins and More

Grandparenting Twins

Grandparents are God's gifts to children.

~Bill Cosby

61

Chicken Soup for the Soul

Grandpa's Necklaces

To me, every hour of the light and dark is a miracle.
Every cubic inch of space is a miracle.
~Walt Whitman

When my husband and I adopted five-year-old identical twin girls from Korea, my father worried how he would ever be able to tell his new granddaughters apart. On the day my dad first met them, he beamed his welcome by picking up the girls and holding one in each arm, his smile as wide as a rainbow. His adoration was clear, but it would take a miracle, he fretted that day, for him to recognize which girl was which.

That miracle came by way of hand-tooled metal. My dad built gas meters for a power company as his living. He was a man of action and few words. His motto was that if miracles didn't fall into your lap on their own, you simply searched them out for yourself. He was forever tinkering, but when he approached me with necklaces he'd made for the twins out of metal scraps from his garage, I was hesitant. How would this go over with little girls who were entranced by what their two older brothers called "all that weird girlie stuff"? The twins marveled at lace and wedding gowns. They loved all things pink. Grandpa's necklaces, dare I say, were way less than dainty. But he was so proud of them—how he'd looped the chains just so, how he'd carved each girl's name on the nameplate with precision—that I just couldn't spoil his surprise.

I should have trusted that, while my girls were in the process of learning English, which left their communication skills limited, they certainly knew the ways of the heart. When Grandpa gave them his gifts, they were wide-eyed and full of appreciative smiles. With my help, the right necklace went to the right girl, and they wore them dutifully. The necklaces even became quasi-teaching tools, aiding them in learning to spell their given English names. All was well... until the day they discovered the joy of playing pranks.

Grandpa, of course, was one of their first casualties. On the instance of that initial prank played on him, my dad greeted each girl by name, only to be met by a duet of funny giggles. It didn't take long for us to realize that the girls had switched necklaces, thereby thwarting my dad's "miraculous" solution to his little identification problem. As time went on, swapping necklaces turned into a favorite game.

Other games were also played through the years. The girls devised an intricate system of hand signals that kept their brothers guessing. They sometimes traded beds before my husband and I tucked them in at night. Later, they worked at the same restaurant and confounded customers when one girl would disappear, only to magically reappear within seconds.

My mother-in-law also experienced the unique nuances of our identical twins. My girls are quite artistic, and my mother-in-law, a fine painter herself, decided to teach them some of her painting techniques. Using oil on canvas, the twins painted a mountain scene, but try as they might, their pictures looked so similar that they could have been the exact same portrait. Those paintings hang where I can see them every morning, and one day, as I studied them, the inherent truth of them touched me. There are definite, subtle differences in the pieces my girls created. You have to look closely and beneath the surface, but there are distinctions in color, texture and dimension that you don't visibly notice at first glance. Just like with my girls.

My dad learned this lesson for himself, I think. Over the years, he began to perceive the mystery of his granddaughters' connection, a mystery that often defies complete understanding. He started to distinguish between the girls by appreciating their subtle differences, of which he grew very fond.

My dad passed away a few years ago, but we still feel his presence every day, and on no day was he felt more poignantly than the day of his funeral. My twins were driving the four-hour trip alone to the town where my parents lived and where the funeral was to take place. My husband and I, our two sons and their girlfriends had already arrived the day before, but because of work commitments, my girls were coming by themselves early the morning of the funeral. To our great dismay, they had a flat tire while traveling on the interstate, which threw their schedule off by hours—and threw us into a panic. This was their first extended trip alone, and our imaginations went wild.

Somehow, though, during that long wait, a calmness came over me. I will always believe that it was my dad, whispering on the wind, telling me that everything would be okay. He was looking out for my girls from his shelter far beyond. Even these four years later, I still think about it. "Couldn't you feel something that day?" I asked one of my girls over lunch not long ago, wanting to hear confirmation of some wondrous happening. "Grandpa's presence? A miracle in the making?"

She gazed at me, eyebrows high. "It's a miracle we got there at all, Mom."

Not quite the answer I'd wanted.

Days later, I went to her sister, ten minutes younger than her twin and therefore my baby, and posed the same question, again awaiting something spectacular. But my younger daughter, much more droll than her sister, only shook her head and gave me her own little smirk. "Dunno, Mom. I was asleep and you-know-who was driving. It's a miracle we got there at all."

I guess that says it, really, about the nature of "twinship."

I was looking for something mystical—clouds lining up in formation, a Good Samaritan with my father's eyes—but my twins, connected as always, each told me a variation of the same thing, albeit it ran along the lines of "Keep it simple, stupid."

And maybe that in itself is pretty miraculous. Maybe my girls have hit upon something. Maybe the miracles we seek in life aren't always the big, drop-your-heart-to-your-stomach kind of things, though there are also those, I know. But maybe your basic, everyday miracle is just as magnificent, too. The simple adventure of a road trip with your sister, the fight-or-flight response of parents worrying about their young, the generosity of a grandmother who shared her time and art with two small apprentices. Or the love of a grandfather who wanted so desperately to know his granddaughters that he fashioned necklaces for them out of metal, and still watches over them from somewhere within the vastness of God's cosmos, his smile as wide as a rainbow.

~Theresa Sanders

62

The Many Colors of Paradise

Perfection is achieved, not when there is nothing more to add, but when there is nothing left to take away.
~Antoine de Saint-Exupéry

I came to Sacile, Italy, for the birth of my twin grandsons, whose mother was stationed nearby with the U.S. Army. I had been in Italy for many weeks, but during the last month of my daughter's pregnancy, we journeyed to Sacile to be around the corner from the hospital, which was attached to Aviano Air Force Base.

During this time of happy anticipation, we explored this exquisite town under a microscope, leaving no stone unturned, no shop or street uninvestigated. We sampled local cuisine with continued culinary expectation, knowing that each meal would be more flavorful than the last. We savored the cobblestone walk to the hospital, crossing over the Livenza River whose banks exploded with the delicious colors of early summer. Gardens were just beginning to come into full bloom; begonias and petunias filled brightly colored window boxes to the bursting. It was a fairy-tale time in which to partake of an extended dream. As I stopped by the local gelato stand each evening, I could not quite fathom the happiness I was experiencing. Living in Italy, the home of my ancestors—albeit a more northern exposure—while awaiting two precious grandsons, was nothing less than magical.

But a storm was brewing on the horizon above the snowcapped Dolomites, least expected and devastatingly brutal.

The babies were growing bigger, nearly full-term, and making my daughter quite uncomfortable. A C-section was planned in a few days, and we immediately realized that now the practical implications of our exile were coming to fruition. Our plans for the remainder of the summer now revolved around babies, babies, babies! Our excitement had reached its peak as the unknown storm continued to travel in our direction.

Four days before the planned delivery, my daughter experienced some difficulty, and we immediately walked the short block from our lodgings to the hospital. Along the way, the mood was somber; somehow this walk was quite different from all the rest. We did not notice the sunshine or the begonias. We spoke little, afraid to vocalize our emotions. However, hope accompanied us on that day for a successful outcome.

But hope only afforded us half a joyous consequence. One twin chose to be born in Sacile that day, while the other chose to stay, never to join his brother in worldly pursuits.

How could a perfect stay in paradise be so divided emotionally? How could two perfect little boys be separated in such idyllic surroundings?

I learned much about perfection that day in Sacile. Perfection, like paradise with its "Garden of Eden," can be taken from us in an instant. Storms can come and wash away that which we thought was permanent, that which we thought was indestructible. It was not unlike the river Livenza, whose banks sometimes overflowed and re-arranged the landscape, scattering the mother ducks and her ducklings to different, unfamiliar locations.

The hope, however, that we felt that day as we walked the cobblestone street to the hospital has re-invented itself. Our sadness will never be completely overshadowed, but our joy in our grandson reaffirms our belief that time has its way of bringing understanding to the most illogical of events.

New growth has once again colored the landscape in Sacile and lovingly sprouted in the precious three-year-old whose birthplace will always conjure up instant recollections of a town whose people took us to their hearts in our grief, and left us with visions of window boxes bursting with begonias on a lovely summer day.

~Norma McCulliss

63

The Stone Collector

Trees and stones will teach you that which you can never learn from masters.
~St. Bernard

Once upon a time, not so long ago, a kindly lady lived in a cottage in the woods with her husband, who acted crabby but had a good heart. Unlike old couples in fairy tales, they were not little nor all that old, even though their sons were grown, had moved away, and had found terrific women to marry.

The couple wished for grandchildren. They pictured little ones running in great circles in their cottage, laughing with pleasure. If only they had grandchildren, they thought, life would be perfect.

The lady, especially, loved children. Weekdays, she traveled downhill from her home into the valley to teach at the local school. She loved her students and her job. The school was like a big family. The staff shared the good and bad that life offered. They grew older together and shared news from their lives. The kindly teacher smiled and hugged her friends as they became grandmothers, and each time she yearned ever more to be a grandmother herself.

Luckily, for one must have interests to keep life worth living, the lady loved stones. Every year she traveled on vacation and collected smooth or sparkling stones from the ocean shore, riverbanks, lakes, deserts or mountain paths. She loved stones so much that she even mailed them home so she wouldn't have to carry them on the airplane. Her friends teased her about mailing rocks, but she smiled and shipped her stones home all the same.

As the years passed, the lady's stone collection grew. She stacked them in small piles in her garden. She set them out in beautiful patterns on her screened porch sills. She remembered the places visited as she dusted her stones and swept away the cobwebs. Her stone collection brought her joy, but still something was missing. Her stones didn't dance or run in circles or hug her.

The lady wished even harder for the gift of grandchildren. She hinted to her family. Sorry. They did not want children now. In fact, they would never have children. She wondered why. Had she been a bad mother? Her students loved her. She loved them. What was the problem?

Some things do not change. The years passed. The kindly teacher grew older. One year, a lifelong dream came true. She traveled to Japan. What amazing places she saw, and what beautiful stones! She had only one suitcase, so she collected only small stones for herself and her sister. One pair was picked up on a golden afternoon when the sun lit the grounds of an ancient samurai castle on the shores of Lake Biwa. The other pair came from a most sacred Shinto shrine in Kyoto, while the rain poured in sheets down the bright orange *torii*. As the lady bent down to pick up two tiny stones from the path, a red umbrella shielded her from the storm and gave an apricot glow to the stones in her hand.

Back at her hotel, the lady carefully packed the small stones in her luggage in a zippered pouch. Of all the souvenirs of her trip, these stones would stay with her longest and have the place of honor in her collection.

When she got home, she unpacked her suitcase but had to leave on another trip in two days, so it wasn't until months later, when she saw her sister, that she remembered the stones. "Oh, I collected two stones for you. But where are they?" She knew she had packed them carefully. She double-checked her stored luggage, but there were no stones. She was so disappointed.

The lady told the story to her son and his wife. They were sorry to hear she had no stones from Japan, but they had some news to cheer her up. They had had a change of heart. They had decided to have a baby! The kindly lady waved her arms, cheered, and hugged her daughter-in-law and son. When the excitement died down, they added, "And it's twins!"

It was then that the kindly lady remembered the Japanese tales she had read to her students before she left for Japan. Some tales told of childless couples finding tiny children in ordinary objects, like cabbages or flowers. In one famous tale, Momotaro, a brave prince, emerged from a peach to brighten the life of a little old couple.

Of course! The missing stones from Japan could have been transformed into her granddaughters. When her sister heard the enchanting news, she rejoiced that her set of twin stones may have served this good cause.

To this day, the kindly lady and her sometimes-crabby husband are much happier. Now they are old, but are still not little. Their twin granddaughters—surely a gift of the stones—are not tiny anymore, but they alone can make the tall man smile. The stone collector, retired from teaching, stays full of joy. When she dusts her stone collection, she always tends to the small space of honor she made for her not-at-all-missing Japanese stones.

~Carol Tremper

64

Mister Golden Pa

Great fathers get promoted to grandfathers.
~Author Unknown

"I can't do this anymore!" I shouted, and crumpled up into a ball on the floor of my office and cried. Three years ago, I told my husband I wanted a divorce. Saying those words to him was traumatic enough, but it was even worse having to tell our children. My twin girls were three and not quite old enough to understand what was really going on. When I explained the situation, they simply thought Daddy was leaving for the night. It wasn't detrimental news to them. My five-year-old son, however, was much different. He sat at the table and cried along with us. He knew Daddy was moving out, but he couldn't begin to understand why. Even after three years, he still asks some pretty tough questions, but he understands completely that it is not his fault.

At the time, I wondered how I was going to manage alone. It just didn't seem possible, but I had to make it work. I was about to change the course of everyone's life. Fortunately, I had my parents every step of the way. If I hadn't, then it's conceivable that the kids and I would have been living in a cardboard box somewhere. My parents never once saw helping me raise my children as a burden, but as a fantastic opportunity to create a lasting bond with their grandchildren. Their assistance also ensured that the kids and I would be able to maintain the same quality of life as when I was married.

My parents began babysitting so I could put in more hours at work. Money was tight between having a mortgage and legal fees. We ran a very tight ship when it came to the kids, manners, discipline, respect, chores, prayers and homework. Consistency proved to be crucial. My son was in school most of the day. The twins attended pre-school part-time and stayed with their grandparents, Pa and Nana, for the rest of the time.

About a year into our new routine, Nana became ill, and it was decided that Pa would watch all three children during the week. Pa had always been fantastic at keeping things orderly, organized, neat and tidy. At times, I joke that he runs my house like a boot camp! But the kids are thriving and having fun with the routine. As soon as I am up in the morning, Pa arrives at 6:00 A.M. Then the kids have their breakfast (which often consists of happy face waffles with apples and bananas). After breakfast, the "face, hands, teeth and fanny" routine begins, which means, "Brush your teeth and wash up! Face, hands, teeth, fanny! Let's go!" The kids laugh hysterically as they get ready.

Then they put out their clothes for the day. The twins have gotten into the habit of laying their clothes on their bed as if a person were actually lying there! It's pretty comical because they have the socks at the end of pants, and when you lift the pants or skirts off the bed, they have their underwear or tights lying underneath, all ready to go!

After my son has boarded the school bus, Pa has the twins begin the daily morning cleaning routine. They begin with dusting all the rooms, mopping the floors and cleaning the "boutique" (bathroom). Beds are made (including mine!), laundry is folded, and dishes are put away. The added pressure of me having to stay on top of my cleaning is relieved greatly. My children do it! After cleaning up for a bit, it's time for play. They rake leaves in the backyard and then jump in them—even Pa! He loves horseplay. They have "tackle time" and play hide and seek. Or if the weather is lousy, they build a fort with Pa, do crafts or watch a movie. Pa and Emily love to play video games together. In fact, she will only play with him!

Now that the twins attend kindergarten in the afternoons, Pa gets a four-hour break. However, at 4:00 when the bus rolls in with all three children, it's time for homework and dinner. Once in a while, I get home from work early enough to join everyone for dinner. Our dinner prayer begins, "God is great, God is good, and we thank him for this food. Amen..." And then we all raise our arms in the air and yell, "MEN!" (The twins couldn't say "amen" for the longest time so it was shortened to just "men.") We'll talk about our day, and Pa will ask the kids if they taught their class the "Pa Song" yet. The kids look at him in embarrassment and say, "Noooo, Pa!" The kids and Pa created a special song a few years ago: "Pa... Pa... Mister Golden Pa... please shine down on meeeeee!"

Table manners are also huge in my house. We taught the kids early on how to hold their utensils correctly while eating. Pa has stayed on them, as well as reinforcing saying, "Please, pass the milk" and "May I please be excused?" Pa has always said that you can get a good impression of a person by how they are at the dinner table. "If they don't have table manners, they don't have ANY manners!"

A few months back, Nana recovered and began babysitting the kids again part-time. This gives both Nana and Pa a little one-on-one time with their grandkids. My son especially adores his Pa, who taught him how to ride a bike, throw a baseball, kick a soccer ball, shoot a basketball, tie his shoes, and catch a fish. After long grandfather-to-grandson talks, my son has learned not only how to respect others, but how to respect and love himself.

Last June, my son came home with a yearbook he created for each month in the first grade. Each month captured what he was doing in his life, from playing soccer to being in the Christmas pageant at church to going to the movies with friends and his twin sisters. And on the inside cover of his book, my son poignantly printed in his seven-year-old handwriting, "I dedicate this book to my Pa." I cried when I saw it, and Pa cried when I told him. It was all he could do to muster the words, "What a good kid!"

Well, that's because of you, Mister Golden Pa.

~Michele Christian

65

The Greatest Love

In true love the smallest distance is too great,
and the greatest distance can be bridged.
~Hans Nouwens

The phone rang.

"Mom, I've been transferred to Seattle," said our youngest son three years after he and his family arrived in Colorado from New Zealand.

Following his Western Samoan service in the Peace Corps, he'd taught in Auckland, New Zealand, met his love, married and had twins—Lina and Leilani. When the twins were eight months old in January 1999, the family moved to the States.

They lived in our walk-out basement for six months. We watched the girls scoot and then crawl across the floor. We caught them as they took their first steps. We heard their first words. Then the family found a house six miles away and moved out.

With the transfer, they'd be more than a thousand miles away. Would our bond be broken? There'd be no more last-minute babysitting. No more sleepovers after a card game with their parents that ran too late. No more dropping in at their house to visit and get my hugs.

On moving day, I brought the girls to my house so they wouldn't get in the movers' way. Great thought, but perhaps not the wisest decision. The next morning, we packed two cars—one for their family and, of course, one for my husband and me—and started out on our two-and-a-half day trek to Puyallup, Washington.

Upon our arrival at the new yellow house, the girls tore up the stairs like tornadoes.

"Where are you going?" I asked.

"To see our rooms," two voices chimed.

Soon, Lina ran to her mother and whined, "Where is my bed?"

Tears filled Leilani's eyes. "I want to go back to the blue house."

I, too, wanted them to go back to the blue house.

A few days later, we returned home alone. However, the phone rang, and two shy little voices said, "Hi, Nana and Papa. What're you doing?" They related all their day's activities and hung up with, "I love you, Nana. I love you, Papa."

Future calls revealed more about their move. They told how lots of children lived in their neighborhood; how they visited the library, church and YMCA located near their home; and how they met John's fellow employees, and gained lots of support and friends. Even though they were far away, we thanked God for their happiness.

The best was yet to come. The phone rang often. Their love continued; they didn't forget us.

"Nana," said Lina's three-year-old voice, "we got new bedspreads." I heard two sets of feet thump in the background. I pictured tiny legs trying to run up the stairs. "Mine is pink with lady bugs and bees. See?"

I laughed and imagined her holding the phone so I could see her treasure.

Feet thumped again. Then Leilani said, "Mine is purple with butterflies and flowers. See?"

A few months later, we answered the phone. "Nana and Papa, we asked Mommy and Daddy if we could come to your house, and they said no. Can you come to ours?"

As Christmas approached, I considered their request. I couldn't stand the thought of the holiday without them. On Christmas day, we flew to Seattle. John picked us up and drove to his house. Arms loaded, we headed for the front door.

"Here," said John, "go through the garage."

"No, the girls don't know we're coming. We'll ring the doorbell."

From outside, I could hear their mother urge them to break a rule and answer the door. At last, it opened, and one little girl peeked around the edge. I knelt before her. She ran into my arms, followed by her sister.

She said, "Oh, Nana, did Santa bring you for our present?"

~Linda L. Osmundson

66

A Letter to My Twin Granddaughters

We all have big changes in our lives that are more or less a second chance.
~Harrison Ford

If I may take a few moments, my dearest twin granddaughters, I would like to tell you about our beginnings, when you first came into my life and stole my heart. On a cold evening in mid-January, my daughter Jennifer, your mother, prematurely delivered my incredible Ashlynn, and then, three minutes later, my perfect Madilynn. From the moment you took your first breaths, you transferred me into the glorious realm of grandmotherhood. With your hurried delivery by caesarean section, I sighed with relief only a mother can feel, knowing that my daughter was no longer in danger and that you both were going to be fine. This short-lived ecstasy was quickly replaced by acute anxiety that your perfectly formed tiny human bodies could not yet sustain themselves, and you would have to stay in the Neonatal Intensive Care Unit.

At first, dear Ashlynn, because you were slightly larger than your sister, you were placed in a more independent baby unit of the hospital. This, however, did not last as you could not maintain your body temperature and were losing too much weight. Within hours, you were transferred to the NICU and placed in the same incubator with your sister. It seemed Madilynn needed you at her side: you added warmth and comfort to her with your touches, rhythmic breathing, and heartbeat. You seemed to help her in her struggle to survive, and as the days passed, you both began to grow, thrive, and show individual characteristics that I will forever hold in my heart.

It was not difficult to tell the two of you apart. Miss Ashlynn, you were a pound larger, with an olive complexion and thick dark mahogany hair. Whereas you, Madilynn, were smaller with a pale complexion and the most beautiful, full and pouty lips. If you will pardon my saying so, you were both so thin you had absolutely no bottoms. I know because I helped change you.

Being fraternal twins, I see some of your mother's and some of your father's characteristics in your faces, hands and toes. You, Ashlynn, have your father's long, graceful fingers and toes. You both have his large eyes and wonderful, lush long eyelashes. Your cute noses and broad smiles have captured part of your mother. When I look closely, I even see inherited adaptations from your grandparents, such as the shape of your ears and the contours of your face. We have all contributed something to what you are.

On every visit, I whispered to you through your plastic walls about how lucky you were to have such wonderful parents who loved you dearly. I wanted you both to know the many disappointments my daughter and son-in-law, your father, had gone through trying to have children naturally, but couldn't. Only in-vitro fertilization would make them parents. You needed to know about the seven months of self-administered daily shots, nauseating stomach pains, and extended days of total bed rest your mother had to endure on your behalf. She also grieved for an earlier baby boy who had been lost due to complications.

I explained to you that your handsome father, Adam, was there, too. He was in the room when the doctors first placed you both inside your mother. He instantly fell in love when you were little more than a hope and a prayer. These visions of you took shape when he saw the sonogram pictures of your early beginnings—the tiny fingers and toes, the small profiles and, most importantly, the beating hearts. Your father's first one-on-one encounters with you occurred when you moved and kicked inside your mother's womb.

This brought your parents even closer together. They were beginning to share parenthood. Your father tried to help your mother by cooking her favorite meals to eat, bringing her pretty flowers to smell and good books to read. He even gave her a little red whistle that dangled from a string, which she was instructed to blow while she was on bed rest if she needed anything. Your mother quickly learned to use it loudly and often.

Peering down at your tiny, thin bodies with almost transparent skin, I felt so helpless. I said so many prayers on your behalf—prayers for your parents, prayers for the doctors and nurses who took care of you, and prayers for the other two babies in your NICU unit. We all prayed for you!

In time, you gained strength, weight and the ability to heat your own bodies. Ashlynn was allowed to go home first. Your mother hated to leave Madilynn behind, but she and your dad took turns visiting the hospital. About a week later, Madilynn was strong enough to come home, too. She was ready to see her sister again.

Your parents had a beautiful pink, white and brown room ready for you. A large pink bear cozily guarded you from his seat in the nearby rocker. Monitors were attached to your beds to record your every move. You have since grown and thrived in your new home.

Your grandfather and I come to visit you as often as we can. I join you in splashing your bath water on the floor. I push you in the swings in the park, feeling a renewed youthful energy in my body. We feed the ducks, and I thrill at the excitement in your eyes. Sometimes I regress to being a child myself when I crawl around the coffee table with you both following close behind. We play peek-a-boo or clap our hands to a favorite childhood song. But what I love best is your laughter and squeals of delight when I enter the room.

I am learning to care for you both on my own. Sometimes your mother needs to get out of the house and run to the store or have lunch with a friend. I must say that feeding you both at the same time took a little training. And coming up with new ways to keep you entertained—making a puppet out of a stuffed animal, using kitchen utensils to make music, dancing around the room like a fifteen-year-old and making all sorts of clownish faces—restarted my creative thought processes. I'm still trying to figure out what to do when you both decide to crawl in opposite directions.

I have also learned to go to bed when you do so that I get up early the next morning with a smile on my face. Getting up early has not always been my favorite thing. However, seeing your sweet little heads pop up as you struggle to your feet to greet me with new words and giggles makes it all worthwhile.

Now I must thank you for my happy regression to childhood. You have kept me young at heart. I am thrilled again to be walking into toy stores, hearing Christmas carols, sharing a cookie, and finding renewed happiness with each moment of each day. Thank you for reminding me of what is important in life.

You are re-teaching me about the wonders and beauty of the world we live in—the simple flutter of a leaf, a blade of grass, the twinkle of lights, the taste of something new, and so much more. And you have managed to do all this in only ten short months. I suspect I have only just begun to learn from your enthusiastic lessons on the thrills of life. You both have given me a second chance.

Some people say twins are "double trouble." I always correct them and say, "Double fun."

~Ann G. Hays

67

Blessed With Boys

Unable are the loved to die. For love is immortality.
~Emily Dickinson

Until recently, my husband, Dan, and I were baffled as to why we were blessed with twins. Stunned, shocked and utterly giddy with joy pretty much describes how we felt when our first ultrasound revealed there were two tiny babies growing in my belly. In fact, the technician administering the ultrasound advised Dan to sit down before she told us the news! Everyone in our combined family was just as surprised as we were, except, strangely, for Nana. I now know why.

My grandmother, whom I affectionately called Nana, was ninety-four years old when she fell in her apartment and broke her hip. Dan and I were playing with our twin boys when my dad called to tell me Nana was in the hospital. I was absolutely devastated. My Nana was one of the most important people in my life, and I knew the prognosis was not good. Not only would rehabilitation be nearly impossible, but it was very likely she would not survive the surgery because her heart was so frail.

Before heading to the hospital to see Nana, I grabbed a photograph of the boys to put in her hospital room. I couldn't help feeling like this was the end for her. My heart ached, knowing our precious time was short, and it was likely she wouldn't see our boys reach their first birthday. In the car, my husband encouraged me to think happy thoughts, which I was relieved to do.

I remembered the first time Nana met the boys after we brought them home from the hospital and how natural she was at holding and feeding them, even though she'd been out of practice for decades! Every time I called her on the phone, the first thing she would say after "hello" was, "How are the boys?" and "Tell me what they're up to!" While the boys' lives involved little more than eating, sleeping and crying at their age, Nana wanted to know every detail and repeated it to anyone who would listen. In fact, just about everyone at her senior living apartment complex not only knew the boys, but also who was who, which boy liked to sleep in his swing, and which one was prone to reflux.

Dan and I arrived to see Nana before they took her in for surgery. She was heavily medicated and looked helpless and frail. Her eyes told us she was scared, and I held her hand and told her how much we loved her. I put the photo of the boys on the table next to her, and her eyes lit up when she saw them. Even though the medicine made her groggy, she asked her usual, "How are the boys? What are they up to?"

All too soon, they wheeled her off to surgery. To distract myself from the situation, I began thinking about the day I told Nana that, not only were we expecting twins, but it was twin BOYS! She was so excited we were naming them Jonathan and James. We picked their names because they were Dan's and his brother's middle names. It didn't even dawn on me that Nana's sons, whom I never got to know, were named John and Jim.

After what seemed like an eternity, the doctor came out to tell us Nana made it through! There were complications with her heart and she was in ICU, but she managed to pull through. I felt as if God had given us the gift of extra time with my precious Nana, and I was so grateful.

After a roller coaster week, Nana was moved out of ICU and into a rehabilitation facility. It was a far cry from the comforts of home, but Nana was optimistic as we helped her settle in. The doctors warned our family that Nana was not out of the woods, but we practiced careful optimism. Before we left for the day, Nana requested the photo of the boys, so Dan found a thumbtack and posted it on the wall next to her bed.

During one of our visits, Nana told me how much she loved looking at the picture of Jonathan and James on her wall every day. She told me that because of the way the boys had "posed" in the photograph, it looked to her like James's tiny, outstretched arm was reaching to her, encouraging her to continue with her painful hip exercises. She told me the boys inspired her to get out of bed each day and work through the challenges of rehabilitation. I couldn't believe it! Nana, a feisty ninety-four-year-old woman, found strength in my four-month-old twins!

Despite weeks of slow, but steady progress, Nana developed pneumonia, the most common, fatal side effect of an older person suffering from a broken hip. Her condition quickly went from bad to worse, and she was rushed back to the hospital. Nana passed away the next day. Our family was devastated. She was an anchor in our family, involved in everything. How were we ever going to live without her?

I found myself struggling to comprehend our loss and make sense of our new world without Nana. And then, like an epiphany, it struck me: "Everything happens for a reason." I'd heard it over and over growing up. I witnessed evidence of this little adage sprinkled throughout my childhood and early adult life, but I never really believed it until now. Our twins, our precious rare blessings, were gifts from God. We were blessed with not just one baby, but two, and I believe this is because it would take two to fill the void Nana left behind. Unlike a lot of twin parents, multiples do not run in our family, and we did not undergo fertility treatments. It was a complete shock and blessing to find out we were pregnant with two. And the fact that we unknowingly gave them the same names as Nana's sons made me smile. Realizing this made it easier for me to cope with Nana's passing. It was as if Nana herself was telling me to find joy in her loss—that she had lived just long enough to know and love them.

We put the photograph of the boys that Nana looked at every day in her casket. I take great comfort in knowing she is watching over our sweet boys, just as they did for her.

~Melissa Wenzel

68

Chicken Soup for the Soul

I'm the Nana—and She's the Nanny!

If you are fortunate enough to find a dependable, nonexorbitant sitter, treasure her, coddle her, ply her with Arpege—and keep her name and phone number a dark secret from your less fortunate friends.
~Stan and Jan Berenstain

"There is no way anyone that young can take proper care of my new grandbabies," I whispered to my friend. "Getting used to the idea of a nanny has been tough enough for a hands-on grandma like me. But now that I've met this twenty-one-year-old, I'm even more concerned," I added.

"She sure looks like she's still in her teens!" my friend said, adding fuel to my frustration.

The two of us had just taken a peek at my day-old triplet grandsons, and we were now sitting on a couch in the hospital waiting room. The young lady under discussion was in the room with my daughter and son-in-law, getting acquainted with her new family.

"Shelle and Bob interviewed a number of potential nannies, and this young lady, Deedee, comes highly recommended," I said, trying to reassure both of us.

For the past eight months, our family, friends and neighbors focused time and energy in preparation for this major event. From the moment big brother, Cole, announced, "We're going to have a baby," our lives changed. Son-in-law Bob laughingly corrected his five-year-old. "Cole and Brady are great, but Shelle and I decided we wanted three children. I guess God thought we meant three at one time. Wow, did we get fooled!"

We began centering our thoughts and prayers on the health of our daughter and those little ones in her womb—plus trying to figure out how we were going to cope with five children under the age of five.

"Well, Mom, it looks like we're going to hire a nanny," Shelle announced as she neared her fifth month. "I've been talking to other parents of multiples, and it's time we start the interviewing process."

Hmm, I thought to myself. Nannies are not a part of my caregiving background—only grandparents and extended family. We all live nearby. We'll do it ourselves! However, under the stress-filled circumstances, I was determined to be agreeable, so I said nothing. But my attitude still screamed, "I'm the Nana... do we really need a nanny?"

Then Deedee became a part of our family. This freckle-faced, pony-tailed young lady taught us how to care for three little bitty babies. She took over night duty while family and friends rocked, fed, and diapered during the daytime. She taught us how to use the ever-present clipboards on the kitchen counter, one for each baby. We recorded each feeding, including the number of ounces consumed, each diaper change, every drop of medication dispensed, etc. Without those clipboards, we envisioned total chaos. Deedee ran a tight ship, and we followed her lead, recognizing in her an experienced nanny.

We all settled into a routine that included my arriving at 5:00 A.M. on Saturday mornings. One Saturday, Bob greeted me with a big smile and asked, "Did you notice the house is totally dark? It's been lights-on 24/7 at this address for seven whole weeks!"

Several months later, Bob and Shelle decided they desperately needed a couple of days away, and Richard and I volunteered for a forty-eight-hour stint over the next weekend. Off we went, excited to spend quality time with our boys, plus take them out and "show them off." The parents were barely out of the driveway when we were challenged to overlook the "accidental nudge" that the two-and-a-half-year-old gave one of his little brothers—who'd stolen all of the attention he was used to getting before they were born. That little "nudge" taught us to stay alert at all times!

"Come on, Nana, let's go out and play ball," five-year-old Cole begged, tugging on my sleeve.

"Would you please take the older boys outside while I feed the triplets?" I asked my husband. "That'll take at least an hour," I added.

The following morning, after feeding, dressing, and loading five boys into the new Suburban (a necessary vehicle for this sized family), we opened the rear door and hoisted the heavy five-foot triplet stroller in the back. Off we went to show off our family celebrities to our friends.

When we arrived at the park, our designated meeting place, we unloaded the stroller and strapped the babies in their seats. "I'll drive this," Richard offered as he began pushing it uphill toward the picnic tables. I tucked a hand from each of the older boys into my hands, put the monstrous diaper bag over my shoulder, and joined our friends.

Within an hour, our little celebrities began fussing and squirming. "I think it's time to go home," I called to Grandpa. "We'd better start loading up."

"I'm not sure that outing was worth all the work," I said as we unloaded boys, diaper bags, etc., back at their house. "Now I see why this family became a stay-at-home family five months ago."

On Sunday morning, when we considered going ahead with our original plan to attend church services, we looked at each other and shook our heads. The thought of bathing, dressing, and loading five little boys in the Suburban was overwhelming. And the lack of sleep from the previous two nights was catching up with two very tired grandparents.

Late morning naps provided us with an opportunity to clean the kitchen, give the house a quick once-over, pack our overnight bags and set them by the front door, ready for a quick getaway.

"What time is Deedee going to be here?" I asked Grandpa.

"Shortly after lunch," he replied.

Preparing lunch meant setting the three bouncy chairs on the kitchen table, warming baby food, strapping in triplets, tying on three bibs, and filling three little mouths. Plus, preparing and feeding a five-year-old and a two-year-old. Whew!

While the little ones rested, I stood by the window and watched for the sight of Deedee's car. When her little black sedan pulled up and parked in front of the house, I heaved a sigh of relief and whispered to my husband, "She's here! We can go home soon!"

As she stepped out of the car, our beloved nanny tossed back her strawberry-blond hair, slung her backpack over her shoulder, and walked up the steps. I opened the door and welcomed her with open arms.

"Hi, everybody!" she called, exuding youthful energy.

"Wow! Are we glad to see you!" I said. "I hope you know what a blessing you are to two tired grandparents. We've concluded from our forty-eight-hour experience that we have enough love in our hearts to go on forever, but our tired old bodies don't agree with our hearts."

We quickly gathered our bags, returned hugs and kisses from the older boys, crawled into our car and headed home. Laying my head back against the seat, I sighed and said, "I'm exhausted! I love being their Nana... but I will be forever grateful for Deedee, their nanny!"

~Betty Johnson Dalrymple

"We have Supernanny on speed dial."

69

Twin Sandwich

Some luck lies in not getting what you thought you wanted but getting what you have, which once you have got it you may be smart enough to see is what you would have wanted had you known.

~Garrison Keillor

I am what you might call a "Twin Sandwich with a Slice of Baloney." I am the only daughter of a twin and, although the old wives' tale (insert "baloney") says twins skip a generation, we skipped two generations, making me the proud grandmother of twins.

My mother loved telling people who found out she had a twin that "the only way you can tell us apart is my brother is taller." However, there were more differences than that.

Mary Loretta and Wesley Lorenz were born the fifth and sixth children of Hugh and Eliza Matilda (Tildy) Cox of Hardburly, Kentucky, a coal mining town in the Eastern Kentucky Appalachian Mountains. I grew up listening to stories about my grandfather, who was a coal miner, and my grandmother, who ran a boardinghouse for the miners. My favorite stories were about Mom and her twin brother.

My mother was born first, which made my uncle the official "baby" of the family. Lorenz was the type of child whom everyone wanted to protect. He was easy-going and expected life to come to him. My mother, on the other hand, was quite feisty. One afternoon, walking home from school, a group of older boys thought they would have a little fun with Lorenz. Loretta immediately jumped to his defense. Lorenz's idea of helping the situation was to tell Loretta, "Hold my books while I run home and tell Momma those boys are beating up on you."

It was during the Depression, but my mother didn't remember hardship until my grandfather became blind. When he developed a brain tumor, the coal miners in their community, poor as they were, scraped enough money together to send him and my grandmother to Rochester, Minnesota, where surgery at the Mayo Clinic saved his life, but not his sight. Mom's older brother, Bob, was living in Michigan, where he had found work in the auto factories, so it was decided that the rest of the family would also move north. They had not been in Michigan long before Grandma died suddenly. The twins were only fourteen. No one had enough room for both of them, so Mom and Uncle Lorenz had to be separated. Though living with different relatives, they attended the same school and graduated from high school together.

By the end of World War II, all of Mom's siblings were married and starting families. My mother was not overly fond of the woman Lorenz married. The special twin bond was never broken, but a gap had widened. When the marriage failed, once again my mother became Lorenz's protector. She helped him get back on his feet and introduced him to his second wife, with whom he would spend the rest of his life. Adulthood and a family had closed the seven-year age gap between Mom and her older sister, Mae. They had the closest relationship in the family, but Mom still had a special feeling for her twin.

When I was grown and planning my own family, I had been told so many times it was my turn to have twins that I began to believe it. I even thought of twin names. My husband, Alex, who was the oldest of five, wanted only two children. But I, being an only child, wanted more. Since our first two, Jennifer and Tracey, were girls, he agreed to try one more time for a son. Darren was born, and we thought our family was complete. Our son Nick was a surprise. I finally had the large family I wanted, but there was not a twin among them.

Jennifer was a senior in high school when Mom, who had a beautiful but weak heart, began to fail. She struggled to hang on to see her oldest grandchild graduate from the same high school she had graduated from fifty years before and twenty-five years after my own graduation. Our three generations of graduates were mentioned as Jennifer received the top honor for a graduating senior. The pride Mom felt gave a little spark to the remainder of her life. She passed away just six weeks later. Uncle Lorenz lived another five years in a blissful state of dementia. Every time his wife or daughters would visit him in the nursing home, he would happily introduce them to staff and fellow patients as "my twin sister, Loretta."

Six years after Mom passed away, our youngest daughter, Tracey, married, followed fourteen months later by Jennifer. Tracey presented us with our first grandchild, an adorable redhead named Courtney. Four years later, Trevor was born, another adorable carrot top. I often thought of how Mom would have loved these great-grandchildren.

Jennifer was involved in getting her master's degree and developing her career. Darren and Nick were still teenagers. The thought of additional grandchildren anytime soon seemed remote until one night in bed. I started dreaming in full Technicolor—or at least in two colors... pink and blue... two babies in pink and blue pajamas. They were Jennifer's babies. It was one of those dreams from which you awaken and it takes a few minutes to realize where you are and that you had been dreaming. It had seemed so real. I mentioned it to Jennifer, who seemed amused and even a little indulgent at her mother's "wishful thinking."

After getting her MBA, Jennifer decided it was time to start a family. When things did not go smoothly I reminded her of my dream and told her that she was not only going to have a baby, but she would have two! I still remembered the dream and convinced myself that I saw the faces of my grandchildren.

When Jennifer became pregnant, I waited anxiously for her to call me after the first ultrasound. She assured me the pregnancy was progressing normally, and I asked the next question that had plagued me since learning she might be expecting: "How many?"

"One," she said. Children are always reluctant to admit when a parent is right.

Christmas was a few weeks later. As we were opening gifts, Alex opened one addressed to Grandma and Grandpa. At first glance, I knew it was a framed picture of an ultrasound. How sweet, I thought, trying to plan the best place to display it, when I heard Alex say, "There are TWO of them?!?" I think I was too excited to hit her with the "I told you so!"

I grabbed the picture of the two little aliens and the inscription that read: "Dear Grandma and Grandpa, WE can't wait to meet you in July. Love, POTUS (President of the United States) and SCOTUS (Supreme Court of the United States)." My son-in-law has high ambitions.

They actually couldn't wait until July to meet us. They came two months early, in May. Maryn was first, followed by her brother, Dylan. My dream had come true, and a new generation of twins was born. That was three years ago.

My dad is eighty-seven and lives with us now. He often says he wishes Mom could see the twins. I swallow the lump in my throat and tell him, "I'm sure she can, Dad."

~Connie Watson

Chapter 8

Twins and More

A Different Path to Parenthood

Two roads diverged in a wood, and I
I took the one less traveled by,
And that has made all the difference.

~*Robert Frost,* The Road Not Taken

70

Chicken Soup for the Soul

First Words

Every language is a temple,
in which the soul of those who speak it is enshrined.
~Oliver Wendell Holmes

The Baltimore-Washington International Airport was quiet on that late night in April 1986. I sat nervously with my husband and two young sons, awaiting an important incoming flight. Our family was about to expand by two. Twins! We had never considered the possibility when, a year before, we'd requested a "sibling pair" from Korea that began our adoption process.

When our social worker told us in January that the adoption agency had located our sibling girls, we were elated. She added the surprise that the girls were identical twins, and that of all the races, Mongoloid twins are most rare. "Such a blessing," she said, and we agreed: We were blessed. Twice blessed, really. I would later often say it was a match made in heaven.

But as I sat in the airport that night, I couldn't help feeling restive. Sudden questions of doubt plagued me: Would our new twin girls accept us? Could love span language and cultures and continents? Would we even be able to communicate that love?

My boys seemed restless, too. It was hours past their bedtime, and they were ready to meet their new sisters and take them home. We had spent months preparing for the girls' arrival. We had moved furniture and organized rooms, bought matching canopy beds and My Little Pony videos. Because the twins would be adjusting to a new time zone, we had anticipated staying up all night on this, their first night in America, which my boys thought a huge excitement.

"Will they know us?" my nine-year-old asked. Always our logical child, he was wise for his years, though we didn't like letting on about that. "They got our pictures, right, Dad?"

"Hope so," answered my husband.

We'd previously sent photo albums to the girls, but my five-year-old was unconcerned with that now. Instead, he puffed out his cheeks and stood tall. He had thick chestnut hair that touched his collar in back and his eyebrows in front, accenting deep brown eyes with the longest of lashes. "And they'll know I'm their big brother, too, right, Mommy?"

"Oh, they will," I told him. "There's no mistaking that, honey."

Our elder son began, logically, to state that his younger brother was technically only ten months older than the twins, who had just turned five in March. But before the brothers could spar in earnest, a rumble of aircraft silenced both boys. We had been waiting with several other families who would meet their new children that night as well, and now we all assembled at the gate. When our girls deplaned, one on each side of an adoption agency companion whose hands they held tightly, I was sure everyone could hear my heartbeat. At last, our twins! They were tiny little girls, indeed identical, with inky hair cut short and a bit unevenly. Dressed in mismatched clothing and tennis shoes, they came right to us. Our boys gathered round, trying to draw their sisters out, but the girls didn't speak, just studied us with shy eyes and curious smiles.

A smile, of course, is a precious thing. It can bridge nearly every gap. We started bridging gaps right away that night. Still, while the girls looked to be soaking up their strange new surroundings, as the minutes ticked into an hour, they hadn't yet attempted to talk. Their companion explained gently to them in Korean that they would soon be leaving with us. I could only imagine how overwhelmed they felt, how frightened. Unlike the infants they had flown with, our girls were old enough to wonder what would become of them with these people whom they had been told were now their family. I was so proud of them, so much in awe. They had traveled so far, and they had been so brave. But as we left the airport and the girls hadn't uttered a sound, I worried again about that language barrier. It suddenly seemed immense.

It was in our living room, with lights aglow, that those first words finally happened.

The girls stood together, holding hands, taking it all in—their first look at their new home. They appeared particularly mesmerized by our family portrait. All at once, they ran over to it, pointed to my picture, then to me: "Uhma." Mommy. They pointed to my husband: "Ah-Pa." Daddy.

We were stunned, and very touched. They had said the words in unison, as only twins could. They had spoken in sweet little voices that brought tears to our eyes. But no sooner had we recovered from this than there came two more words. "Op-Pa." Old brother. Perfect. The girls had accurately identified our nine-year-old. And then, amid frowns and head tilts and a couple of silly giggles, they peered at their other brother. "Uhn-Ni." Old sister.

Oh, no! So much for big-brother dreams!

My five year old took it in stride, though, and with the later help of a translator, we corrected the twins' first faux pas. Since then, our family has shared many joyful firsts and, as with all families, a few bumps along the way. Those first words in Korean led to first words in English, first school days, first report cards, first friends and first boyfriends. There have been bedtime routines ("Time to kiss my favorite spot," I'd announce to each girl as I tucked them in, nuzzling the soft, flat bridge of their noses), and inventive communication ("All gone poo-poo towels," one girl proclaimed one day when encountering an empty toilet paper roll). As they grew, the girls went through the typical twin machinations. They wanted, as children, to dress alike, and then, as teenagers, to dress differently. They fell into swapping clothes, and sometimes personas, vexing teachers and grandparents. Our twins didn't have a mere privately devised language. They also had, in those early years, the added use of their native tongue, which they infused with their own inflections and gesticulation. It was how we all learned to communicate, with gestures and head shakes and a whole lot of pointing, a kind of unique familial game of charades.

And so the end of my twins' journey was also the beginning. Somehow, together, they found their way to us from halfway across the globe. How providential that they had each other, that they had such a special connection. I have always believed God puts people in our lives at just the right moment, for just the right purpose. My girls have been the one constant, the one sparkling light in each other's world. Together they discovered that the sun would still rise in America as it had in Korea, that the stars would still shine as bright as their eyes, that a smile was still and always a smile.

Today, my children are grown. My twins are beautiful young women who wear their connection well and remain vastly protective of each other. But I will forever get tears at the memory of that enchanting spring night, and of two little girls who found just the right first words.

~Theresa Sanders

71

A Love Like No Other

A baby is born with a need to be loved—and never outgrows it.
~Frank A. Clark

Dear Babies,

As our time together draws to a close, I want to express how you both have changed my life. Soon you each will be born and will finally meet your daddy, who has waited ever-so-patiently to hold you in his arms. While your birth day will be a day of joy and happiness for all of us, there will be a part of me that will miss you both... your kicks, your rolls, your hiccups and the occasional knees under my ribs. Our time together, carefully planned from the beginning, has been a blessing in my life. I feel privileged to have carried each of you until the time when you will join your daddy and feel all the love he has waiting for you.

I'll never forget that first sonogram—"two embryos, two heartbeats"—at which time your daddy nearly fainted! He always wanted to be a dad, but two at once? I was thrilled! That is, as excited as a non-biological mom can be. You see, I am your gestational surrogate mother.

From the time the doctor placed you both inside me, we've experienced many things together. You've heard the voices of my two daughters as we've discussed homework assignments, sleepovers, boyfriends and dating, as well as the occasional disagreements that every family has. Besides my voice, you most often hear that of my partner, who talks to you every night and shares a love of music with you both. You are the center of attention when the grocery clerk or postman or the bank teller learns that you are a boy and a girl, and then is oh-so-surprised to learn that you are not mine. That takes some explaining, but my younger daughter, always up for the task, explains in her matter-of-fact nine-year-old way, "Oh, these are not *our* babies!" She then goes on to explain how you are your daddy's children and that you will go home with him once you are born.

Food is always a large part of my pregnancies, and this one is no different. I have very intense cravings for fresh sub sandwiches, and we typically enjoy them at least three times a week. Perhaps you'll each have a love for fresh veggies since I pile them on my subs!

While not yet born, both of you stole the show at your daddy's baby shower! As a guest, I was able to meet the many family members and friends who are anxiously awaiting your arrival. They were filled with giddy excitement that was freely expressed and devoured. Oh, what a life each of you will have! Your lives will be filled with much joy, laughter, opportunity, security and love.

I love each of you. It's a love that is unique and unlike the love I have for my own children. When people ask, "But don't you love them? How could you give them up?" I say, "Of course, I love them. I have felt them move inside me for many months, and I will care for them until they are ready to be born. But they are not mine to 'give up.'" You are your daddy's children, and you will always hold a very special place in my heart as my surrogate babies.

While you have been busy growing and getting strong, your daddy has been busy preparing for your arrival. Two of everything... cribs, car seats and a stroller built for two! He's read every parenting book he can get his hands on, and we share what he's learned in our weekly e-mails and phone calls. He also travels to Florida for our doctor appointments and sonograms, and has joined my family at our local pumpkin patch. We've shared our family love of boiled peanuts with him, something he had never tasted before.

As the last few days we will share together come to a close, I protect you as I always have... questioning each procedure and medication that is given, ensuring that neither of you is harmed. I rest and stay relaxed so as not to stress either of you. My belly rubs are often as are my trips to the bathroom. Yet, all of it I will miss. I look forward to hearing your first cries and counting each of your fingers and toes! I also want to know if you have hair. But, most of all, I can't wait to see your daddy's face when he sees each of you for the first time and then holds you both in his arms... next to your spot in his heart.

Birth day: The day has finally come for the two of you to enter this world and meet all those who have waited for your grand arrival. Soon, you will leave the warm comfort and coziness, albeit cramped, of my body in exchange for your own place in this world. It will be a bit strange at first—cold, bright and filled with crisp noise—but don't you worry. Your daddy will soon wrap you in his arms that are warm, safe and filled with wondrous love.

I hear your cries and see your small bodies, and my heart swells with pride and much love. Wrapped up like papooses, they place you both on my chest. My partner and I cry with overwhelming pride and joy. Your daddy snaps away with his camera, making sure to capture your first few moments. He is so excited; I swear he is walking on air! Bringing life into the world—a life that is not biologically mine—is a tremendous event and a life-changing journey. For this, I thank each of you and your daddy for allowing me to be a part of your special journey to becoming a family.

Update: It's been five years since your births, and while you are not close to me in location, each of you is still very much a part of my life. We see each other once a year, and your daddy keeps me posted on your activities and growth through e-mails, photos and phone calls throughout the year. The best visit was last Christmas when I was able to hear, directly from your four-year-old mouths, "You carried us in your belly until we were born. Then we went home with our daddy!"

The three of you have blessed my life beyond measure. Being your surrogate mother was and still remains a sacred and cherished time in my life.

~Stacie Lykins

72

The First Time Ever I Saw Your Face

A baby is God's opinion that the world should go on.
~Carl Sandburg

The torrential downpour did not surprise us as we awoke on that chilly October day. It was the day we thought would never come, but the day that finally did.

Almost without exception, it rained on the days we were scheduled to visit our adoption agency. Whether it was attending pre-adoption classes, support groups for waiting parents, or informational meetings, it never failed to pour. The dark and stormy weather reflected the inner turmoil we felt as each month drifted into another and no baby was placed with us.

But that Wednesday, the dark clouds and gray sky could not block the sunshine that radiated in our hearts. After years of lying awake at night dreaming of holding my precious child in my arms, fantasizing about what that moment would be like, it was finally happening, although it bore no resemblance to what I had imagined. Now we had two babies coming—two tiny people whose combined weight was less than the chicken I cooked each Friday for Shabbat. Two babies slightly larger than a ruler. Two babies who had come into the world twelve weeks too soon.

My husband and I could not contain our excitement, and we arrived at our agency a half hour before our appointment. We were met by the staff with smiles and greetings of congratulations as they came out to ask the babies' names and how we were feeling.

Once our social worker arrived, we went into a private room with her and the other social worker who had actually seen the twins. We were told what to expect in the NICU, which was nothing like our daughter's arrival into the world seven-and-a-half years earlier.

After signing the papers, we jumped into our car for the wet ride to the hospital. The excitement mounted as we followed our social worker's car through the city streets that would soon become all too familiar.

An NICU nurse met us, and we were led into the room where my husband and I were taught to do a surgical scrub hand washing. We hurriedly walked down the hallway to Room A, where the tiniest babies were kept.

My heart was pounding, and my breathing became more rapid. The sounds of the NICU assaulted my ears—the whir of the respirators, the "beep beep" of apnea monitors—until I was taken to an Isolette containing a little boy wearing many tubes and wires, a diaper, and an orange knit cap way too big for his head. Then it all became silent... until my sobs resonated throughout the room.

I am not one to openly display emotion. My reaction—tears of joy at my dream coming true, tears of gratitude for G-d letting us arrive at this day, tears of relief that the six-and-a-half-year journey to become parents again was now over—surprised me. The deep depression that I had been mired in for so long was gone. I saw the light once again in that Isolette.

My son. My tiny miracle. My baby boy. It would be days before my husband and I were permitted to hold him, but we were allowed to stroke him through the Isolette's holes. "Mommy's here," I whispered to him. "I'll always be here."

A few moments later, my husband and I were led to another Isolette across the room. Inside lay an even tinier baby. Like her brother, she wore only tubes, wires, and a diaper. But unlike her twin, she wore a tiny pink ribbon KY-jellied to her head.

Tears again came to my eyes, but the sobs did not. Her skin was so translucent, and the four ounces less that she weighed than her older brother seemed to make her tinier, more fragile. She had previously had a few apneas—trouble breathing. The thought of loving her and then losing her after waiting for so long was unbearable. Despite the well of love overflowing in my heart, I was afraid to love her. It would be days before the dam broke and I could love with the confidence that all would work out fine.

After endless photos and video recording, it was time to leave. We had to go home and tell our dear daughter, our family, and our friends that our family of three was now five.

As I lay down to sleep that night, my dreams were different. I lay awake visualizing the faces of my pink and blue miracles and the day they would be able to come home forever.

~Marla Feldman

73

Chicken Soup for the Soul

The Gift of a Stranger

Gratitude unlocks the fullness of life... It can turn a meal into a feast, a house into a home, a stranger into a friend.
~Melody Beattie

The gift of twins. What combination of forces produces such a miracle? Luck? Family history?

In my case, the formula looks like this: Ten Years + Sacrifice of Complete Stranger = Twin Boys

My story started with a miscarriage. My doctor assured me that many women lose pregnancies on the way to parenthood. "Try again," he advised.

Fast-forward seven years and six more miscarriages. I had been to countless fertility doctors. Participated in medical studies. Received injections and IVs. Endured surgery.

But miscarriage number seven sealed my fate: I would never carry a child to term.

I sobbed.

My husband Joe and I floundered. We had to be parents. What could we do that would be as important?

Trying to shake off despair, we attended a workshop on adoption. Faces of gorgeous babies smiled up at us from brochures. Adoptive parents spoke of their dreams being fulfilled. How lovely it all sounded.

But our workshop folder also bulged with handouts on legal requirements and waiting periods. After seven years of heartache, adoption seemed like starting all over. There was so much to learn.

So many steps. My husband was in his forties, and I was close. How long would adoption take? The tick of the clock never felt louder.

Then our fertility doctor made a suggestion: gestational surrogacy. Another woman could carry our embryos to term. He enthused at the prospect. He was sure my eggs were fine. The problem had to be something about my uterus.

Joe was 100 percent on-board from the start, but I balked. Biology and science had always failed me. I had suffered through years of physical and emotional pain. I couldn't imagine this process would be any different.

Yet...

We knew the world of fertility treatment. We even knew an agency that worked with gestational surrogates. One of the people at the agency was a high school friend of Joe's. Another was an attorney in fertility and adoption law, someone we knew and trusted.

We could simply call the agency and sign up.

We did.

And then waited an entire year.

Our agency had just opened its doors to gestational surrogacy and had to build a pool of candidates. Though we were thrilled that their screening process was thorough, the ticking of the clock felt deafening.

Finally, we were presented with a candidate: Sally. The agency gave us a questionnaire she had completed. We loved all of her answers. Giddy with excitement, we called the agency and said we wanted to meet Sally and her husband.

As the big day approached, nerves set in: I was about to meet the woman who might carry my child. Would she like us? How would we know if she was the right person? I called the agency. "What should I wear?" I asked. "Is this considered a 'business casual' situation?!"

I needn't have worried. Sally and her husband were open and kind. We all decided to move on to the next step.

Sally went through a "test cycle" with our fertility doctor. Because my menstrual cycle would need to be in synch with hers, the doctor needed to be sure her body would respond well to the various medications involved.

It was a miserable failure. After three test cycles, our doctor gave us the news: medically, Sally was not a candidate.

Joe and I were crushed.

Another year went by.

Then another questionnaire: Angie. On paper she was funny and down-to-earth. We tried not to get too excited. After all, anything could happen. Yet we felt giddiness returning.

Joe and I met Angie and her husband, Felix. After two minutes, we were all laughing. Our personalities meshed beautifully.

Angie moved on to the test cycle.

Perfection.

I couldn't believe it. In our nine-year quest to have a child, nothing had ever gone perfectly.

Our fertility doctor synchronized our cycles and then, on the day of the "embryo transfer," he nestled four embryos into Angie's uterus.

I'll never forget that afternoon. We were all there for the procedure: Joe, Felix, Angie, and I. We had spoken with Angie a few times on the phone since our initial meeting, but we barely knew her.

After the doctor finished, he left the room. Angie had to lie flat on her back for a bit to increase the odds that the embryos would latch on. Joe, Angie, Felix and I looked at each other.

"Soooooooooo...." I said. "How 'bout those Cubs?"

Over the next two weeks, we spoke to Angie every few days. We didn't want to call too much and drive her nuts. Or call too little and have her think we didn't care.

On the day of her pregnancy test, I focused on not hyperventilating. The doctor's office said we'd be notified by 1:30 P.M. At 1:45, depression set in. "They already called her," I thought, "and they're just figuring out how to break it to me."

At 1:55 the phone rang. "I've got good news!" the nurse sang.

That moment is forever crystallized in my memory: The pool of afternoon light on my dresser. The sense of weightlessness I felt.

Two weeks later, Joe and I stood open-mouthed in front of an ultrasound screen: two white dots pulsed in a sea of black.

Their hearts in synch with ours.

Our boys.

Deep down, I had yearned for twins. Though I knew one healthy baby would be an unbelievable gift, I wanted two. I loved growing up with siblings. I loved the laughter and the fights and the way a brother or a sister knows you better than anyone.

We began calling Angie our "guardian Angie."

For the next eight months, she and I spoke daily. I discovered she was hilarious, smart, and strong.

That strength came in handy. I still can't believe what she endured:

Fourteen weeks of twice-daily progesterone shots to fortify the pregnancy. Shots that left her hip black-and-blue long after the pregnancy was over.

Thirty-nine weeks of two babies, growing, then kicking, inside of her.

Serious lack of sleep.

Five weeks of contractions.

And a C-section.

When the boys came squalling into the world, one word summed up my feelings: surprise.

After ten years, one would think I'd be anything but surprised, but I was.

My boys actually existed, no longer dots on a screen.

I was a mom. Finally, finally, finally. A mom.

Four years later, the sense of awe lingers.

How can those bubbly, giggly smiles be real?

How can their soft arms around my neck be any sweeter?

How can someone decide to help a complete stranger in such a fundamental, personal, and selfless way?

I don't know, but I'm lucky to have found out.

~Sara F. Shacter

74

A Different Kind of Triplet

A family is a patchwork of love.
~Author Unknown

A typical day in our home can include several decimated rooms, a pond of orange juice, and a new wall mural—in crayon. There is often raucous screaming, pushing, shoving, throwing of food, and uncontrollable giggling. Our house is often crazy. Any family with triplets could say the same. Well, I guess you can't really say they're triplets....

Let me start from the beginning. I was born sixteen years ago, followed by my brother fifteen months later, a sister three years after that, and another sister six years later. We were very happy. We four siblings grew up together, likening ourselves to the original four in the Narnia series or the four sisters of *Little Women*, an idea unappreciated by our sole brother. We were the perfect family unit. And that wasn't ever going to change.

Yeah, right.

When I was thirteen, my parents came to a seemingly random conclusion that they wanted another kid. Every thirteen-year-old's dream come true, right? A baby. They sat us down and told us of their decision to adopt a baby from Guatemala. I was distraught. I was confused. I was angry. I scowled at the social worker. I refused to look at bassinets. I yelled at my mother, and I cried. I didn't understand why my parents wanted another baby. They had me, after all. Once all the paperwork was done, the waiting game began. My parents and siblings were anxious. I was sullen.

The July I was to turn fourteen, my mom got a call about two babies born three days apart. They weren't biologically related (one was of Mayan origin and the other more Spanish), but they needed to be placed in a good home. "They'll be almost like twins!" my mom said, telling us over spaghetti that she had accepted the offer. I wasn't pleased.

We found out in September that Mom was pregnant.

The next year of our lives was difficult. We were all running around trying to get things ready, and making sure that Mom was okay. I almost didn't notice between running to the kitchen to make peanut butter milkshakes and meeting more social workers that my feelings of anger at the impending additions to our family were ebbing. I was growing accustomed to the idea. I was growing to love these soon-to-be-arriving babies.

Sam came home from Guatemala City on Thanksgiving Day, and it was like we had known him all along. Maria came home in January, with Josie following in February. Once they had all arrived, it felt to me as though we were complete. Our numbers had swelled from six to nine, but somehow it didn't feel like there were too many of us.

These days, we like to joke that we only hit the *Brady Bunch* number for a few months, but now we've got the perfect number for the Weasley family from the Harry Potter books and *The Sound of Music* gang. People pass us on the street with our huge triple stroller and say, "Look, triplets!" Even though they are not biologically related—they are all different sizes, have different birthdays, and are of different ethnic backgrounds—we don't correct them. In our house, a triplet is not the way you were born, but how you were raised in relationship to your siblings.

We have these three babies whom I honestly thought I would always resent. But living with "triplets" has made our whole family more patient, loving, and closer. The triplets will always have us, and we will always have them. Most importantly, Sam, Maria, and Josie will always have each other, and that's what really makes a multiple. I like to say that our family wasn't made by DNA or genes or heritage, but we were made by love.

~Mary Margaret Fessler

75

Miracles in a Military Family

The reproduction of mankind is a great marvel and mystery.
~Martin Luther

Infertility. I never thought I would have to experience it. Frustration, loneliness, anger, depression, and feeling inadequate are just a few words to explain the emotions I felt when my physician explained that I had Polycystic Ovarian Syndrome. My first appointment with a reproductive medicine specialist was in January. My husband, a naval officer, was deployed, so I walked into the clinic alone, with no one by my side.

My husband would return home in May if his ship came in on time. But the war in Iraq had started in January, which meant it could be eight months before Chris could finally return home. I was so sad, not knowing when my husband would be home and wanting to have the children he always wanted and deserved. I knew he would be a great daddy.

The staff at the clinic was very caring and informative. They explained all the tests I would need to go through before the actual procedures to get pregnant could begin. I had blood draws, vaginal ultrasounds, cyst aspirations, a hysterosalpingogram, and many other tests. I also had abdominal surgery, which my physician believed was an important step in the fertility process. My reproductive insides were all messed up and needed some clean-up. I had never had surgery before. My friends were my support system and brought me to the appointments that required sedation or the more intensive appointments when I needed someone to hold my hand. A person really finds out who her true friends are at times like these.

My husband did return home on time, a week after my surgery. I watched the *USS Oscar Austin* come into port. I couldn't run to my spouse like the others, but I held my hand across my abdomen and walked slowly up the dock to greet my husband.

After months of further treatments, including ovulation-inducing medications and artificial insemination, my doctor explained that we had been unsuccessful. She recommended in vitro fertilization as our next step. She rarely recommended such an invasive procedure for a twenty-five-year-old, but I had many problems. Disappointed, I told her it wasn't an option due to our financial situation. But my husband and I prayed about it and decided that we had come so far that it would be detrimental to stop now. We took out a medical loan and proceeded.

My husband's ship had to pursue testing in the Atlantic Ocean and would be gone again for three weeks. I had started the injections needed for the in vitro process. My husband had to deposit his sperm in the private clinic room before he would leave. The technology seemed to take the excitement out of getting pregnant. My friend Steph took me to my appointment, and the physician retrieved fifteen eggs. Four eggs were of excellent quality, and the physician decided to implant two eggs due to my age. I was given a picture of the two eggs in a Petri dish before implantation.

Two weeks passed, and I visited the clinic once again to have my blood drawn for a pregnancy test. Later that day, they called and told me that I had to return because the laboratory was unable to pick up my blood due to time issues. Around 5:00 P.M., I sat in the waiting room wondering when my name would be called. Finally, the door opened. My doctor and the nurses walked through it with balloons in hand, announcing, "Everyone in this room is pregnant!" Fifteen impatient women smiled, cried, and screamed in disbelief.

My wonderful and compassionate doctor walked over to my

chair to congratulate me and tell me one more secret. "Marcy, I believe you are having twins." My heart dropped into my stomach. How did she know this? Apparently, my hormone levels were so high that it indicated multiples.

Two weeks later, I went in for a vaginal ultrasound with my husband. Yes, he was finally able to attend an appointment with me—the one appointment that really mattered, when we found out that two embryos had indeed implanted. I finally saw the light at the end of the tunnel.

I will always have an interesting story to tell my children, family, and friends—I got pregnant with my husband's children when he wasn't even home! Life as a military family can be quite interesting.

~Marcy DeHaan

76

Chicken Soup for the Soul

Our Version of Family

Biology is the least of what makes someone a mother.
~Oprah Winfrey

"I am sorry, but I can't find a heartbeat."

The doctor's words stung. My friend, Kim, stared into the cold, harsh light above the exam table, unable to wrap her head around what her heart felt. She longed to be anywhere but in that room. How could the doctor be so matter-of-fact? He spoke the words mechanically, unaware of what they meant to her. More devastating than his words was the fact that Kim had heard them before, four times before.

• • •

Five years earlier, Kim and her husband David had made the decision to try for kids immediately. No better time than their honeymoon! "Are you sure we should take this test so soon?" David had asked. "It could take months." But Kim was certain she was pregnant.

The paper bag crunched while her shaking hands pulled out the skinny box. Fear and excitement flooded over her. After taking the test, she twirled her dark hair between her fingers, impatiently waiting for the results. David's strong hand rested on her shoulder to stop her from pacing.

"If this doesn't tell us what we want, it will be all right. We have plenty of time," he assured Kim.

Two lines dazzled them. Were they seeing the result accurately? Tears ran down Kim's face. Laughter shook her body. Her fingers ran rapidly over the buttons of the phone. Everyone had to know her news. I was overjoyed when Kim told me about her pregnancy!

Ten weeks into the pregnancy, things started to go wrong. Kim told me about the agonizing doctor's visit—how the large clock on the wall of the office seemed to taunt them with its ticking while they waited for the doctor to reveal their fate. "You were pregnant with twins."

Were! They wondered how such a small word could pack so much punch.

"One of the twins didn't make it, but there is no reason why you can't carry the other one to term." The doctor's icy words held little emotion.

Kim wondered how she could go on living knowing she would never hold one of her children, but she put on a brave face and ignored the tremendous emotional pain she felt over her loss. Only those of us who were closest to her knew what she was really going through. Then, days before entering the "safe zone," cramping grabbed Kim's uterus, claiming the second little life she had tried so hard to protect.

"You can try again," the doctor told her in his usual cool tones. "This is nature's way of taking care of something that wasn't meant to be."

"Not meant to be? Tell that to my heart," Kim replied. Her head hung in an attempt to keep from meeting the eyes of the women in the office—women who still possessed their hopes and dreams.

"How could God do this to us?" she cried, clinging to David's shirt.

Kim and David rode this roller coaster time and time again, learning to control the excitement and guard their secret every time they discovered Kim was pregnant. But getting pregnant came easy; staying pregnant was impossible.

•••

Walking out of the doctor's office after losing her fifth baby, Kim knew she could never put herself through that kind of pain again. "Why don't we adopt?" she asked David. "I could love any child."

"But wouldn't you like to have one of our own? Don't you want to see what our baby would look like?"

Kim would have loved that, but she couldn't handle another loss. She prayed for God to give her an answer.

Months later, I realized that I could be the answer to Kim's prayers.

"Let me carry a baby for you," I offered, while Kim and I sat enjoying our coffee. Kim later told me that the sun shining off my hair created the sudden appearance of a halo.

"I don't know. David would never go for this."

"Why not? This way he could have the biological child he wants. We know that you can get pregnant. You just need someone who can carry to term."

"I can't ask you to do that."

"Don't be silly. All I have to do is carry the baby for nine months; you have to raise the child. Just think about it."

At first, Kim thought it was a crazy idea, but her mind constantly wandered back to it. Finally, she shared the idea with David. To her surprise, he went along with it.

I underwent in vitro fertilization, using only two embryos. Ten days later, we got good news. I was pregnant—with twins! We were all surprised that it had happened so quickly, with very little effort.

Kim spent every spare minute with me, watching my belly expand. She admitted to suffering moments of envy, wishing she could personally experience the growth of her children, but she quickly replaced them with appreciation as I made every effort to include her in everything. Nonetheless, I could see that she was keeping her expectations in check. How could she be happy? She had been there before, and it always ended in loss.

During a sonogram appointment in the third trimester, it finally hit Kim. "I am going to be a mother! I'm going to have a baby. I can't believe it." Her feelings of excitement and joy refused to be controlled or guarded any longer. She realized that this was really happening.

"You're not having a baby; you're having two," I teased. The excitement in the room was contagious. It was moments like this that reassured me I was doing the right thing.

Weeks later, the nurses wheeled me into the delivery room while Kim and David followed beside the gurney. Time slowed down in the delivery room, but sped up all at once as the twins' birth neared. Kim and David never dreamed they would experience the birth of their own children. The doctor spoke to Kim, but she could focus only on my face while I held her hand, reassuring her with a tender smile.

Within minutes of each other, their twin boys were born. The nurses started to hand them to me, but I refused to take them. "Kim is their mother; she should hold them first. She has been waiting a long time to see them."

Next thing I knew, Kim was holding her twin boys—the twins she had longed for since her first miscarriage. Kissing the tops of their downy soft heads, the sweet baby smell lingered under her nose. Removing their blankets, she counted all twenty toes and fingers. They were perfect gifts from God.

Tears filled her eyes as she leaned toward my ear. Her voice shaking, she spoke barely more than a whisper, "Thank you. Thank you."

While admiring what we had done together, Kim added, "Will you be their godmother? Together we can tell them our special story of how much they were wanted and loved."

I knew that I would always be part of their lives. We had created our own version of family.

~Helen Zanone

Chapter 9

Twins and More

Double Trouble, Double Fun

It's double the giggles and double the grins,
and double the trouble if you're blessed with twins.

~*Author Unknown*

77

The Best of Intentions

Remember, people will judge you by your actions, not your intentions.
~Author Unknown

"Jim, dit down and dit me down!"

Those are among the first words that our parents remember hearing us say. Upon that request, my twin brother would bang on the railing of his baby bed until the hinge gave and the side slid to the ground. Then he'd hop out of his bed, walk to mine, and fiddle with it until I was free as well. That's when troubles began for our household.

We boys were always inseparable in those early years. Jim and I also tried to be helpful to our mother with the household chores that she somehow managed to squeeze in between caring for our older brother and us. In fact, our parents found that the only way they could get a moment's peace was to place Jim and me in a fenced area in the front yard. It looked strikingly similar to a dog run. We circled the perimeter of the enclosure in search of an escape until the grass had worn thin and a dirt trail ringed the lot. If a toy was passed to us through the chicken wire, we'd manage to destroy it in record time. What might be considered child neglect today was nothing more than survival in the 1950s.

Jim and I must have sensed the hardships that Mother faced, and on several occasions we tried to help out as best we could. Even as toddlers we looked for ways to lighten the load for her. On one occasion, Jim and I decided to help with diaper detail. After a bit of coaxing, a hamper filled with soiled cloth diapers overturned. "The boys," as family and friends called us, spread them out on the floor. The vacuum cleaner, assembled and ready for use, sat in the hallway, and we wrestled it into the room. With a flick of the switch, Jim and I managed to remove all the foul content from those diapers. Upon completing the vacuuming, we folded the diapers and stuffed them in the chest of drawers with the other clean ones. For some reason, Mother's response to our hard work was less than grateful.

Times were tough in our home. Daddy worked at a paper mill and brought home a paycheck that never lasted the month. In those days, daycare was nonexistent, so Mother spent her days riding herd on us, sewing for other women, and canning, freezing, and preserving foods for her brood. One of my mother's prized possessions in those days was a velvet-covered couch. It was one of the few nice things she'd managed to place in the house.

Being children who loved and appreciated their mother, Jim and I decided to clean the couch for her. We fetched a large jar of Noxzema cleansing cream from the bathroom. Then we crawled upon the couch and began to apply the product to every square inch. At some point, Mother realized how quiet the house had become, and as alarms sounded in her head, she knew that something must be wrong. She found us at work, but not before we had emptied the entire container and massaged it into the velvet fabric. Before long, the couch was junked and replaced with something more durable. Evidently, our hard work had gone unappreciated again.

Jim and I had identical teddy bears, and we kept them with us at all times. Our older brother Dal would torment us by grabbing the stuffed animals and hitting or kicking them. Our anguished cries poured from the room as he pummeled our bears. The toys took on almost human qualities to Jim and me, and we looked after them as if they were alive. So, it was only natural to bathe them. However, we weren't tall enough to reach the sink or to turn on the faucet in the bathtub. Yet, we could reach the water in the commode, and without hesitation, Jim and I dunked our bears into that small pool and then lathered up our stuffed friends with a bar of Dial soap. Again, Mother noticed the absence of chaos in the household and searched us out. With a disgusted "Yuck," she retrieved the bears, washed them out in the sink, and took them outside. Jim and I stood at the back door, looked on in terror, and wailed as our little friends hung by their ears on the clothes line as the sun and wind dried the water and soap suds.

Times have changed since Jim and I were kids. Children are under constant surveillance by moms and daycare workers. Jim and I were twins who needed to be busy at all times. Our actions were completed with the best of intentions; they just always seemed to backfire. Fifty years later, we still try too hard to help out. Now our wives and children have to deal with the overzealous acts of a set of twins who haven't changed all that much.

~Joe Rector

78

A Twin Bath

Childhood is that wonderful time of life when all you need to do to lose weight is take a bath.
~Author Unknown

My son had screamed his way through six months of life when I declared to my husband, "We need to have our second child now." He thought I was crazy, but I explained that having two babies close together would surely help our situation because the two children would entertain each other. Therefore, there would be less screaming. Less screaming was our immediate goal, so we went forth with "The Plan."

I got pregnant immediately, and as life would have it, twin girls were on the way. My fourteen-month-old son was still screaming when they arrived. We knew they were ours because the girls screamed just as much as our son did. They screamed at each other, they screamed at their new brother, and they screamed at us. My son reacted by screaming. I screamed at my husband, and he gently reminded me of "The Plan." Oh, yes, "The Plan."

We loved our little screamers, and as time passed, the screaming did subside, and they did entertain each other. They entertained each other so much, though, that they were never very interested in my words, especially when they were used to try to put a stop to any of their entertainment. Big people are not nearly as entertaining as little people we learned, and my voice never seemed to penetrate their eardrums. In fact, my constant "Don't, don't, don't..." was met with an immediate need by them to perform the action following the word "don't."

•••

So here I am one day, home alone with the three. An afternoon bath is needed after the high chair feeding frenzy. The girls are about eighteen months, and my son is two-and-a-half. All three have to be in the bath at the same time because, if not, the free-range child left out of the bath will surely find some furniture to pull down or a ceiling fan to ride. So all three are in the bath, wet and naked. Ding dong! Someone is at the door. I run the ten feet from the bathroom to the door, grab the package from the UPS man and turn to slam the door. However, one of the naked, sudsy little people scampers by my leg, running full speed into the front yard. It's the boy. I run to grab him, yelling, "Don't you run out there!" It takes both my arms to wrangle his slippery little body back to the door. The sudsy twins only hear, "You run out there!" Remember, they are compelled to perform the action after the word "don't." So they, too, slip past me and streak down the street.

Panic sets in. The choices aren't good. Do I run the current wet one into the house, taking my eyes off the twin runaways? I can't lock the door because I'll lock myself out. But if I don't lock it, the initial escapee will reopen the door. I go with Plan B: run after the twins, carrying Offender #1 in my arms.

We are ten houses down the street now, and they are still running, screaming their little naked heads off. I am running after them yelling, "Don't! Don't!" carrying my son like a foamy, kicking football under one arm. I catch up to them. Their twin mind reading goes into action, and they immediately sprint in opposite directions.

Where is everyone? I need help! Please, someone come out of your house and help! Don't you see two streaking twins running by your windows followed by a crazed, wild-eyed mom carrying a naked football?

One girl makes a dash for the street, and I decide to go for that one. I tackle her, but her wet body squirts from my grasp. I do a Jet-Li-style karate move and pin her in between my legs, still holding the squirming boy. I yell a futile, "Don't! Don't!" at the last free child, and she mocks me by running figure eights in a nearby yard.

Then, for some strange reason, the free twin stops running and screaming. A puzzled look takes over her face. All of a sudden, she is contemplative. I see her bend her legs ever so slightly and assume a wider stance. Oh, no. Please, no. But, alas, she uses the yard as her own personal potty, defacing the yard that Stella, the owner, proudly prunes and preens every weekend. Right as this is happening, help arrives in the form of Stella emerging from her front door. Everyone freezes and looks at her. She stares in amazement. The pottying twin continues her "business" on the yard. "Help!" I squeak.

Looking back, I remember Stella watching the kids as I cleaned up her yard with the dog's pooper-scooper. Then she helped me walk all three of my naked hoodlums back to my house. Fortunately, she was also a mom, and she told me stories of her parenting adventures. She assured me that, especially with twins, there would be many more adventures around the corner. Boy, was she right!

~Shannon McCarty

Something has gone terribly wrong...

Reprinted by permission of Enoch Pyle
©2008

79

Losing a Bet

Man is a gaming animal.
He must always be trying to get the better in something or other.
~Charles Lamb

We have three active kids—twin boys, who are twenty-one months old, and our daughter, who is three. My husband, Rob, jokes occasionally that if it weren't for me, we would be shut-ins and just get delivery for everything. He claims you can get anything off the Internet, so therefore there is no reason to go anywhere... ever. It's just too much work with three young children.

In fact, I had overheard him confessing on many occasions that he has never taken all three children out by himself. He has taken one or even two at a time, but never three. It's hard to believe that a grown man of forty would be scared to take three smiling little critters out to run errands, but I found a way to use this fear for my amusement.

Rob and I occasionally make bets. (Usually, they're about silly things, like which movie will earn more money—*Sex and the City* or *Batman*?) I always seem to lose, and Rob finds it fun to make the penalty something that will make him laugh. One time, I was required to sing karaoke in front of a crowded room (which I really think is audience abuse)!

Well, a few months ago, Rob finally lost a bet. Unfortunately for the kids, the penalty was that he had to take all three of them out on a busy Saturday to go grocery shopping at Costco... by himself. Poor guy. I now know what the term "deer in the headlights" means.

Saturday arrived, and Rob had his "game face" on. Diapers changed... check! Kids dressed... check! Kids fed... check! Diaper bag packed... check! Coffee downed... check! With that, we started loading the kids in the car.

I plopped our daughter in her car seat, latched it and told her to have fun and be good for Daddy. (All the while, I am thinking, "Oh, if only I could be a fly on the wall for this one!") I gave each kid a kiss (including my sweet husband) and then handed over the grocery list. Rob took one look at the page and said, "I thought you were going to give me a short list."

"That is the short list!" I responded with a smile and then quickly walked back inside.

While they were away, I went up the street and had a pedicure. Every time I thought of Rob at Costco with all three kids, I would start giggling. It was great!

"How was it?" I asked as I met them back in the driveway two hours later. As I walked up to Rob in the driver's seat, I could tell that he had been sweating. "Oh, fine!" he replied with a smile that appeared to be forced.

Later, in the house, I got more of the story. Since Saturdays are the busiest at Costco, Rob had to park far away from the front door and somehow deliver the children from the car to the closest shopping cart. He managed to accomplish this, and they made it through the door and started to cruise the aisles in search of the items on the list.

Apparently, they had made it through only half of the grocery list when our daughter announced that she had to go potty... now! One of the downsides about shopping at Costco is that their gigantic shopping carts cannot be easily left anywhere near the bathrooms, and in many cases they cannot be taken to the bathroom without going through the checkout. And poor Rob not only had to deal with our three-year-old, but also to figure out what to do with the twins (who are not yet walking well enough to be set down in a restroom without having icky consequences).

Now, most parents of twins will, at one time or another, be in situations where they think, "Somebody help me!" They'll look around pleadingly, hoping that their mother will magically appear and tell them how to resolve the situation, or that someone else's mom will recognize the signs of distress and make everything all better. Such was the situation in which Rob found himself.

When the "I have to go potty" announcement was made, Rob decided that the shopping trip was complete. He raced to the closest checkout stand and hurriedly dumped the contents of the cart onto the conveyer belt while our daughter wiggled the pee-pee dance next to him. While waiting for the cashier to complete the order, he informed her that they were in an emergency bathroom situation and that he was too frazzled to answer her question about whether the boys were identical or fraternal and all of the other normal twin-related questions. Instead, he pleaded with her to hurry. By this time, both boys in the cart were on the opposite side of the checkout stand, crying and attempting to stand up since Daddy was out of reach. Apparently, this is where Rob really started sweating.

After they made it through the checkout, he hurriedly escorted our daughter—who was telling him that she couldn't hold it any longer—into the bathroom with a boy held like a football under each arm. All four squeezed into a tight stall in which our daughter proceeded to go potty. Just in time.

Of course, not wanting to admit to his frazzled state, Rob played down the situation quite a bit when he got home, and only gave me part of the story. He also jokingly picked on me for giving our daughter a cup of juice before the trip. I certainly hadn't done it on purpose, but it was a great idea for the next time I sent him out with the kids!

The next day, I got the rest of the story when I arrived at Costco with only one of the boys, Ryan, to pick up where Rob had left off. As I went through the checkout, the clerk looked at Ryan and said, "Hi again!" When I asked her what she meant, she said, "Oh, he was here yesterday." I was surprised that she recognized my son when she must help at least a hundred people a day, but she explained that she remembered both boys, along my husband and daughter. She laughed and said, "Oh, your husband was a hard one to forget. He was a mess! The boys were crying and trying to escape from the cart, the girl was about to pee her pants, and all he could say to me was 'Hurry, please!'"

When I got home, I told Rob about the clerk remembering him. He sheepishly told me the rest of the story in its entirety. He hasn't made a bet with me since.

~Stacey Vandell

80

The Glamorous Life

Home is the one place in all this world where hearts are sure of each other.
~Frederick W. Robertson

Whenever I tell someone that my husband is a professional golfer on the PGA Tour, they have an image of five-star hotels, room service being delivered at 10 A.M. and leisurely walking around the most beautiful golf courses in the world. Well, for Tom and me, it did start out that way....

We exchanged vows on the island of Maui at sunset, with Vince Gill singing as my father walked me down the aisle. Tom's three beautiful blue-eyed, blond-haired children—whom I am now blessed to call my stepchildren—were standing by our sides. We returned to Scottsdale, Arizona, and almost immediately began dreaming of conceiving children of our own. Six months later, I was pregnant and ecstatic! Liza Jane (named after Vince's famous song) was born on February 10, 1996.

After adjusting to living on the road with a little one, we decided to have another. I had my first ultrasound four weeks into my second pregnancy because I just knew something wasn't the same as my first, and I learned that I was carrying twins! I was floored. I didn't even know if there were twins in my family. But after a difficult pregnancy, Jay and Jennifer (named after friends Jay Haas and Jennifer Johnson) made their appearance on May 7, 1998.

We were so thrilled and yet so tired. Two days after arriving home, a friend of mine brought over dinner. Tom greeted her at the door wearing a V-neck puffy-sleeved maternity top of mine, to which she simply said, "Nice shirt!" I still laugh at that image. We survived the all-night feedings, although Tom and I were known to put gallons of milk in the pantry and pencils in the dishwasher.

That is when my life as a tour wife abruptly ended. I was happy to put up my suitcases except for special occasions. Motherhood was my new career. Tom reluctantly went back on tour. We missed each other terribly when he was away and cherished each moment together when he was home. The kids were literally like branches on a tree when Daddy came home. He was smothered, and he loved it!

As the next three years passed, the older children were in college, the little ones were starting pre-school, and Tom was moving on to the Champions Tour. We were finally starting to live easily on a schedule, absolutely surrounded with laughter and love. With six happy and healthy children, there was only one thing left to do: have just one more "bonus" Purtzer to round things out. This time I was in for an ultrasound at just two weeks, and guess what they found... yep, I was again pregnant with twins! Tom didn't believe it until he saw the picture from the ultrasound with his own eyes. I can't blame him because we make a habit of teasing each other relentlessly. On August 25, 2002, Robin and Juli were born. Tom refers to them as his "hall of fame twins." They were named after two of his closest friends, Robin Yount and Juli Inkster. Both are hall of fame members in their respective sports.

Since then, we have repainted our house several times over. We have original artwork in black Sharpie on the furniture and under the dining room table. And on any given day, there is either something stuck in the garbage disposal or the dogs are getting makeovers along with the dolls. We have had some very original haircuts come out of the "double-trouble room" (my five-year-old twin girls' bedroom). One of my favorite memories is catching Jennifer in her footed pajamas finger-painting peanut butter throughout the walk-in pantry. No matter how messy or hectic each day begins, it always ends with clean, sweet-smelling children making the rounds of good-night hugs and kisses, and a read from the Bible. Our gratitude cups are definitely running over.

My definition of the glamorous life has definitely been rewritten, but it is all the more beautifully made, sticky kisses and all. Just think, grandparenthood is just around the corner!

~Lori Purtzer

81

Hank Has Just Left the Building

When my kids become wild and unruly, I use a nice, safe playpen. When they're finished, I climb out.
~Erma Bombeck

I had turned down a couple of invitations from a friend of mine to take my twin boys to story time at our local library. I was afraid of the unknown, and I knew that sometimes I got over my head when I took them on outings by myself. My instincts were telling me this was that type of situation, but I finally decided to ignore my little voice and go. Besides, it seemed like the perfect day to take them. It was winter time, but we were having mild, beautiful weather. What could possibly happen on such a gorgeous day?

We got there, and I explained to my friend and the storyteller that if things didn't go well, I would put the guys back in the stroller after the first story. Well, it became apparent even before the story began that my little guys were not going to be entertained by a storyteller. The other children sat quietly with their moms or dads and listened while the story was being told. But my guys were running around the library (thank goodness, it is a small library) and standing on the cute little activity table set up for coloring or reading books.

When I realized this situation was totally out of control and the story was near the end, I started packing the boys back into the stroller. I caught Jack and was strapping him in when I saw little

Hank dart across the library. I finished strapping Jack into the stroller, knowing that the library was not that big and I could easily find Hank. Not so. He was nowhere to be found!

I checked with everyone I could find. People said they saw him running, but they didn't know where he went. The man at the front desk said there was no way that Hank could have gone through an exit door because a bell rings when the doors are opened, and he had not heard the bell ring. He came out from behind the desk and began looking for Hank for me.

After what seemed like an eternity, I heard someone yell, "I found him!" I ran in the direction of the voice and found that Hank had gone through an exit door to the basement of the library and tumbled down two flights of stairs. A lady working in the basement had caught him!

I do not remember much after that point except that I held little Hank tightly, tried to keep from crying and vowed to myself that I would never take my twin boys anywhere again!

I learned from this experience that parenting twins is different. Perhaps some twins might have gone to that story time every Tuesday morning and been fine. But my twins, I now realize, need a more active outing that involves climbing and running—preferably in a completely enclosed area! Raising twins requires a double dose of mother's instinct... and sometimes a catcher's mitt!

~Jean Hale

82

My Pesky Twin Brothers

Big sisters are the crab grass in the lawn of life.
~Charles M. Schulz

There's nothing like Mom giving birth to twin boys to make a big sister feel like chopped liver.

It was bad enough each time she disappeared into the hospital and brought home a new sister—twice. The more kids, the less attention for me. But two boys? Only eight years old, and already I felt invisible.

This was back before the plethora of fertility drug-induced multiples. Twins were rather a rarity, and everywhere we went, people gawked at Bob and Don. Chucked them under their fat little chins. Waved. Cooed. And completely ignored me.

Named for Mom's older brothers, my fraternal twin brothers upstaged me at every turn.

And as they grew, they created work. As the eldest, I was in charge of Donny, who tended toward trouble. Sal got sunny Bobby, the cheery one, who'd later send Mom into fits of laughter by picking her up and putting her in a closet. Jill, the third sister, opted for pets, from cats to "horny toads."

It was my task to fish Donny out of the tub first (Bobby wanted to stay in to swim laps), stand him on the toilet seat to dry him off, and wrestle him into jammies. I taught him to pee straight. And the day he ran away from home, it was my neck on the line.

Mom and Dad were off on errands, and five-year-old Don, as usual, was not cooperating.

"I'm leaving home!" he announced.

"Go ahead!" I dared.

Matter-of-factly, he spread himself a peanut butter and jelly sandwich, and tossed a carrot into a paper bag for good measure. He slammed the door behind him.

Where would he go? What if he didn't come back? What would he do when it grew dark? Worst of all, how much trouble would I be in for letting him skip?

I decided to follow him, trailing at a discreet distance. Up Donna Lane he went, and around the corner. Two blocks straight ahead until he came to Chapman Avenue, a busy Southern California thoroughfare.

As the cars whizzed past, Don settled on the curb and took out his lunch. Halfway through the carrot, I edged over to him and asked about his plans.

"I was going to Gramma and Grampa's," he said.

"That's way far away in Glendale, and you can't walk on the freeway," I ventured wisely.

"So?" he sneered in defiance, sputtering carrots. "My real problem is... I'm not allowed to cross Chapman."

Saved by the bell, er, the busy road, I thought with relief. Donny finished his carrot, wadded up his lunch bag and stuffed it in his pocket. Together, we walked home.

And together, we grew up and became parents ourselves. I became a grandparent before Don did, and eventually, gramma to twin girls. The day I helped my daughter cart them in for their first doctor's appointment, I was suddenly eight years old again.

People beamed at the babies. Chucked them under the chin. Cooed. And ignored me.

Hey, I thought, what am I—chopped liver?

No, I reminded myself, I'm the big sister, the mother, the delighted grandmother. Bob and Don are now grandfathers.

And to this day when I see twins, or sometimes triplets, I still speak to their big brother or sister first. You're still important, I want to reassure them.

I just hope they live near a busy street.

~Jann Mitchell

83

Surprise! No Surprise!

Each day comes bearing its own gifts. Untie the ribbons.
~Ruth Ann Schabacker

Think back to your childhood. Remember when you and your siblings opened piles of birthday and Christmas gifts, surprised and thrilled by the wondrous contents placed inside each package?

You do?

Well, I don't. It wasn't that we didn't receive presents on those special days or that we didn't experience some pretty impressive hauls. I just never was surprised because my twin brother, Ron, always spoiled the bombshell by prematurely opening the brightly wrapped boxes. One isn't exactly elated when one knows what's inside the gift box prior to the "opening ceremony."

To his credit, I must say that my pre-adolescent brother, barely out of his primers and coloring books, could wrap up a gift with the skill and dexterity of the most seasoned department store clerk. Nor did he tamper with presents other than his own; he never touched a single package marked "To Al."

Still, the damage was done, for my parents, in their infinite wisdom, bought each of us the exact same thing throughout much of our childhood, at least until about the age of nine or ten. Their reasoning was practical—sort of "preventive maintenance." Although the philosophy escaped me during my youth, I have since realized that buying for twins presented a potential risk: What if one of the little guys thought the other's present was better and began to fight over it? Why not prevent this by purchasing them the same thing? Surely that would circumvent any potential squabbling.

It makes perfect sense to me... now. But at the tender age of six, my point of view was less evolved than it is today. All I could see was the spoiler effect, the fact that my brother was ruining my surprise by ruining his.

Don't get me wrong. I enjoyed the companionship of my brother; never was I at a loss for a playmate or, depending upon the activity, an accomplice. I only wished that he would suppress his curiosity and allow for both his—and my—surprise.

The genesis of his remarkable talent remains unknown to me. I suspect the overload of after-school classic TV sitcoms had something to do with it. Even at an early age, as far back as first or second grade, he must've figured, 'Why not?' After all, Lucy Ricardo was doing it, as was Herman Munster, the Brady Kids, Fred Flintstone, and any number of syndicated TV icons.

Nor do I believe that Ron meant any malice by this act; he simply had to know what providence had provided for him. His only crime was selfishness that he didn't consider my feelings in this matter. After several anti-climactic holidays, I finally asked him to stop ruining the surprise. (I think my exact words were something like, "Open up another present and I'll tell Mom!") But no amount of pleading or threats worked. When the matter was brought to our parents' attention, they reacted by scolding my brother and finding new places to hide the gifts. However, neither punishment worked since Ron also possessed the sleuthing skills of Sherlock Holmes and could sniff out a present from the deepest bowels of the earth.

Finally, at about the age of nine or ten, our personalities and tastes began to form, which ultimately solved the dilemma of the spoiled surprises.

Ron developed an early interest in music. Classic rock, rhythm and blues. Especially the Motor City stuff Everything from Marvin Gaye and Smokey Robinson to The Temptations and The Supremes. In those days, almost forty years ago, everyone collected 45s (singles) and records (vinyl albums). This was before the advent of compact discs and iPods.

Me? I preferred books, laboratory kits, and whatever I could use to further my knowledge and curiosity.

The differences in our hobbies made birthdays and Christmases more exciting. Ron still opened his gifts before the actual gathering, but at least the activity didn't spoil my surprise, as I was certain to receive something totally different from, say, Smokey Robinson & the Miracles' *The Tears of a Clown* or Diana Ross & The Supremes' *Greatest Hits*, Volume 3.

At last, I could enjoy the thrill of total amazement!

In the years since, I have often guilted my brother—playfully, of course—with my assertion that this early trauma helped to shape my blasé attitude toward the gift-exchange experience. Basically, he ruined Christmas and birthday surprises for me. But I'm only teasing him. The real reason I abhor birthday gifts is because they remind me of my advanced age... which is another story.

Looking back, I must admit that receiving the same gifts as your twin brother—even if it is not a surprise—is much more preferable than receiving no gifts at all. Besides, how wonderful it was to have a twin brother to share not only my childhood days but my whole life with. I can still recall the handful of classmates who used to confide in me that they wished they had a brother or sister to play with, their voices so sad and lonely.

It may have taken many years, but today I realize the truth: Having a twin has been a real blessing to me... even better than the surprise contents of a box.

~Al Serradell

84

Happy Birthday to a Mother of Twins

The one thing children wear out faster than shoes is parents.
~John J. Plomp

On my birthday, my three-year-old twin boys slept in until 9:00 A.M. What a great present, I thought, to be able to sleep in and wake up on my own. Little did I know that it would be the boys' only present to me!

Since it was my birthday, I thought it would be fun to have a picnic lunch downstairs—the Wisconsin Winter kind—while watching a cartoon movie. Before the movie ended, I snuck upstairs to take a quick shower. I must have overestimated the remaining length of the movie to keep them occupied.

I came out of the shower to find both boys on the living room carpet—with an entire gallon box of instant mashed potatoes dumped all over the floor! They were throwing it around by the handful. It looked like snow everywhere! As punishment, I sent them to their room for a nap after giving them a bath. What a waste, I thought to myself, as I sorted the potatoes from the toys and vacuumed. Luckily, the chocolate milk mix container that lay on the floor next to the empty box of instant mashed potatoes had not been opened.

After maybe ten minutes of cleaning, I heard the boys again. Obviously, they were not sleeping. Opening their bedroom door, I literally choked at the sight. It was snowing baby powder—a whole bottle of baby powder to be exact! There was powder all over their beds, the floor, their toys, and my boys. My twins have dark hair, skin and eyes, but at that moment they looked like ghosts. They must have tasted it, too, because it was all around their mouths like clown paint. What a mess! I wanted to scream, shut the door, and ignore them, but I still had eight more hours before my husband came home.

And so the clean-up began again. I had to put a fan in their open window to try to ventilate the room. (Unfortunately, it was about twenty degrees outside.) I put the boys in the bathtub for the second time that day. Afterward, I stripped their beds and took all the clothes and bedding to the wash. Being so tired, and knowing that the cleanup of their room had only just begun because all that powder needed to settle first, I took the boys downstairs for a nap. This time, I was napping with them to make sure they did not get into anything else.

With naptime over and a small supper eaten, I decided it was time to finish cleaning up their room. Trying to keep the boys out while I cleaned was difficult, but at least when they kept running up and down the hall to check on me every two minutes, I knew they were not creating another mess... or were they? It was eight o'clock at night, bedtime for the boys, and I was not even halfway through wiping the powder off their bedroom furniture. Suddenly, I heard something strange cracking.

Oh, no, I thought. Is there something worse than baby powder and instant mashed potatoes? Yes! The boys had gotten into the refrigerator and taken a full egg carton into the living room. When I found them, one was rolling the eggs down a little slide onto the carpet, while the other was riding over them with his tricycle. Anger is an extremely nice word for what I felt at that moment! I did not even have the strength to punish them. It was already after 8:00, and I still hadn't finished cleaning up the baby powder.

It was time for their third bath of the day—this time to remove the eggs smeared all over them. Meanwhile, I grabbed the paper towels and another bucket of soapy water and wiped up the eggs as much as I could. Leaving the egg mess, I went back to finish cleaning up the baby powder so the boys could sleep in their room that night.

Finally, my husband came home to what was left of the messes and spent at least an hour and a half trying to get the remaining powder out and removing the eggs soaked into the carpet. The boys went to bed around eleven that night.

Believe it or not, I found out it could have been even worse—unopened syrup and mustard bottles were found under the slide when my husband began cleaning up the eggs! I do not think my husband fully comprehended the extent of my horrible day until he saw the pictures I had taken of our twins in the middle of their messes.

My final thought for the day, besides wishing it was midnight so I could say it wasn't my birthday anymore, was that no one would believe me if I told them this story—except, maybe, for a mother of twins!

~Jana Malkan

Campbell.
"IT WAS AN EARTHQUAKE. A TWO ON THE RICHTER SCALE."

85

The Switch

Let us be thankful for the fools. But for them the rest of us could not succeed.
~Mark Twain

It is more fun to switch than it is to change.

April Fools' Day was getting close, and Dot and I were supercharged with excitement. She was my partner in crime, and we were on the eve of our annual event. Maybe it was just our Irish ancestry demonstrating itself, but we looked forward to any opportunity to have fun, joke, laugh, and tease.

As identical twins, we loved to switch classes. April Fools' Day was the perfect time for this caper. It gave us a chance to have a little fun with teachers and classmates. We planned our strategy with precision. We choreographed our outfits with matching shoes and decided how to style our hair. Timing and planning were crucial to this clandestine operation. We confirmed that we knew at least one person in each class. If we didn't, that would be a dead giveaway. Only a few close friends were aware of what we did each year. We were called mirror twins, as we were identical in looks, always dressed alike, and our voices sounded alike. That made it relatively easy to fool people. However, we always had to be on the outlook for the kid who was a tattletale.

It was hilarious to sit in a different class and watch a variety of expressions on kids' faces. Not everyone picked up that something was happening right away. However, a few were perceptive enough to distinguish the subtle differences between Dot and me. Others remembered us from the previous year and quickly caught on. Soon, word buzzed around the class like bees collecting nectar, but the teacher never saw through the ruse. I sat there with a giggle hanging dangerously just under my breath, about to burst out loud. It was exciting. I felt like Nancy Drew going undercover on one of her mystery adventures. Suspense was in the air like a heavy cloud. If the teacher asked me a question about the lesson taught that day, I was up a creek without a paddle. I tried to appear nonchalant as I concentrated on blending into the class.

Dot and I hurried and met at the end of school to compare notes. We screamed, laughed, and congratulated each other on another successful switch. Our hoax worked. We were fortunate and never got caught. That was the biggest thrill of the day.

As we grew up, we perfected the switch in other situations. We experimented once on a double date. My boyfriend, Gene, was driving in from out of town and bringing his friend, David, for Dot. As we had never met him, it was the perfect time to play our special game. When we got ready to get into the car to go to the restaurant, I got in the back seat with David. Dot went in the front with Gene, who was already aware of the arrangement. I talked and acted like everything was normal. About fifteen minutes later, Dot and I started laughing. The poor guy had no clue what was happening. As we laughed, we let David in on our little secret. Gene stopped the car, and Dot and I exchanged places. At least David was a good sport and laughed, too. That was his first encounter with twins.

Later, when Dot married, we tricked her husband, Ken, more than once. The first time it happened was when she was at my house and Ken called to speak to her. While they were talking, I indicated that we should play the switch. That was before speaker phones, so she quickly handed me the phone. I continued the conversation for a few minutes and returned the phone to her. We repeated this process several times. Finally, at the end of the conversation, she told Ken how we tricked him. As he could not tell us apart on the phone, he laughed and knew the joke was on him.

Dot and I not only were able to switch places and trick people with our voices, but we were able to change thoughts at the drop of a hat. We would be talking together for a few minutes on a particular subject and in midstream take off on another tangent. It was like we played hopscotch in our minds and just skipped to the next move. One time, my husband tried to follow our conversation and got thoroughly confused. We would phone one another and just start talking without a lot of detail. Dot always knew exactly what I was talking about. It was like we had a special form of verbal shorthand. To anyone else, this sounded like gobbledegook. It sure made for some wild conversations.

Switching was much more fun than changing. It added a lot more flavor to everyday living. Variety is the spice of life, and twins definitely enjoy it!

~Donna K. Hogue

86

Chicken Soup for the Soul

Romance in Steel

While we try to teach our children all about life,
our children teach us what life is all about.
~Angela Schwindt

My twin boys have become intimate with vehicles of all kinds. They are just shy of two years old, yet their passion is as tenacious as the heartbeats that fuel their little bodies. I thought I could steer clear of the emotional pang of that particular word, intimacy, until it knocked on the door in the form of my sons' first serious girlfriends or some other consuming love that causes older boys to return home after hours in a vague, inebriated sweat. But no, the darlings have arrived in the undying form of four wheels and a chassis. The whole affair began one morning in the parking lot of Costco, when my son, Luke, pointed to the SUV beside us and declared in an arresting Boston accent, "Caaahhhh." It was his first word.

When Luke uttered the word again with such conviction and exuberance, we knew what he wanted—resounding confirmation from his parents that, yes, the colossal thing next to us was a car. Instead, we lost the chance to bestow praise because of a dizzying wave of parental angst. Soon Julian joined his brother in pointing and shouting "car" for every vehicle, and it felt like a clash of values.

For one thing, my husband and I have always prided one another on our compact cars. If our jobs permitted us, we would have abandoned our cars completely for the more earth-friendly option of commuting by bicycle. Suddenly, through that mysterious process of physical sensation and developing brain to his first articulation, Luke gave voice to the word "car." Was it really true that all the impressions our son gathered from the time of infancy culminated in this word? If we had lived in the woods or on a farm, we wondered, would our son's first word have been "tree"? Or "cow" maybe?

Perhaps our culture of commerce had already begun to affect our children's sense of self in relation to the world. We agonized over the few times we turned on the television when the boys were present. During those times, one of the boys inevitably abandoned *Green Eggs and Ham* and froze in front of the screen as the electric glow of a sedan glided along a Pacific highway. The loving voiceover, always god-like, assured us, "Yes, this can be your life."

My husband and I made a decision. We looked at the parking lot sprawl in our lives and vowed to introduce the boys to the verdant landscapes of nature. At the beach on Cape Cod, we took off our shoes and led the boys through sand and tide pools. Instead of chasing the waves on that gleaming summer day, however, Julian insisted on traipsing back up the dunes, past the flowering beach plums, to stand on the pavement and observe the summer vacation traffic.

We tried visiting the local farm. Enthusiastically, we showed the boys how to pick berries from the bush and smiled when Luke filled his mouth with blueberries as if he were storing them for the long winter ahead. Suddenly, some mysterious radar engaged that part of his brain in tune with the mechanisms of things. Luke began pulling me vigorously by the hand, berry juice trickling down his mouth and neck, my freshly picked quart of blueberries spilling over. My son became a little blue pit bull, moaning and tugging, until he reached the far corner of the orchard. His destination—an aging excavator, rusting beside a pit of rotting apples. Perhaps we should have considered that if we did live on a farm, our son's first word might have intuitively been "tractor."

We are aware of the fact that many boys and girls regard cars with awe. Friends tell of their children's toy car and truck collections, overflowing from toy boxes to basements. We have seen toy store aisles dedicated entirely to the likes of Tonka and Matchbox—those corporate giants that make billions of dollars by melding plastic into trains, trucks, and cars, season after selling season. Now each morning at about seven A.M., we hear the joyous twin shouts of "Buuuuuuus!" when a tired, municipal bus drives by. My husband and I love reading, art and languages. The boys' grandfather is a poet, for crying out loud, so we must ask, "Where did this passion for cars come from?"

Studies conjecture that children's attention to cars may be affiliated with early man's use of tools, an interest in the way inanimate objects work together for a purpose. A colleague of mine added that it's about making sense of the world. "They like to categorize things," she said. "They'll order their cars by color and model. Then just wait until they start up with dinosaurs."

Whatever the meaning behind this love of cars, one thing I know is certain: In the boys' faces, there is joy and, sometimes, heartache. At the moment, they do not seem to be absorbed in disassembling their vehicles to uncover the parts at work, nor have they placed all their Matchbox cars in color-coordinated rows. Instead, the boys are wide-eyed at the call of police sirens or garbage trucks driving in reverse. They look longingly at the postal truck, and then cry out when the mail carrier drives off into the sunset. Hours of contentment are found when playing with cars in their Fisher-Price garage as if the boys' imagination assures a place of closeness with their beloved. Often, there is simply a wildly contagious joy of fans for their team of diggers, dump trucks, and motorcycles by day, and tenderness when choosing a toy car to cuddle in the crib by night.

When I finally stopped projecting my own interests onto the twins, some curious things happened. During a summer walk on the boulevard, I followed the boys, and we discovered that it was "Motorcycle Night" along the Merrimack River. We saw the shiniest Harleys and the sleekest Japanese models you could ever imagine.

One afternoon, we stopped to admire a majestic red fire engine in front of a fire station. When the firefighters came outside, they smiled at us and said, "We've been looking for you guys!" Then they reached into the truck and gave us three kid-sized fire hats. On the interstate highway, we caught the eye of a bandana-clad trucker. Through the flash of headlights and side-view mirrors, we could see that the Mack truck was proudly named "Miss Nanci" in a display of purple script on the metal frame. When Julian and Luke reached up and cried out, "TRUUUUUCK," the trucker reached up, too. And as our vehicles drove at high-speed side-by-side, Miss Nanci returned the glory in the long, sustaining thrill of a steel horn.

~Jennifer Moglia Lucil

87

Chicken Soup for the Soul

Santa Has a Twin!

Our hearts grow tender with childhood memories and love of kindred, and we are better throughout the year for having, in spirit, become a child again at Christmastime.

~Laura Ingalls Wilder

The Christmas season was upon us, and once again the department stores filled their shelves with festive items to tempt the shoppers. Christmas had always been my favorite holiday, and now with children of my own I was eager to build those perfect memories that children remember forever. From my own childhood, I fondly recalled popcorn balls hung by red and green ribbons, sword fights with empty wrapping paper tubes, a Christmas mouse, and a ceramic Christmas tree. I so wanted to create those kinds of memories with my kids, and I did with one Santa figurine that stills holds a very special spot in our hearts today, many years later.

As a young family at the time, our Christmas decorations were a bit on the sparse side, and I was just beginning to build my now bursting-at-the-seams Santa Claus collection. I am also quite partial to unique things, so when I found this particular Santa, I knew he was coming home with me! He was a sixteen-inch robust Santa figurine, but this Santa was clad in a green suit (rather than the common red suit) from head to toe, complete with the fur collar. I was so thrilled when I found him. Once home, I located the perfect spot for him on the corner cabinet.

My identical twin boys were four that year, and I was acutely aware that they were old enough now for their memories to begin. They were little sponges, absorbing something every minute of every day. I had been anticipating the holiday season for months, laying out my plans for baking Christmas cookies and stringing the popcorn. We had taken the official Christmas card portrait, with the twins in their color-coded matching outfits, one in red and one in green.

We had relied heavily on color coding in their early years, which allowed friends and family to identify each without the hanging question, "Is that right?" Quinton had always worn red, and Zachary had always worn blue. But, for the Christmas season, Zachary got a break and was switched to green instead. Every Christmas to that point, my beautiful boys would dress throughout the Christmas season in red and green.

Later that month, my parents came to share the holiday season. After the initial oohing and aahing over the decorations, meal, and especially the grandchildren, we settled in the living room to continue our visit. The boys were cuddled in the laps of their grandparents, dressed in their red and green Christmas pajamas. As we discussed Santa's impending arrival to the wide-eyed boys, my father caught a glimpse of the newest Santa figurine in the corner.

"What kind of crazy Santa is that over there?" he asked. "Santa Claus doesn't wear green!"

Zachary, without missing a beat, looked up and said in his most matter-of-fact voice: "Grampy! Can't you see? That is Santa's identical twin!"

~Yavonne Field-Bagwell

off the mark.com
by Mark Parisi
RUDOLPH WENT ON TO HAVE TWINS,
LEIF BLINKER AND WRIGHT BLINKER
MARK PARISI 12-17

88

Chicken Soup for the Soul

Me First

It's too big a world to be in competition with everyone.
The only person who I have to be better than is myself.
~*Colonel Potter,* M*A*S*H

My twin brother, Ron, and I have always competed.

Round One, which occurred shortly after our birth, went to me. According to family members, I was the first one to crawl, to babble words, to stand up and stagger to adults. It wasn't that my brother, Ron, was slower to develop. Hardly. He simply would hold back and watch me perform the latest trick as if to assess the outcome. Once he saw the attention I received, he would then perform the same feat and enjoy his own reward.

Pretty clever, actually. I mean, why jump out in front of traffic before deciding whether it would hurt?

Growing up, these were my bragging rights, being the first to do this or that. Of course, that's what siblings—especially twins—do; they compete.

But Ron had his own strategy. After all, he was smart enough to play it cautiously, since not everything on my list of "firsts" was positive.

I remember a couple of my stunts that caused an incredible reaction—and not the good kind. One day, I decided I didn't need to take the afternoon bus home from school. As an eight-year-old, I could chart my own path, literally, and talked my brother, Ron, into walking home with me. This misguided act of independence would seem dangerous enough in a small town. Factor in the actual locale as Los Angeles, and the potential for disaster takes on epic proportions.

Only now, as an adult, many years later, could I even begin to imagine my parents' horror when the afternoon bus arrived at the corner and their precious twin boys failed to get off. Frantic, Mom and Dad contacted the school, the police, relatives, friends—anyone who might have seen us. Thankfully, a cop spotted us trying to cross the highway (who says we don't have guardian angels watching us?) and brought us safely home. I cannot remember what my punishment was, but it was obviously severe enough for me never to do it again.

Another horrendously bad idea occurred when I talked my brother into re-enacting a scene from one of our favorite horror movies, and we set the backyard on fire. The blaze extinguished, one of the firemen informed my parents that they had a juvenile delinquent on their hands. (I'm pretty sure they were talking about me.)

In high school, Ron's competitiveness proved successful as he made better grades than I did, while we both competed for who joined the most campus clubs and received the most party invitations. My vindication occurred when I was the first to be accepted into a prestigious college, a victory that surprised even me.

But as the Brat Pack of the eighties would say, "That was then; this is now," as I saw my so-called lead (however slight) vanish over the years. As adults, Ron always seemed to land the better jobs and have the nicer apartments.

Today, my brother battles multiple sclerosis. When I first learned of his condition, I panicked and flew to California to see him, expecting the worst. Fortunately, I was surprised to see that the disease had not dampened his spirit or his competitive streak. He took his medication without complaint; he even suggested we drive to the beach so he could take a long walk along the piers.

I told him I was proud of how well he was handling the situation. He didn't even seem to mind wearing the leg braces that slowed him down on the long hike along the beach. In fact, he kept scolding me for slowing down when I began to tire out. "Can't you keep up, old man?" he laughed.

Ron's attitude was inspiring. He said—and showed—that he refused to let the disease win. During one of our conversations, he said that the disease was a blessing, since it reminded him of how much he possessed in life, of how lucky he was to have so many family members and friends around him. He admitted that he, like so many of us, had taken life and all its activities for granted.

But no more.

Each day has become a gift to him, a potential for great things to happen. He told me he could live with the disease, but he would not let it control his life. Whatever he wanted to do, he would do it and celebrate in the knowledge that he could.

As I contemplate these conversations, I believe Ron has won Round Two over me. He's faced serious illness first and has shown me that he isn't afraid; that there is no need for fear; that faith and acceptance can help carry him through this difficult journey.

This reminded me of how, when we were toddlers, Ron would wait for me to crawl, and then walk first. Now, I can see that it is Ron who has raised the bar of competition. Because of his desire to win, he has moved into first place, and I am the one who must now catch up.

~Al Serradell

Chapter 10

Twins and More

Lessons Learned

You learn something every day if you pay attention.

~Ray LeBlond

89

The Fire Department, an Angel, and One Big Rock

When someone sings his own praises, he always gets the tune too high.
~Mary H. Waldrip

My husband, Noel, and I were competent individuals before we had twins. We quickly met our match in the form of two tiny infants. Despite arriving early and spending time in the NICU, our daughters, Sarah and Keegan, were small, but healthy girls. We were thrilled to have them home and finally start functioning as parents. Being a first-time mom, I had no idea how to pace myself. The girls were on a schedule, but complications around feeding, reflux, and colic left little time for sleep. My excitement quickly morphed into a bedraggled alertness, and I seldom left the house.

One of our big milestones was Keegan and Sarah's first pediatrician appointment. We found a fantastic pediatrician who is a twin himself, and we were brimming with pride as we walked into his office. The visit went swimmingly. There was satisfactory oohing and ahhing over the girls by the office staff. Our pediatrician was impressed with the girls' progress and told us we were doing a fine job as parents. We beamed at the news. Despite our physical exhaustion, there was a spring in our step as we bundled our babies in their infant seats and headed out to the family truckster, our small SUV that Noel refuses to admit closely resembles a station wagon.

We placed the girls in the car, popped their binkies in their mouths, and shut the doors. Noel and I shared a tender moment looking into each other's eyes over the top of the car. We were proud parents with two beautiful daughters. Then Noel and I both tried to open our doors. The smiles left our faces in tandem as we realized that, like our babies, our keys were securely locked inside the car.

I would like to say that we immediately sprang into action, but our lack of sleep led us to spend the next few minutes looking dumbfounded and repeatedly trying to open the car doors. Attempts to get our two-month-olds to unlock the doors were equally unsuccessful. My head began to clear enough to take in small chunks of information about our situation. I noted that Sarah and Keegan were both dozing comfortably covered in their blankets. Unfortunately, this would probably not last long because that day was turning out to be the hottest day that fall. We needed a new strategy, and we needed one quickly. Noel pulled out his cell phone and called the fire department. They were a bit delayed due to an actual fire as opposed to a foolish parenting misstep. Thankfully, the girls were still sleeping, and I tried to cover one of the windows with my body to keep out the sun.

Soon, we heard the sirens and saw the lights. The fire truck could not fit into the parking lot so it ended up blocking most of the street. The firefighters ran over to the car with a jimmy and a trailing crowd of onlookers. The lunch hour was approaching, and people began to dribble out into the little parking lot. Bits of the spectators' conversations filtered through my head: "New parents," "They must feel awful," and, of course, the inevitable, "Twins... they must have their hands full!" I was too relieved and exhausted to feel the mortification. One of the firemen began working on the door while another tried to joke with us to lessen the tension. I was beginning to relax a bit when I heard one of them say, "Uh, we have a problem over here."

Apparently, if you wanted a vehicle that could withstand the most experienced car thief, our family truckster would be the way to go. All of the firemen's attempts to open the door were stymied. This was no longer funny; it was beginning to get hot. I looked around on the ground and found a suitable rock with which to break a window. Noel pleaded with me to wait just one more minute while he ran inside the pediatrician's office to get the number of a locksmith from the phonebook. I stood outside, blocking the sun from my babies' window, avoiding eye contact with the crowd, and trying to decide which window would be best to break. If I broke the window in the front seat, the glass might end up on the girls. If I broke our back window, I was unsure if I could get past the newly installed dog gate. After several weeks of little to no sleep, deciding which window to break was proving as difficult as an SAT question.

Noel ran back to the car. "The locksmith will be here in less than five minutes!" he reported. Then he added, "Um, could you put down the rock, honey?" "No!" I growled. The rock was dirty and unwieldy, but it was a solid representation that a solution would come. At this point, our beloved pediatrician came out of his office. He heard that we were still in the parking lot and came out to investigate. The good doc quickly assessed the situation and gave his recommendation: If the locksmith was not here in a couple of minutes, break a window. My grip on the rock tightened. Just then we heard tires squeal as an enormous truck with the picture of a lock on the side pulled up. Everyone in the crowd, even the firemen, drew silent, as the door of the truck swung open with an ominous creak.

Out of the truck stepped an imposing woman. Picture for a moment a tough, no-nonsense woman—the type who could intimidate firemen, the type affectionately referred to as a "broad." A slight gasp ran through the crowd as the firemen shrank back, but all I saw was an angel. To this day, I swear that she was surrounded by a halo of light; then again, that could have been the sleep deprivation. "Let's get them babies out," she confidently announced. In less than fifteen seconds, we had Sarah and Keegan back in our arms. The crowd cheered, waking our girls, who finally began to cry. After thanking our guardian angel profusely and taking her picture with the twins on her cell phone ("Twins! I've got to show this to the guys back at the shop!"), we headed back inside so our pediatrician could check out the girls once again.

Our family's triumphant strut out of the pediatrician's office was now replaced by a walk of shame. Other parents looked at us with derision, pity, or bemusement. The doctor assured us that Keegan and Sarah emerged from the ordeal unscathed, then set about trying to comfort us. "This happens to a lot of parents," he said. "Someday, you'll look back on this and laugh—well, not today, of course!" he quickly added, noting my icy stare. It turns out, he was right. Not only can I now laugh at our story, but I can also look back on that day with fondness. It is comforting to remember that when I felt lost and helpless as a parent, grasping at straws (or in this case, a big rock), our family was sent our very own guardian angel.

~Anne K. Jacobs, Ph.D.

90

Twins Impact a Culture

We shall require a substantially new manner of thinking if mankind is to survive.
~Albert Einstein

[EDITORS' NOTE: Identical twins, Janice and Faye Rostvit, have traveled to more than ninety countries in an international singing ministry. Since they have visited Papua New Guinea a number of times, they have witnessed changes taking place in cultural views and treatment of twins.]

Palms swayed in the breeze. Dugout canoes were moored by the shore of the muddy Ramu River. The year was 1984. As my twin and I walked into the village of Garati, which was situated on a rise above the banks of the river, we were overwhelmed by the reaction we received. Men and women swarmed around us, touching our long hair, pointing to our eyes, our identical clothes and shoes. They buzzed in frenzied bewilderment. We were unaware of the fact that they had never seen adult twins. In their cultural beliefs, twins were a bad omen. When twins were born, they would separate them, taking one to a distant village to be raised by someone else. The family who took the infant would be told that its mother had died, rather than divulge that the baby was a twin.

God was at work among these people. Bible translators, David and Sharran Pryor, were in the early stages of their work in Garati.

Six months before we came, an old man named Ruri was the first of the village "Big Men" to fully abandon evil practices and declare his faith in Jesus. He had been the leader of their ancestral spirit worship and remembered the killing raids their people had made. When young men who were not yet Christians asked Ruri to teach them how to call up the spirits, Ruri refused.

"Those were evil ways," he said. "We always lived in fear when we worshiped the demons. Now we must follow God and His ways." Within months, half of the villagers followed Ruri's example and were baptized in the Ramu River. Ruri counseled the believers, "We need to let God's Spirit teach us what areas of our thinking and behavior need to change."

We were in Garati for more than a week, singing morning and evening and always being seen together. We enjoy our twinship. We had no idea what the people were thinking as they observed us—but it would soon change their treatment of twins. A few weeks later, a lady gave birth to twin boys. She and her husband decided to break custom and raise their sons together. They reasoned, "It was evident that the American twins enjoyed being together. Our boys will be happier if allowed to grow up in the same village. Maybe one day they will also serve God together."

It was rewarding that God used us to help other twins experience the joy of "oneness" in their "twoness."

•••

In another village, situated up in the highlands, one lady feared she was pregnant with twins. Being more cumbersome than usual, she was receiving unkind remarks from others in her village. "Only dogs or pigs should have litters." Here, too, it was considered a bad omen when twins were born. They believed that only one baby was the true child. The other was an impersonating spirit come to destroy the family. However, their treatment of twins was even more severe. Being unable to determine the true child, both infants were usually killed at birth. This lady hoped her pregnancy would result in only one baby. Expecting the delivery to be a difficult one, she chose to walk over the mountain ridges to a mission hospital.

There, her greatest fears were realized—a multiple birth. And, it was not only twins, but triplets! How shameful! She wondered what she should do. How could she return to her village? In her despondent state of mind, she was not producing breast milk. Her three tiny daughters were being fed intravenously as they lay in incubators. A couple of days later, two other women came to the hospital and gave birth to twins. Was there some consolation that she was no longer alone in her dilemma?

One day, a nurse entered the maternity ward and announced that American twin ladies would be singing in the hospital. The three mothers of multiples sat up with intense curiosity. TWIN LADIES? Twins never reach adulthood!

As the two of us came into the ward and sang Christian songs, we were unaware of the questions whirling through these three mothers' minds: Who are these ladies? How can they sing in our language? They are twins, but which one is the bad Spirit? How can either of them be evil when both are praising God? The following morning, the three mothers summoned us back to the ward. When we arrived, we were greeted with smiles. Two of the women sat on their beds holding their twins. The mother of triplets sat cross-legged on a mat on the floor, two infants on her lap and the third held to her breast. The change in the mothers' attitudes was evident. They were eager to tell us that they were determined to keep their multiples, even if they would face reproach in their villages.

•••

Over the next two decades, we have returned to this South Pacific island several times, each time for a two- or three-month tour. In nearly every village, we are greeted by people who are eager to show us their twins. They say things like, "Because of seeing you, we are now letting our twins live."

In this culture, a baby is carried about in a woven string bag slung over its mother's back. The strap of the bag is just above the mother's forehead, with the full weight bearing upon her head. At least in this aspect, one might say it's a "headache" to care for twins, especially when both are suspended in their hammock-like bags!

On one return to the village of Garati, everyone was eager for us to meet some ten-month-old twin girls. They were the granddaughters of Ruri, the patriarch of the village. As the mother handed the girls to us, she happily told us, "I have named them after you. This one is Janice, and that one is Faye. I hope they will grow up to sing for God just like you do."

What an honor. As singers, we always felt that singing in the languages of the people was our ministry. Little did we know that God would use the fact that we are twins to impact a culture and help save twins.

~Janice and Faye Rostvit

91

Two Turkeys

You don't get harmony when everybody sings the same note.
~Doug Floyd

Sometimes, it seems as if our four-year-old twin boys have only two things in common: their parents and birth date. When I was pregnant, I could already tell the difference in their energy levels. Nick was the calm one, scaring me more than once because he stayed so still in my womb. While Henry, it seemed, kicked from conception.

Years later, little has changed. Nick is easygoing, and Henry is in constant motion. Still, he can focus for long periods of time on activities of interest to him. Sometimes, when Henry's playing with his train set, it is almost impossible to get his attention.

One day last May, when they were three, we went to a local playground. They played follow the leader with another little boy. At one point in the game, Henry hugged the boy and began turning in circles faster and faster with him. The boy cried out, and his mother and I rushed to intervene. I took Henry aside, reminding him to be gentle.

That summer, Henry began to act strangely around other children. He'd chase them, stare into their faces, push them down or bump them. It wasn't intentional or mean; he just couldn't seem to help himself.

I wondered, was it because Henry was a twin? He'd hugged, kissed and pushed Nick right from the start; there's no such thing as personal space in the womb. They had slept in one crib until they were three months old. To me, it appeared as if Henry was behaving around other kids the way he did around his twin.

To the other children and their mothers, however, Henry was too physical. Going to playgrounds became a source of stress for me. No matter how many times Henry and I went over the rules ("don't push," "be nice"), his energy could escalate like a tornado gathering speed. Caught up in chasing the other children, he'd barrel into them, knocking them down. All the while, Nick played normally.

Following Henry around on the playground, I wasn't sure if I was protecting the other children, my son, or myself. It was exhausting, and I found myself staying home with the boys, rather than face the disapproval of the other mothers. I knew they were thinking, "Why can't she control her kid?"

I hoped that Henry would settle down in preschool, but the notes from his teacher started coming home right after the school year began.

"Henry has made improvements as far as being able to sit still during circle time and focus on classroom activities," said one, "but by the end of the afternoon, he has run out of patience and cannot remember to keep his hands to himself and not bother the other children."

I did what any self-respecting mother would do: I blamed myself. Nick was doing well in school. I'd messed up with Henry somewhere. My thoughts swung from what's wrong with me to what's wrong with him and back again.

At a parent-teacher conference, Henry's teacher did not come out and say it, but I knew what she was thinking: Attention Deficit Hyperactivity Disorder (ADHD). She asked that we have Henry tested through the county's preschool diagnostic center. Knowing how focused Henry could get on puzzles and books, I didn't think he had ADHD, but the teacher's concerns had me second-guessing myself.

She's the expert, I told myself. She's seen this type of thing before.

It was strange driving to the testing center with only Henry in the backseat. I couldn't remember a time when it was just the two of us. Henry felt special to be on this outing with Mommy, asking a dozen times where we were going and why.

"A nice lady is going to play games with you," I told him, feeling like a liar.

Why us? I thought to myself as I led Henry into the diagnostic center. Why can't we be normal?

I had never gotten used to being in the spotlight because we had twins. Now I felt like all eyes were on my family because we had a "problem child."

Mary, the examiner, allowed me to observe as she asked Henry to throw a ball, stack several cubes, and wiggle his thumb. All of these tasks he accomplished easily. His hearing and vision tested normal.

"Now we'll measure his reasoning skills," Mary said.

She opened a workbook in front of him, pointing to the first problem: pictures of four articles of clothing—a hat, pants, a sneaker, and a scarf—and below, a foot. Catching on quickly, Henry pointed to the sneaker, choosing correctly that it was related to the foot. More problems like this followed, each more difficult than the last, but Henry solved them all. At one point during the testing, Mary grinned at me, as if to say, "Are you watching this?"

Next, she gave Henry a pile of foam squares with sides of yellow or black, and asked him to duplicate a picture in the workbook of similarly colored squares in a pattern. Of all the tests, Henry enjoyed this most, fitting the squares together like a puzzle. Even when the patterns became more complex, he concentrated hard, trying different combinations until it matched. With each success, he turned to me, "Mommy, look!"

How had I missed this? How could I have been so blind? I'd gotten so caught up in what was wrong with Henry that I'd overlooked everything that was right about him. I never felt more inadequate as a mother... or more proud.

"I have to score these numbers," Mary said when the test was over, "but between you and me, they're extremely high."

High enough, it turns out, to place him in the ninety-eighth percentile for cognitive development.

Henry didn't have ADHD or any other learning disability. And the examiner said that he would eventually outgrow his "personal space" issues. Wonderful news, but we were right back where we started. Except that now I knew Henry better. I promised myself that I would never again let others' impressions inform me about my own child. I was his mother, and I had obviously done something right.

At school a few days later, the twins made turkeys out of construction paper for Thanksgiving. Looking displeased, Henry's teacher took me aside at pick-up. "His turkey is sideways," she said.

Instead of pasting his turkey on the paper in a portrait arrangement like his brother and every other student, Henry had pasted it in landscape.

A few weeks ago, I might have felt like a failure as a mother. I might have wondered why Henry couldn't follow directions like the other kids. But the testing had not been for nothing.

I never felt as proud of both boys as when I hung those two turkeys on the wall—one portrait, one sideways—both perfect—the two turkeys similar and yet so different.

~Denice A. Jobe

92

Humility

Humility is the only true wisdom by which we prepare our minds for all the possible changes of life.
~George Arliss

TWINS! When I heard that word, I felt such a mixture of emotions. First, there was denial. "No, this is a mistake! Maybe it is just a smudge on the ultrasound screen." This quickly led to panic. "Oh, my gosh, how am I ever going to handle twins? I am thirty-eight years old with a two-year-old!" And, finally, elation. "This is great! My family is complete on my second shot!" I began to convince myself that I could handle this. "I am a woman of thirty-eight. I have a good head on my shoulders. I am a classic over-achiever. I am a teacher. I can work with large numbers of children. I can keep them in control. Yeah, I can manage this situation. I can complete my family and continue with my professional goals!" Little did I know how much the next two years would rock my world and change my perspective.

Control is such a funny word. To have control, one assumes that one is in charge of a situation. Now I know who really has control over everything, but at that time I was bound and determined to try. I had the schedules decided on. I had the clipboards to implement those schedules. I had all the twin books to refer to. I had the baby gear. Finally, I had the plan. I was going to be one of those mothers who did it all. I would work full-time as a teacher. I would be a full-time mother and manager of the household. I was going to maintain my friendships, keep a clean house, cook nutritious meals that everyone would eat without fuss, organize play dates, take the kids on community outings and run the kids to various activities. Through all of this, I would keep my sanity.

After the twins arrived, I held strong through the three-and-a-half-week stay in the NICU. I held strong through the apnea monitors and medication regimes when the babies came home. I held strong through the sleepless nights and constant feedings. I held strong through potty training my oldest while home with the twins on maternity leave. If I could do this, I felt, I could easily add working to the mix. I was confident I could do anything. Remember, I had the clipboards and the printed charts. I was in control.

Truthfully, I had a meltdown on the second day back to work. I did not realize that I was maintaining the status quo while at home—balancing the aspects I had perceived control over in the safe environment of my home—but I did not have that luxury at work. It became apparent rather quickly that maintaining the household and my career was impossible at the level I had set for myself. I could not be the teacher or employee that I was before twins, and continue to be the mother that I had become now that they were born. This became an emotional struggle for me on every level.

And it still is. The bags of ungraded work travel home with me, but often remain ungraded. The glorious lesson plans that took hours to create and prepare have become mundane. All the after-hours of parent communication are left unfinished each night in lieu of dinner, bath time and bedtime stories. My dreams of becoming Department Chair and then possibly an administrator have taken a back seat to parenting. A cosmic shift in my priorities occurred while I was home with the kids on maternity leave. Since staying at home permanently is not a financial option for our family, I had to succumb to letting go of my professional aspirations for my parental responsibilities.

Slowly, over the past few years, the meals have become less elaborate, the house is not as clean as I like, and friendships have fallen by the wayside. The job, although still full-time, has changed to allow more freedom in my daily schedule to deal with life's unexpected surprises. I have jumped off the fast track and changed the career path I had originally planned to refocus my priorities. Most importantly, I have traded in overachieving at work for being a better wife and mother. The "exceeds expectations" I used to strive for on my work evaluations has been traded in for just "meets expectations" on the job. My performance at home now takes precedence over the evaluations at work. I decided to excel in my personal life instead of professionally.

Doing it all is no longer the priority; doing what is right for my family and myself is. Now that the twins are exploring toddlerhood, I am reminded daily that control is an illusion. Temper tantrums, public outings, illnesses and mealtimes take on an entirely different meaning when there are two. Just when I think I have covered all the bases in these areas, my children remind me that I could not possibly be that clairvoyant. Twins changed my life in every possible way. Most importantly, they taught me humility. It is the most valuable lesson I continue to learn every day.

~Jackie Gaston

"I've always been an overachiever."

93

I Will Not Forget

We do not remember days; we remember moments.
~Cesare Pavese

"Mommy, will you rock me please?"

One of my four-year-old twins looks up at me with his big blue eyes, pleading for me to let him get out of bed and rock with me in the glider in his room. He's my little Night Owl. His fraternal twin snoozes blissfully, as always, in the top bunk.

Even though they're almost five years old, my twin boys still love to rock with me when they're feeling scared or tired.

I think about the work that awaits me on the computer. The twins' bedtime is when I get a lot of my writing done. But his tearful eyes are my undoing.

"Sure," I tell him, taking the stuffed animals off the cushioned seat. "Climb aboard."

His long legs stretch nearly the whole length of mine as he puts his arms around me and snuggles his head into my shoulder.

What happened to the baby I had seemingly yesterday? I glance up at his brother, who easily fills the twin mattress on his bed. Where did both of my babies go?

As I gently rock my "big boy" to sleep, my mind travels back in time. More than eighteen years ago, I was blessed with my firstborn son. My second one followed almost three years later. Both "boys" are more than six feet tall now, and I can barely remember what they looked like when they were small. Looking at their childhood pictures in our photo albums feels almost like I'm looking at children I do not know—children who are in high school and college now. Where have the years gone?

I was a single mother for much of their growing-up years. I spent so much time worrying about making a living for my boys that I somehow forgot to live for the moment. I was so focused on the destination that I didn't enjoy the journey as much as I should have.

I recalled their passion for Teenage Mutant Ninja Turtles, Pokémon, Star Wars and Harry Potter. The Legos they'd sift noisily through on Saturday mornings, thinking they were giving me a little extra time to sleep. Their enthusiasm for going to reptile shows and bookstores. One day, we were buying Matchbox cars. The next, we were giving them all away to some other little boys with a passion for cars.

Then, out of the blue—as often happens—God brought a special man into my life. And then I received an even greater gift in the form of "two little men"—fraternal twin babies. I felt as if I'd been given a "do-over."

So now, once again, I'm raising two little boys—doubly blessed with twins! Like their older brothers, they love cars and Legos, Star Wars and reptiles. They will certainly be my last sons, and I'm taking the trip nice and slowly this time. I want to memorize their faces and their sweet little voices.

I feel the warmth of my little one's breath on my shoulder. I smooth his sweaty brow and rub circles on his back. I hear his breathing become slow and even as he settles into sleep. I breathe in the scent of him and savor the moment, etching it into my mind. This time, I vow, I will not forget.

~Susan M. Heim

94

Left Out

A suburban mother's role is to deliver children obstetrically once, and by car forever after.
~Peter De Vries

It was a beautiful summer evening. Everyone was glowing with the look of having spent the majority of the day at the beach. The kids had all jumped into the pool once we returned home to get rid of the sand and get ready for their basketball game. The girls had been together all day long and were busy planning the all-important sleepovers for the night. I think I had a total of twelve kids in my van, and nine of them were 101 percent giggly, loud girly-girls!

The girls quickly dressed in their brilliant red, black and white shiny basketball uniforms. The travel basketball coach had put together a summer league that met once a week for a game. Our town has two nice basketball courts with lights, so the games were in the evenings, and other towns would travel to play us. My triplet daughters, Brittany and Brandi, along with their group of friends, enjoyed running around and playing basketball at night under the lights. The parents enjoyed it, too, because we didn't have to worry about dinner or rushing someone off to another sport since our day was almost done. We would bring blankets and coolers to the games and often serve dinner right there to the kids on the team while their siblings played and ran around in the other fields.

It was the summer before sixth grade for my triplets. They seemed to have grown up and turned into preteens overnight! I dropped off the kids at the courts and then went to find a parking place for my fifteen-passenger van, otherwise known as the "Pacemobile"!

The girls were out warming up when I began to set up camp. Two of my friends were already there and had their territory established, and they had saved a spot for me and another friend. Once I was seated and spread out, my friend Cate leaned over to me and said in a quiet voice, "There may be an issue Brandi needs to talk to you about after the game." She went on to explain that one of their teammates, Tracy, had passed out her birthday party invitations, and Brandi didn't get one. I said, "What?!" Tracy has been friendly with both of my daughters since kindergarten. She had played on Britt's soccer team for several seasons, and I even coached her for a year or two. All of the girls were on the same basketball team, and Tracy had always been invited to our parties and sleepovers. Through the years, she had always been in one of my children's classrooms. Cate then went on to explain that Tracy had passed out the invitations in front of the team, and Brandi was the only one who didn't get one. Apparently, Brandi's face had dropped when they were all handed out and she didn't get one.

I felt awful. I wanted to cry. I wanted to jump through the crowd and go hug my daughter and mend her broken heart. How did she keep it together? How was she able to not cry in front of everyone? To make matters worse, her sister, Brittany, had received an invitation and not her! My mind raced to search for reasons. I said to Cate, "Perhaps they could only invite a few friends because they are going out to the movies or to get their nails done." Cate said, "No, it is a swimming party and sleepover at her house." I said in a matter-of-fact voice, "Perhaps Tracy forgot her invitation in the car, or it fell out while walking to the courts?" Cate said that when Tracy was handing them out, Brandi had leaned over when Britt got hers and said, "Oh, am I invited, too?" because people would often just write both names on one invitation. But Tracy just shook her head and said, "You're not invited."

What did Brandi do to Tracy to not be included? I continued to search my mind for answers. Brandi is my most happy-go-lucky kid. She doesn't have a mean-spirited bone in her body. Everyone likes her, and she is fun to be around. Why didn't this girl like her? Why did the mother allow her to invite the whole basketball team and leave one girl out?

The buzzer sounded, and the game began. I think I was in a zone for the next hour, although I did manage to clap at the appropriate times and cheer the team on. In front of my friends, I tried to act like it didn't matter, but it did. After the game, as the girls came out, Brandi came over to me and said, "Mom, I want to go home." Their suitcases were already packed and ready to carry on the summer fun with a sleepover, but Brandi had changed her mind. Britt said, "Yeah, I think I want to go home, too." I knew right away what this was all about, and we needed to get to the van as quickly as possible. Their friends also knew what was going on. We said our goodbyes and apologies for the change of plans and made our way to the safe haven of the van.

Britt was the first to blurt out her protests. "Mom, Tracy is so mean! She invited the whole team except Brandi to her birthday party!" By this time, Brandi was red-faced and sobbing in her hands. Her brothers were in the back seat of the van and seized the moment to try to break the ice. The girls' triplet brother Steve hollered out, "Tracy probably doesn't want Brandi to hog all of the covers at the party!" Brother Ben chimed in, "And she snores really loud!"

"Enough!" I said as I shot them my devil look that says not another word if you know what is good for you! I asked Brandi if she and Tracy had perhaps had a falling-out over something. Brandi said, "No, Mom, we're friends as far as I know."

Brandi went on to say, "I was so embarrassed!" then she went through the chain of events I had missed while I was parking the van. All I could say was, "I am so very sorry, honey! It's been a long day. Let's go home and try to get some sleep." I gave her a hug and sent her off to clean up before bed.

The next day, first thing in the morning, three of my good friends all called before I had finished my first cup of coffee. They all felt as awful as I did. They were so kind as to offer suggestions on how or what I should do, if anything. "Call the mom and explain what happened," one said. "Do nothing, and don't let Britt go either," another one said. "Just let it play out," still another said. "I am sure she will get invited."

My mother's heart wanted to lash out. I said to my husband over coffee, "We have always invited this little girl to our parties. Never again!" As soon as the words left my mouth, though, I felt stupid and silly, like I was back in high school. I looked at him and smiled, "I know, I know... two wrongs don't make a right." He nodded with approval of my response.

Brandi woke up the next day and began making plans with her friends right away. I asked her if she was okay, and she said yes. When Britt woke up, we talked a little about it. I asked her what she wanted to do about the party, and she said, "Well, all of my friends are going, but I think it is wrong the way Tracy treated Brandi." I was happy that Britt felt that way and had compassion for her triplet sister.

In hindsight, I think Brandi was more embarrassed about the way the invitations were handed out than the fact that she didn't get an invitation. Many times, my triplet girls are not invited to everything together. They shouldn't be. I have always encouraged individuality between them. They are individuals, and have separate friends and separate lives. But, in this instance, this was a friend they thought they shared together.

The rest of the week was busy and fun with summer plans. There were play dates, sleepovers and fun to be found. We actually forgot all about the party until the actual day of the party came. Britt and Brandi had spoken to several of their friends during the day and had been reminded of the party. I left it up to Britt whether she wanted to go or not.

Later that day, we were out shopping and actually ran into Tracy and her mom shopping for the big event. I gulped when I saw them. I had no idea what to say, how to act, or what they would say. Did they know by now that Brandi was terribly hurt by not being invited? Did the mom even have a clue? Why did I feel weird? I hadn't done anything! A little voice spoke to me and said, "Deep breaths, let it go. Just smile and be cordial. Let the girls do the talking."

Brandi said, "Mom, look who is here. It's Tracy and her mom!" Brandi waved with excitement, and then ran over to Tracy and began talking. Brandi had remembered that Tracy had a hamster cage for sale at a yard sale, and she was interested in buying it with her babysitting money. Brandi returned and said, "They still have the cage, Mom. I think I'm going to buy it!" We then went on our merry way shopping, and not another word was said.

Brandi rolled with the punches and recovered like a trooper, and I learned a valuable parenting lesson. I realized that we shouldn't fight our children's battles for them. Left alone, they can usually work things out for themselves. Sooner or later, they will get their feelings hurt and need a hug or a kiss from us, but we don't need to fix everything for them.

I am sure Tracy had a lovely party even though my girls weren't there. No big deal. Tracy will continue to be welcomed at any party or function we have. Life is way too short to get all upset over the small stuff.

~Pam Pace

95

Don't Drink the Water!

Water is the giver of life.
~Proverb

When I was growing up in rural America, I can remember having two sets of twins in my life. The Hamilton boys went to my church, and unless you were familiar with the family, you would have never guessed they were twins. They were opposite in both appearance and personality. One was blond and outgoing, the other brunette and reserved. The Bailey girls, on the other hand, were identical twins in every way. Well, that's not entirely true. One of them had a birthmark, more like a super-sized freckle, next to one eyebrow. That was about the only way to tell them apart, and to this day I can never remember which one has the birthmark! So when I started working at Richmond School, I was amazed to discover the many sets of twins associated with this school.

Almost every school has had the occasional set of twins enroll, but over the past two decades, this small rural school in northeastern California has had twenty sets of twins connected to it in one way or another. That's right, over twenty sets. Now this school is not large; its enrollment in that time has ranged from one hundred seventy-five students to its current enrollment of about two hundred and thirty. That means the twin population has averaged about three percent.

Not all of the twins have been students, but rather the offspring of faculty and staff. Richmond School has had six members who are parents of twins. And it doesn't stop there either. One member, who has since retired, has twin granddaughters, and another member, a mother of twins, has twin brothers-in-law. There was even a staff member who was the daughter of a twin!

At one point, the first-grade class, which had about twenty-six students, had three sets of twins. Even more astounding, each set consisted of one boy and one girl. However, only one set managed to stay in the area long enough to graduate from the eighth grade.

People have often marveled at and even wondered why there are so many twins connected to Richmond School. Some claim it's "in the water," and others say it's just a coincidence. All I know is that I began teaching at this school in 1992... and in 1996 I gave birth to twin girls. And yes, I drank the water!

~Lynne Sella

96

Odd Man Out

Certain is it that there is no kind of affection so purely angelic as of a father to a daughter. In love to our wives there is desire; to our sons, ambition; but to our daughters there is something which there are no words to express.
~Joseph Addison

Our twin girls, Morgan and Chloe, are forever waiting for Mommy to get home. There used to be practical reasons for that, but lately it seems all they want to do is share secrets with her while openly keeping them from me, their father. My wife Erika revels in this. "Girls together, stormy weather," she will say as they peer at me from the corners of six twinkling eyes. I've gotten used to this. Stormy weather...

But then...

Last week, we packed up the girls and took them to "Aunt Marianne and Sarah's house," where their Aunt Marianne and older cousin Sarah live. Of course, Uncle Rick lives there, too, but he apparently is not worthy of mention. Anyway, upon closing our garage door on the visit to Aunt Marianne and Sarah's and the fifty or so miles between us, we woke the girls from their slumber.

"Okay, girls, we're home. Mommy and Daddy will carry you up to bed."

"Can we go to Aunt Marianne and Sarah's?"

"Girls, we just got home from Aunt Marianne and Sarah's."

This was last Saturday. Since then, at every turn, we have been besieged with the plea, "Can you take us to Aunt Marianne and

Sarah's?" I'm not quite sure how many times we've heard it, but it's safe to say that had we caved and dropped in uninvited on Aunt Marianne and Sarah (and Rick) at each request, we'd have spent more time there than at our own home. We'd have, in fact, spent all of our time there.

Eventually, the question had to be asked, and Erika asked it. "Why do you love Aunt Marianne and Sarah so much? What is it about them? Do you love them more than Mommy and Daddy?"

"Don't worry," Morgan assured us. "We love you, too. It's just that..." She didn't complete the sentence.

"It's just that what?" Erika demanded. Morgan hummed and ambled off in deep thought (probably to Aunt Marianne and Sarah's). "Mor-gan, it's just that what?!" No answer would come. "Nothing, Mommy." I put my arms around Erika, kissed her and bid her a warm welcome to fatherhood.

This morning, precisely one week after our now infamous visit to you-know-who's (and Rick's), Morgan was galloping around singing songs (they sing constantly) about being tricked and how she was supposed to have gone to Aunt Marianne and Sarah's, but that we, the parents, had somehow concocted a great lie.

She sang in tortured tones, "All I thought was that we were going to goooooooooo!" Rather than play along or delve as I normally would, I took out the video camera and began shooting her, thinking it would make a nice video to send to Aunt Marianne and Sarah. However, upon seeing me with the camera, the passion suddenly dissipated, so I put the thing away. I decided, though, that Marianne and Sarah would be too appreciative of the recent trend for me to just allow it all to slip between the cracks. So I went downstairs to my computer to convey it (the old-fashioned way) through e-mail. Not two minutes after plopping down in my chair, Morgan came gliding into the room with news. Her expression told me it was big, so I began typing as quickly as I could in an effort to get a complete and accurate translation.

"Daddy, here's the truth. If you don't take me to Aunt Marianne and Sarah's, we have to stay here forever. That's your choice."

"We have to take you?" I asked, while typing feverishly and speaking s-l-o-o-o-w-l-y so I could get it all down.

"That's the deal. This pink magical diamond shows me the reflection of Aunt Marianne and Sarah. TWINKLE!" (Note: The "twinkle" and dire theatrics are an ode to the mystical Barbie movies and fairy godmothers from Disney. A lot of twinkling has been going on in our house lately.)

So I got Morgan's little (twinkling) gem and sent a nod to the heavens for having been seated at the keyboard as it came down. Now Aunt Marianne and Sarah would have a proper account of the State of the Family.

Ten minutes later, as I arranged the whole tale in text for the aunt/cousin dynamo, I had to break away as Morgan returned with Chloe and what appeared to be further serious and important news. I had a feeling I knew what it was going to be about, and I was happy for Aunt Marianne and Sarah as I poised my fingers over the keyboard:

"We've got a magic cornstalk, a magic leaf, a magic treasure chest, and a magic Hershey's Kiss, and we need them for the magic spell to make Aunt Marianne and Sarah come here."

"Yes," said Chloe, "I have a green magic twinkle, and in its reflection I can see Aunt Marianne and Sarah."

"Yes," Morgan said. "And if they don't stay at our house, we should stay at their house."

"Yes," said Chloe. "That way we can be around Aunt Marianne and Sarah forever."

Forever... The word hung out there for a moment, and I considered it as the girls lilted up and away from the basement and me. For the week, I'd lost my daughters. They were now in the emotional custody of their aunt and cousin, and apparently there was nothing I could do about it. It would normally be an unsavory little bite to swallow, but in sharing it with Erika, I'm a little ashamed to admit that I've choked it down with surprising ease. Yes, I have been copiously aware that while Erika and I have been nudging and giggling about the twins' Aunt-Marianne-and-Sarah infatuation, deep down inside she is a little troubled by her slipping stature. But, in my defense, when one is five years old, forever lasts for about five minutes. At ten years old, forever is ten minutes, and teenager forever is over in the length of a song. Likewise, Erika would soon resume her place at the top of the family food chain, while I would again be the odd man out. But, for now, I would just sit back and enjoy a little spousal solidarity.

With her effortless timing, Erika returned home from her Saturday morning run. Cued by the sound of the door, Morgan and Chloe descended upon her, brimming with the kind of passion that is obvious from a floor below. This would normally be some kind of twinkly-eyed secret session, and I would be excluded and feeling that familiar twinge. But not this time. This time, I had a pretty good idea of what it was all about. Twinkle!

~Chris Tremper

97

The Perfect Sex

History is particularly important in throwing light on the source of our attitudes about sex because many of the assumptions we make are not necessarily scientific or rational but holdovers of past belief systems that are no longer held by modern society.
~Vern Bullough

In Somalia, children die at an alarming rate. Especially twins. Few people expect both twins to survive pregnancy, labor, delivery or the first five years of childhood.

"Mataano! Alxumdillalah!" was the daily response received when I told people my children were living, breathing, healthy two-year-old twins. Twins! Praise God!

The conversation inevitably moved to which parent they resembled. Justice was declared to be a photocopy of his daddy, while Blessing was the exact replica of her mommy. Words dissolved into giggles and hushed whispers at these declarations. It took me months to discover what the joke was.

Over those months, I also began learning about female genital mutilation (FGM). More than 90 percent of Somali women had endured the rudimentary procedure, effectively rendering them incapable of sexual pleasure. Despite this, watching MTV and performing lewd dancing were two of the most popular leisure activities for young women.

They laughed at the television images and imagined feelings they would never experience. This gave the world of men and women in bed a strange aura of mystery, attraction and revulsion. An uncircumcised woman was dirty, yet she could enjoy herself. But, as they had been taught by generations of older women, she probably shouldn't. Everyone in town knew I was uncircumcised, a stigma I had never expected to be branded with before living in Somalia.

"We believe," my neighbor, Halimo, said, "that a child will look like whichever parent enjoyed conception more. If a boy looks like his father, the husband enjoyed it more. If he looks like his mother, she enjoyed it more."

"Then when people say Justice looks like Jeff..." I started.

"That's a good thing," she said.

"And when they say that Blessing looks like me..."

"Shame on you!" she said. She glanced at me, peeked out the window at Jeff, who was fixing our water pump, and smirked.

"And that," she said solemnly, pointing at my twins, "was the perfect sex."

—Rachel E. Jones

98

The Prayer Blanket

Those who sleep under a quilt sleep under a blanket of love.
~Author Unknown

My nephew Chris and his wife Betty tried having a baby for over a year, to no avail. After dozens of tests and consultations, the doctor recommended hormone injections. My brother Dave and his wife Andrea e-mailed the entire family requesting prayer.

Several weeks passed. We were sitting down to dinner one evening when the phone rang. "Chris and Betty are pregnant," my sister-in-law cried. "Please keep those prayers coming though. It's still awfully early in the pregnancy!"

The next day, I drove to our local Wal-Mart for a few necessities. Heading for the shoe department, I made a wrong turn, ending up in the craft department. Bins and bins of pastel-colored yarn caught my eye. Suddenly, Chris and Betty's baby came to mind, as well as my sister-in-law's plea for prayer. Reaching out, I thoughtfully ran my fingers across a soft ball of multicolored yarn in pink, lavender and white.

Suddenly, I felt a gentle nudging from somewhere deep inside. "Cover the baby in prayer," it seemed to say. Frozen in place, I tried protesting.

"Lord, if that's you talking, I don't even know if it's going to be a girl or a boy yet. Isn't it a little early to be thinking about crocheting a baby blanket?"

"Prayer is needed NOW!" the nudge continued more urgently.

Swallowing any further words of protest, I immediately filled my arms with the soft yarn.

"You'll need enough to make two blankets..."

By this time, I was certain I'd had one too many cups of coffee for breakfast. I doubled the amount of yarn. The necessities I'd come for were forgotten. I hurried to the register at the front of the store.

That evening, I settled into the porch rocker clutching the crochet needles and yarn. Crickets chirped in the distance. The neighbor across the street beckoned her children inside.

As one stitch followed another onto the needle, I whispered a chain of prayers straight to heaven for the precious baby yet to be born. Next were prayers for the expectant parents and the proud grandparents. One prayer followed another until my lap was suddenly covered with a lovely bit of warmth.

Weeks later, I was folding the finished blanket when the phone rang. My brother's excited voice instantly caught my attention. "Guess what? Betty's going to have twins!"

I clutched the blanket to my chest, feeling the sudden laughter rising to meet it.

Glancing across the room at the extra balls of yarn, I sent a silent prayer of gratitude to heaven. "Thank you for supplying all our needs before we even know about them, Father!"

I'd begin crocheting the second blanket that very night... along with another chain of prayers to heaven.

Grace and Olivia Terry were born December 19, 2006, blanketed in soft, warm prayer... and love.

~Mary Z. Smith

99

First Day Jitters

Somehow our devils are never quite what we expect when we meet them face to face.
~Nelson DeMille

My kitchen smelled of pancakes while the sun cast its light through the windows to start the day. This was a big day in my house. Our almost-six-year-old twin girls were starting kindergarten, and this was their first day. The girls sat side by side at the table, excited about all the projects they would do and the new friends they would make. They were growing up, no longer wearing the cute matching outfits I used to pick out. A bottom tooth was already missing from each blond-haired, pony-tailed girl.

I sat their chocolate-chip pancakes in front of them, and they both dug in. A few bites later, I noticed that Lauren was softly crying. I knew why, but the mom in me had to ask, "What's wrong?" She dug her face into my side and muttered, "I'll miss Nicky." I took a deep breath as the pain on my heart tugged in my chest. I couldn't breathe.

Was I the worst mom ever for separating my twins? They were so young, but I wanted them to find their own strengths and learn to make friends without leaning on each other. But now, in a moment of weakness, I was regretting my decision. I looked down and saw that Nicole was crying, too. When her eyes caught mine, she said, "I'll miss Lauren. I don't want to be in a different class."

Oh, Lord, help me! A million thoughts ran through my mind.

I'm ruining their lives. I've taken away the one person they could always count on! Do I have a right to make this decision for them? Please, God, tell me I'm doing the right thing...

I wrapped an arm around each of them and pulled them into me with hugs. "It'll be okay," I said in a crackly voice that threatened to reveal my uncertainty. "You will make new friends. They will know your name and not call you 'Which one are you?' each day. You will see each other at lunch, and you can play together on the playground."

I wasn't just trying to convince them. I was trying to convince myself, too. They talked it over and began to look at it from a positive point of view. Even so, they were a little sad at the bus stop.

After I waved goodbye to them, I went into the house to secretly cry in my guilt. I anxiously met the girls at the bus stop that afternoon. Much to my surprise, they told me they'd had a wonderful day at school, only missing each other a little bit!

With each passing day, it got easier. Within a week, they had adjusted, and now they are both thriving in their own classrooms. A month into school, Nicole was invited to a birthday party by a classmate. I worried that Lauren would be hurt at not being included, but I was surprised to find she had come to terms with the fact that they wouldn't always be together and would have different friends of their own.

I thanked God for blessing me with these two wonderful children! I would be lying if I said it wasn't still difficult for me to separate my twins. Sometimes, I still experience a twinge of guilt. But my twins' happiness has convinced me I made the right decision for them.

~Donna Sullivan

Logistics Manager Needed

Any mother could perform the jobs of several air traffic controllers with ease.
~Lisa Alther

When you first see two heartbeats on the ultrasound, you experience both overwhelming joy and sheer panic. Twins! You start reading all the parenting books, especially those with advice about twins. The one skill you really need, though, you won't find in any parenting book. What you really need is to be a logistics manager.

Let's say you need to be at Gramma's house for dinner by 6:00 P.M. You need to start getting ready no later than 4:30. When our girls were infants, a typical outing required bottles, bibs, diapers, wipes, diaper rash cream, extra clothes, toys, and blankets. This might sound like a typical list, but remember you are packing for two. You don't need four bottles; you need eight. You don't need three diapers; you need six. Traditional diaper bags are not designed for twins. We had an extra-large beach bag we'd fill.

We used to pack everything we could the night before and leave the bag near the garage door. You learn, usually the hard way, that the more you can do in advance, the better for everyone. Why? As you are walking out the door, one baby will wet her diaper and need a complete clothing change. And the other one will start screaming for a bottle. No matter that you planned the outing at a time when neither one usually needs a diaper change or a bottle. They know you are trying to get out the door. It's their job to make it difficult.

When our twin girls were eight months old, we decided to spend a week in Wisconsin. We stayed at a fully stocked house, so we didn't have to worry about cereal bowls, plates, silverware, dishwashing soap, etc. It also had a washer and dryer, so I only had to pack half the clothes as we planned to do laundry. We created a packing list that looked something like this:

Two pack-and-plays
Two portable high chairs
One double-stroller
Two cases of diapers
Two walkers
100 jars of baby food
Two bags of books/toys
Two suitcases
One set of golf clubs

At the time, we had two four-door cars. One was a mid-size; the other a sedan. Both were fine for getting the girls around the neighborhood or perhaps for an occasional overnight stay with Gramma. Neither was big enough for vacation packing. We borrowed a mid-size SUV. Even with such a large vehicle, we barely packed everything. The entire ride there, my husband could not see out the back window. The ride home was a bit easier as we had used all the diapers and baby food. For the next trip, we bought a mini-van with a folding third row. We learned our lesson.

Now that the girls are in preschool, we don't need pack-and-plays and portable high chairs anymore. Those items have been replaced by bikes with training wheels and scooters. Getting out of the house is easier as they can put on their own shoes and dress themselves. The basic lessons, though, stay with you. We still start early. Now, instead of needing a bottle, one girl always seems to get something on her outfit as we want to walk out the door. We anticipate needing to change clothes, brush hair, fix socks, etc. And they need to accessorize with necklaces, bracelets, and purses. They are girly-girls. Rather than getting upset, we just build in the time.

We wouldn't trade our twin experiences. It's been an adventure and a joy. Plus, we have a new skill set to add to our resumes. What more could you ask for?

~Shari L. Schmidt, APR

Wanted: Mother of Twins — No Experience Necessary

One of the biggest complaints about motherhood is the lack of training.
~Erma Bombeck

How often have I wondered why we need a license to drive, cut hair, and even go fishing, yet not to parent children. Shouldn't there be some sort of test? Or necessary training? Perhaps the concept is that parenting should come naturally, no experience necessary. Perhaps that concept is ridiculous.

Once again I had forgotten to bring my two-and-a-half-year-old twins to the restroom before my cart was half-full on the other side of the grocery store. After finding a place to stash the cart, gathering up my purse and the washable bag full of hand sanitizer, sippy cups, diapers, extra clothes, Band-Aids, toys, and a spare binky or two, we headed into the oversized family stall. My son, Spencer, quietly sat down, perfectly content to rely on his trusty diaper so he could look at his truck book. I had been a twin mom long enough to no longer ponder the floors in public restrooms. My daughter, Rhiannon, had recently decided that diapers were yucky and only wanted to wear big girl panties like her older sister.

Quite the chatterbox at a very young age, and still not big enough to make it onto the growth charts, she was quite a sight: chatting away while carefully balancing her very small self on the toilet. I simply waited and listened, proud of my expert parental guidance of conversation, not noticing the woman who had entered, used the restroom, and was now washing her hands.

As we exited the stall, the woman was visibly startled and brought her hand to her mouth with a sudden "Oh!" at the sight of my teeny, tiny talking toddler. After a moment of awkward silence, she laughed and explained that she had been listening to our conversation and expected to see someone much... taller.

I spent the next few moments relishing the praise about my daughter being so advanced in her speech. Failing to mention how she was small for her age and not as young as she looked, I accepted every compliment as an affirmation of my success as a mother. I felt confident and appreciated. As the woman and I left the restroom—her praising and me glowing—my daughter began to tug at my clothes. I hushed her with several smiling just-a-minute-dear-mommy-is-too-busy-getting-her-ego-stroked kind of gestures, but she demanded my attention. Through my fake smile, upon returning to my grocery cart, I finally asked, "What is it, honey? What are you trying to tell me?" I could not imagine what this two-year-old had to say that was more important than me soaking up my well-deserved praise.

Looking at me with utter confusion, she pointed back toward the restroom. Oh, no... Humiliated, I excused myself, walked back into the restroom stall and retrieved her content and silent twin brother, still looking at his truck book, while the woman curiously looked on. "That my brother," my daughter explained to the woman. "My mommy forget him." The woman stifled her laughter. So much for my shining moment.

Soon after this humbling experience, I complained to our pediatrician that Spencer was just too quiet, and Rhiannon always seemed to translate for him. Rhiannon assured me Spencer did speak, but I rarely heard him. I feared his words were only babble, or "twinspeak," and I questioned whether or not she actually understood him, since the rest of us found it difficult.

"It's not a problem," the doctor said. "She's an early talker. Maybe he's not. No big deal." I squinted my eyes at him. Then he added, "He's obviously communicating, especially to her, so don't worry." Not satisfied, I insisted he investigate further.

Accustomed to my demands, he smiled and looked at Spencer. "Can you talk?"

Before he could open his little mouth, Rhiannon said, "He can talk. He talk to me all the time."

With the patience of Job, the pediatrician thanked her for her insight and asked Spencer more specifically, "Can you talk to me?"

Again, Rhiannon replied, "He can talk to you, but he won't. He most time just talk to me." Then the twins hugged each other and sat down to rearrange the brightly colored magnetic gears on a new toy they had never seen before.

Amused, their pediatrician smiled at me and whispered, "I think I may have found the problem."

Just then, clear as a bell, Spencer quietly instructed Rhiannon, "No, do it this way... like this." Our pediatrician looked at me, mouth agape, and then laughed out loud as I lowered my head in shame. He patted me on the shoulder, and then left the room as I nodded silently, eyes closed... absolutely certain that my chances at Twin Mom of the Year were pretty well shot. Perhaps, in my case at least, it's a good thing we don't need a license to parent. If we did, I'm sure I would still be childless.

~Sherry L. Emerson

Chicken Soup for the Soul®

Meet Our Contributors!

About the Authors

Acknowledgments

About Chicken Soup

Share with Us

Meet Our Contributors!

Julie (Cantwell) Armstrong has been a professional journalist for fifteen years. She earned her Bachelor of Science degree from Eastern Michigan University. Nothing matters more to her than her twins, Malinda and Alissa, and her husband, Don. Julie's story is dedicated to her mother, Linda (Elkins) Snider (1954-2001).

Aaron Bacall has graduate degrees in organic chemistry, as well as educational administration and supervision from New York University. He has been a pharmaceutical research chemist, college department coordinator, college instructor, and now a full-time cartoonist and illustrator. His work has appeared in most national magazines, such as *The New Yorker, Reader's Digest, Saturday Evening Post*, and *Barron's*, as well as several cartoon collections. It has also been used for advertising, greeting cards, wall and desk calendars, and corporate promotional books. Three of his cartoons are featured in the permanent collection at the Harvard Business School's Baker Library. He can be reached at ABacall@msn.com.

Dot Beams is a published author, an editor, a certified English tutor, and a business material/resume writer. Dot coordinated the first U.S. Aerospace Outplacement Center in 1973. She is a Christian women's speaker and loves using humor when speaking to single parent groups. Dot may be reached at polkadot19@sbcglobal.net.

Melissa Blake, a freelance writer and newspaper columnist, lives in DeKalb, Illinois. She hopes to work for a magazine one day. Until then, she continues to enjoy spending time with the lovely triplets.

Sage de Beixedon Breslin, Ph.D., is a licensed psychologist and intuitive consultant. She is also an accomplished author. Her latest publications have been written to inspire and touch those who have struggled with life's challenges. Her books and courses are available on her website at www.healingheartcenter.org. She can be reached at Sage@HealingHeartCenter.org.

Isabel Stenzel Byrnes is a social worker and public health educator. She volunteers for the cystic fibrosis and transplant communities and lives in Northern California with her husband. Together with her twin, Isabel has co-written the twin memoir, *The Power of Two: A Twin Triumph over Cystic Fibrosis*. See www.stenzeltwins.com.

Martha Campbell is a graduate of Washington University, St. Louis School of Fine Arts, and a former writer/designer for Hallmark Cards. She has been a freelance cartoonist and illustrator since leaving Hallmark. She lives in Harrison, Arkansas.

Michele Christian currently has two other published short stories in *It's Twins! Parent-to-Parent Advice from Infancy Through Adolescence* by Susan Heim, and *Twin Connections: Stories That Celebrate the Mysterious Bond Between Twins* by Debbie LaChusa. Michele plans to continue writing children's stories. She can be reached at michelechristian819@yahoo.com.

Linda S. Clare of Eugene, Oregon, has published three books: *Lost Boys and the Moms Who Love Them; Revealed: Spiritual Reality in a Makeover World*; and, *Making Peace with a Dangerous God*. Her debut novel, *The Fence My Father Built*, will be released in August 2009 from Abingdon Press. Visit her blog at http://godsonggrace.blogspot.com.

Gayle Allen Cox caught the writing bug at age fifteen when a song burst forth while riding in the family sedan. Her songs have appeared on Southern Gospel's Top 40, and her byline has appeared in *The Dallas Morning News*, the *Houston Chronicle*, and in various other newspapers and magazines. She enjoys hearing from readers. E-mail her at gac@awesomenet.net.

Margaret P. Cunningham is honored to have six previous stories published in *Chicken Soup for the Soul* books. Black Lyon Publishing has recently released her first novel, *Lily in Bloom*, a quirky love story set in a renowned Southern garden. Margaret lives with her husband, Tom, in Mobile, Alabama.

Betty Johnson Dalrymple is a freelance writer of inspirational devotions and articles, and a contributor to numerous popular devotional books. She facilitates a grief-support group, and enjoys traveling, playing golf and spending time with her husband and their large blended family consisting of nineteen grandchildren—including triplets.

Mia LeBlanc Daveline lives in Sherman Oaks, California, with her twin girls. She is completing a book and appeared on *Oprah* to tell their story. Mia also devotes time to the Melanoma Research Foundation and the celebrity golf tournament held in her husband Kerry's memory. Her e-mail is daveline@earthlink.net.

Marcy DeHaan received her Bachelor of Science in Nursing with a minor in Psychology from Grand View College, Des Moines, Iowa, in 2001. She has been a hospice nurse since 2003 and knows it is her calling to help those at the end of life. She has lived in four different states due to her husband's past military service, and currently resides in the Norfolk, Virginia area. She enjoys traveling, music, and spending time with her husband and twin sons. She feels blessed to have a great family and career. Please e-mail her at redlexi@hotmail.com.

Deborah A. Ein is managing editor of a weekly community newspaper

(*The Grapevine*), where she has her own column ("Gleanings"). When she's not writing or editing, she is likely to be shuttling one or all three of her children here and there. You can contact her through her website at www.writermomz.com.

Sherry L. Emerson lives in Lawrence, Kansas with her husband Tim and their three children. She and Tim are small business owners who enjoy spending time outdoors with their very active family. Sherry spends her free time volunteering and enjoys freelance writing when she can find the time.

Marla Feldman lives with her husband of twenty-one years and their three children. Previously an elementary school teacher, Marla can now be found working part-time in her synagogue's religious school. She enjoys being home with her family. Her work has appeared in the books, *Twice the Love: Stories of Inspiration for Families with Twins, Multiples and Singletons* and *It's Twins! Parent-to-Parent Advice from Infancy Through Adolescence.*

Mary Margaret Fessler is a junior in high school. She is adjusting well to life as the oldest of seven. When not chasing two-year-olds, she loves reading, running, cooking, gardening, and knitting.

Yavonne Field-Bagwell is the very proud mother of identical twins, Quinton and Zachary, born in 1991. Her first children's book, also written about her boys, was published in 1999. Yavonne is an internal auditor who loves to travel, scrapbook, and write when she can, which is not nearly often enough.

Laurie M. Ford writes a bi-weekly column, "Twin Spin," for her local newspaper in Mokena, Illinois, where she and her husband (and unofficial editor) Michael raise their family. Laurie is a member of the Midwest Writers Association and The International Women's Writing Guild. She can be reached at twinspin@ymail.com.

Rosemary Francis enjoys writing in many genres, mostly as a children's writer, but also about teas, herbs and history. She has always worked in the medical field, and in her spare time she enjoys singing, swimming, traveling and visiting local historical locations in the Northern Neck of Virginia.

Rachel Furey grew up in Smyrna, New York, and will complete her MFA in creative writing at Southern Illinois University at Carbondale in the spring of 2009. Her work has appeared or is forthcoming in *Women's Basketball Magazine, Press 53 Open Awards Anthology*, and a Main Street Rag short fiction anthology.

Jacqueline Gaston graduated from the University of Connecticut in 1989 with a Bachelor of Science degree and received her Master's of Education from George Mason University in 1996. She is currently a Transition Teacher at Chantilly High School in Virginia. She is a proud wife and mother of four children.

Freelance writer **Marian Gormley** has been published in regional, national and international publications, including publication in a number of *Chicken Soup for the Soul* books. She has a background in software engineering, public relations, marketing and teaching. Residing with her family in Virginia, she writes primarily about parenting, family life, education, health and the arts.

Karen H. Gros is a freelance writer from the South. Karen has been published in national magazines and is a regular contributor to *Teen Trend Magazine* and *Multiples Magazine*. She also enjoys traveling and camping, as well as spending time with family and LSU sports in her free time. You can e-mail Karen at lsu_is_number_1@yahoo.com.

Jean Hale is a Domestic Engineer and works primarily for her twin boys. She loves to travel, swim and sleep, but raising her twins is her most favorite hobby. Please e-mail her at hankseal@earthlink.net.

Jonny Hawkins sells cartoons to magazines, book publishers and companies all over the world. His latest book, *A Joke a Day Keeps the Doctor Away*, and calendars, *Medical Cartoon-A-Day, Fishing Cartoon-A-Day* and *Car 'Toon-A-Day*, are available online and at bookstores everywhere. He can be reached at jonnyhawkins2nz@yahoo.com.

A certified appraiser and auctioneer, **Ann G. Hays** served as a doll appraiser for the television program, *Antiques Roadshow*. She authored many articles for collector magazines. Ann and husband, Ken, created a weekly insert for children entitled *The Peanut Butter Journal*, which was included in her state's largest newspaper. E-mail her at annhays@haysauction.com.

Patricia Hoff is owner of Move it! Fitness, Inc., a family fitness mobile gym, and co-founder of It Takes a Village Foundation, a non-profit organization dedicated to helping families in the third world. She lives in Milton, Massachusetts, with her husband and four children. Please e-mail her at patti@moveitwithpatti.com.

Donna K. Hogue is retired. In 2006 at the age of sixty-three, she wrote her first book, *An Oasis Moment*, a daily devotional. Her second book, *Divorce Happens... Even to Christians*, was written the following year. Donna is very active in Women's Ministry. Please e-mail her at DKTWIN@aol.com.

Betsy Jackman worked in advertising for ten years before switching to development in higher education with a focus on human resources. Betsy is a certified coach and holds a B.A. in Psychology from Michigan State University. She lives in Chicago and is passionate about photography, travel, and inspiring others.

Anne K. Jacobs, Ph.D., a clinical child psychologist, works with the Terrorism & Disaster Center. She has authored more than two dozen scholarly publications and is now trying to write works of a more personal nature. She and her husband, Noel, enjoy raising their twin girls, their Dalmatian, and seven tarantulas. Contact her at akzerg@yahoo.com.

Denice Aldrich Jobe is a writer whose features and essays have appeared in national publications, including *The Washington Post* and *Preemie*, and the books *Twice the Love: Stories of Inspiration for Families with Twins, Multiples and Singletons* and *It's Twins! Parent-to-Parent Advice from Infancy Through Adolescence*. She lives in Virginia with her husband and twin sons. Visit www.denicealdrichjobe.com to learn more about her work.

Rachel E. Jones lives in East Africa with her husband and three children. She serves women in the areas of English teaching, micro-enterprise development and athletics. She enjoys swimming with whale sharks, studying languages (currently on #6) and writing about her experiences overseas.

Sally Kamerling is a retired nurse educator. Since retirement she has pursued her long-time interest in writing. Her discovery of a treasure trove of letters from her grandmother led to a desire to learn more about family history and honor some of those forgotten relatives by telling their stories.

Joanne C. King is a wife, mother and author of the multi-award-winning book, *Answers and Answers CDROM*. King created *Answers* so all children could have a permanent record of their parents' unconditional love and wisdom regarding faith, education, relationships and more. King may be reached at answersbook@aol.com and www.joannecking.com.

Cheryl Kirking is the mother of nearly-grown triplets, an award-winning author, songwriter, and conference speaker who inspires audiences nationwide through her Ripples of Encouragement(™) Keynotes in Concert. She has written seven books, including *Crayons* *in the Dryer*, and has recorded six CDs of original songs. For booking information, visit her website at www.cherylkirking.com.

Amy P. Knight received her Bachelor of Arts from Vassar College and a Master of Fine Arts in fiction from the University of Arizona. She lives in Tucson, Arizona, with her partner and her two dogs, and is at work on her first novel.

Jacqueline Davidson Kopito received her B.A. Degree from Syracuse University and a Master's in Corporate and Public Communications from Seton Hall University. She and her twin sister, Amy Davidson Lombardo, are currently working on getting their first book, *Tales of the Twins: Life Stories of Identical Sisters*, published. The twins are simultaneously developing a line of greeting cards for twins and multiples of all ages. Jacqueline lives with her husband and two sons in Short Hills, New Jersey.

Susan Lack is an identical twin. She lives in New Mexico while her other half lives in California. She is a registered "research twin" with SRI International, and has fun writing fiction and first-person essays. This is her first non-fiction piece. Her plan is to finish her novel and retire to a beach.

Elaine A. Lederman is a single mother of three girls—eleven-year-old Sophia and five-and-a-half-year-old twins, Naomi and Jillian. She is a self-employed CPA.

Amy Davidson Lombardo received her B.A. Degree in Communications from the University of Hartford, and a Master's of Science in Counseling (with Honors) from Pace University. Amy currently practices social work in Ridgefield, Connecticut, where she lives with her husband and two sons.

Patricia Lorenz is an art-of-living writer and speaker, and the author of eleven books, including *The Five Things We Need to Be Happy*. She's one of the top contributors to the *Chicken Soup for the Soul* books with stories in more than forty of them. To inquire about having her speak at your next function, visit her website at www.PatriciaLorenz.com.

Jennifer Moglia Lucil received her Bachelor of Arts from Smith College in 1994 and her Master of Arts from Brown University in 1995. Before her adventures with twin boys began, she taught at a Montessori school outside of Boston. She currently sneaks away at nap time to write.

A former police officer and 9-1-1 operator, **Stacie Lykins** was blessed to have carried twins twice as a gestational surrogate. She resides in Florida with her family and Abby-cat. It's her life-long dream to start a non-profit organization to fund education for single mothers. Please e-mail her at StacieLykins@aol.com.

Jana Malkan, a 2002 Marquette University Alumni, is Vice President of the Waukesha Mothers of Twins Club and Editor of the Wisconsin Organization of Mothers of Twins Clubs. Jana is a Tupperware manager and an antique dealer. She and her husband have identical twin boys born in 2004 and a third son born in 2008. Contact her at janasdukan@gmail.com.

Sara Matson lives in Minnesota with her husband and eight-year-old twin girls, Leah and Chloe, who enjoy celebrating their brother Luke's birthday every April. A freelance writer, Sara writes for various children's, parenting, and family magazines.

Tamara Mays is a school counselor and loves to write. She has her Master's degree in Education and Counseling.

Shannon McCarty received her Master's in Rehabilitation Counseling from the University of Texas Medical Center in Dallas in 1994 and currently resides in Austin, Texas. She writes humor pieces about parenting, and receives much of her inspiration from her twins, Tess and Tabitha, and son, Riley. Please e-mail her at smccarty@austin.rr.com.

Jeffrey McCracken is a reporter for *The Wall Street Journal* in New York covering bankruptcy and distressed companies. He received a bachelor's degree in journalism and a law degree from Wayne State University in Detroit. A Michigan native, he currently resides with his wife and three-year-old twins in New Jersey.

Norma McCulliss is a mother of five and grandmother of nine. She has lived for thirty-plus years in Florida and has published articles in both local and national publications. She is currently awaiting the publication of her first children's book, *Violets for Mary*. Her e-mail address is nmcculliss@hotmail.com.

Donna Milligan Meadows is the mother of six adult children—including triplets. She worked for many years as an elementary school librarian and hopes to write a children's book someday. She loves reading, traveling, gardening and especially reading to her grandchildren. Please e-mail her at meadowsdonna@hotmail.com.

Stacie Roth Miller earned her B.A. in psychology, graduating summa cum laude, from Huntington College in 2001. She was recently enrolled as a professional writing student at Taylor University, Fort Wayne. Currently, Stacie is a stay-at-home mom to her three children. She may be contacted at stacieleigh88@hotmail.com.

Jann Mitchell is an American writer and quilter married to a Swedish HIV/AIDS specialist. They live in Stockholm, Sweden, and in Portland, Oregon. They work part-time in Tanzania, East Africa, where she helps AIDS orphans and the grandmothers raising them. You can reach her at jannmmitchell@aol.com, or visit her website, www.bibijann.org, or blog at http://bibijannhelps.blogspot.com.

Lois Muehl has a B.A. from Oberlin and an M.A. from the University of Iowa, both in English Education. Retired from running a UI Reading Lab for nineteen years, she has also taught in North Carolina, Thailand, Korea, and China. She enjoys family, doing folk art, and writing. Her latest book is *DARK/LIGHT*, a collection of serious and whimsical poetry.

Janice Flood Nichols holds a B.A. from Seton Hill College and a M.Ed. from the University of Pittsburgh. As the author of *Twin Voices: A Memoir of Polio, the Forgotten Killer*, she devotes her time to speaking about the importance of polio eradication. Visit her website at www.twinvoices.com.

Linda L. Osmundson lives in Fort Collins, Colorado, with her husband of forty-three years. She writes for parent, grandparent, teacher, religious, travel, and children's publications, *Family Circle* and six other *Chicken Soup for the Soul* books. She enjoys golf, reading, art, crafts, travel and Dixieland Jazz.

Pam Pace is the mother of triplets Brittany, Brandi and Stephen, plus Bailey and Benjamin. She is co-founder of Keeping Pace with Multiple Miracles, a non-profit support organization for multiple birth families. Pam is a certified lactation counselor and writer. She has been married to Stephen for twenty years. E-mail: keepingpace.multiplemiracles@verizon.net.

Mark Parisi's "off the mark" comic, syndicated since 1987, is distributed by United Media. Mark's humor also graces greeting cards, T-shirts, calendars, magazines, newsletters and books. Lynn is his wife/business partner. Their daughter, Jen, contributes with inspiration (as do three cats and a dog). Check out: offthemark.com.

Vi Parsons is a genealogy researcher, teacher and author of her family history book, *Jacob Dragoo and Our Susanna Bright Side*. She is the co-author of *Double Take*, a book of her childhood memories.

She and her twin sister are the creators of Carr Twins & Co. Visit www.carrtwins.com.

Stephanie Piro lives in New Hampshire with her husband, daughter, and three cats. She is one of King Features' team of women cartoonists, "Six Chix" (she is the Saturday chick!). Her single panel, "Fair Game," appears in newspapers and on her website: www.stephaniepiro.com. Her new book, *My Cat Loves Me Naked*, is available at bookstores everywhere. She also designs gift items for her company, Strip T's. Contact her at stephaniepiro@verizon.net or 27 River Road, Farmington, NH 03835.

Kathleen Whitman Plucker lives and writes in the Midwest. She holds degrees from the University of Virginia and enjoys photography, scrapbooking, and volunteering. You may reach her at kplucker@earthlink.net.

Denice R. Porchia graduated from Wayne County Community College as a Certified Occupational Therapist Assistant. She also has a business degree in Office Management. Her first published book was called *Pure Gold*. She is currently writing her own greeting card line. She is also working on a book on domestic violence.

Kalynne Hackney Pudner holds a Ph.D. in Philosophy from the University of Virginia. She lives with her husband and nine children in Alabama, where she teaches ethics and philosophy of law at Auburn University. Her uniquely philosophical approach to motherhood can be found at www.phdwithninekids.blogspot.com.

Lori Purtzer is the wife of PGA Tour Professional Tom Purtzer. With their five children, including two sets of fraternal twins, and his three children, their very large family is complete. No matter what, Dad is always a champion at home. Lori is busy compiling family stories. Contact her at Purtzy5@aol.com.

Enoch Pyle currently works as a freelance cartoonist from his home in Southwest Missouri. He lives with his wife, Darrah, and two sons, Aden and Noah. Enoch is now developing a historical comic strip based on his Christian roots and family values. You can find more information by visiting www.EnochPyle.com.

S.R. has an Associate of Arts and a Bachelor of Science degree. She is a working mom enjoying small-town living with her husband and three sons. She enjoys cooking, a rare quiet moment, opportunities for creativity and, most of all, spending time with her family.

Samira Rao has a Master's of Science in Health Education. She published a Health & Wellness newsletter subscribed to by hospitals, health facilities and homes. Her second book, *Leaps of Faith*, will be completed shortly. For information on her books, online newsletter or latest health/healing/spiritual resources, please visit www.samirarao.com or e-mail her at samirarao@yahoo.com.

Janell M. Rardon, author of *Rock-Solid Families: Transform an Ordinary Home into a Fortress of Faith*, faced a huge life change in Fall 2008 when she sent her twins off to college. She resides in Virginia with her husband, Rob. Visit Janell's website at www.janellrardon.com or e-mail her at janellrardon@hotmail.com.

Chris Rathje is working on his first two books and is continuing the path to his dreams as a member of Lakeshore Demolition wheelchair rugby team and Lakeshore Athletics team. He would like to thank his friends and family for their wonderful support. He would especially like to recognize his hometown of Downers Grove, the University of Illinois, Northwestern Medill IMC, the Lakeshore Foundation and his adopted home of Birmingham. Chris's writing can be followed at http://chrisrathje.blogspot.com. E-mail him at chris.rathje@gmail.com.

Joe Rector is a freelance writer who writes columns for two local newspapers and other magazines. He has made other contributions to *Chicken Soup for the Soul*. Joe retired from teaching high school English after thirty years. He has created a website for teachers, www.teachertales.net. Please e-mail Joe at joerector@comcast.net.

Bruce Robinson is an award-winning, internationally published cartoonist whose work has appeared in numerous consumer and trade periodicals, including *National Enquirer*, *The Saturday Evening Post, Woman's World, The Sun, First*, and *Highlights for Children*. He is also author of the cartoon book, *Good Medicine*. Contact him at cartoonsbybrucerobinson@hotmail.com.

Janice and Faye Rostvit, identical twins, are international singers. For forty years, they have performed in ninety countries, singing in 116 languages. They compose and record songs, and authored the book, *Twin Reflections*, highlighting God's providential care. Their college honored them with the "Outstanding Alumni Award." E-mail them at rostvit@juno.com.

Lee Rothberg, a freelance writer and former nurse, currently works at the Matawan Aberdeen Library in New Jersey. While a medical staff writer for *The Woman's Newspaper of Princeton*, she received several awards from the National Federation of Press Women. She wholeheartedly appreciates the exceptional nurturing skills of her parents.

Theresa Sanders grew up in Springfield, Missouri, graduated from the University of Maryland, and has worked as a technical writer and consultant. She loves the message of the *Chicken Soup for the Soul* books, and has contributed to several. Mom to four beloved grown children, she lives with her husband near St. Louis.

Shari L. Schmidt, APR, is an award-winning marketing communications professional with extensive experience working with corporations, not-for-profit agencies, and trade associations. Schmidt chronicles life with twins on her award-winning blog, Two Times the Fun, at http://twotimesthefun.blogspot.com.

Lynne Sella lives in California with her husband and twin daughters. A teacher at Richmond School, she has written children's stories, humorous anecdotes about living with twins, and a series of stories about the misadventures of a female deputy sheriff in an isolated region of northern California.

Al Serradell, a native of Los Angeles, California, is a life-long writer of inspirational, motivational (managerial issues) and Young Adult fiction, and is the proud "parent" of the original Beverly Hills chihuahua.

Sara F. Shacter is a children's writer. Her articles have appeared in publications such as *Highlights for Children* and *World Book's Childcraft Annuals*. She recently made her fiction debut with the picture book, *Heading to the Wedding* (Red Rock Press). A former teacher, she loves speaking at schools. Please visit her at www.sarafshacter.com.

Mary Z. Smith resides in Richmond, Virginia, with her husband, Barry, and rat terrier, Frankie. They have four children. Mary enjoys writing for *Angels on Earth* and *Guideposts* magazines.

Jean Haynie Stewart enjoys parenting twins and now grandparenting with her husband of forty-seven years in Mission Viejo, California. She's an award-winning writer, and her family stories can be found in numerous *Chicken Soup for the Soul* books and other anthologies. Her articles are in the *Orange County Register, ByLine, California Living, Aviation Life Styles*, and *Christian Communicator*.

Donna Sullivan graduated from The University of Alabama in 1995. She is a stay-at-home mom to elementary-school-aged identical twin girls and a preschool-aged son. Donna lives in Mechanicsville,

Virginia, where she spends time with her husband and three children in their numerous sporting and after-school activities.

Karen Talcott has a master's degree in education and taught elementary school for fifteen years before becoming a stay-at-home mother and author. Her book, *Moms of Multiples' Devotions to Go*, will be published in fall 2009. A children's book, *Cora McFee, the Picky Eater*, as well as a women's devotional book, are also in development. She and her husband, Leland, have three children—a daughter and boy/girl twins.

Kent W. Tarver is a native Oklahoman for forty-three years. His interests include singing, writing and traveling. Kent is currently working on motivational books for the workplace.

Christina Baglivi Tinglof is the creator and editor of talk-about-twins.com, a website devoted to twins and twin relationships. She's a contributing writer to *Twins Magazine*, and has authored five books, including *Parenting School-Age Twins and Multiples* and *Double Duty: The Parents' Guide to Raising Twins*.

Carol Tremper earned her Master of Education of the Gifted and Talented from Widener University. Professionally active, she taught for thirty years while creating national student challenges, conducting teacher workshops, editing newsletters, and writing professional articles and books. Now retired, Carol relishes writing, poetry, art, family, travel, and photography. E-mail her at zeearts@ptd.net.

Christopher Tremper earned a Bachelor's in Liberal Arts (Music) from Kean University in 1988. He has authored several (as yet unsold!) screenplays, an (as yet unpublished!) novel, and he writes and records (as yet unheralded by *Billboard Magazine*!) music. He currently works as an engineer for NJ Transit, but prefers creative pursuits to actually making money. Feel free to e-mail him at ChristopherJamesTremper@comcast.net.

Stacey Tyser received her Bachelor of Science at George Mason University in 1997. She is an IT professional and a mom to three-year-old identical twin girls, Camryn Grace and Emma Catherine. The Tyser family resides in Rockville, Maryland.

Stacey Vandell and her husband Rob are the proud (and crazed) parents of Jake and Ryan (21 months) and daughter, Regan (age three). The Vandells are founders of A lot'o'tots at www.alototots.com, which caters specifically to parents of multiples by giving automatic discounts when more than one of the same item type is purchased. Contact them at customerservice@alototots.com.

Ann Vitorovich, a first-generation American, attended Columbia Union College and worked as a legal secretary. She enjoys anything creative, including painting, sewing and making hats. In retirement, she enjoys cooking, walking and writing. Ann has two books, including *Whom Shall I Fear*, and a second to be released in 2010. E-mail her at voyann1959@cox.net.

Chela Newton Wallace received her Bachelor of Arts in Music from the University of Oregon in 1982. She taught piano and played professionally for many years. Chela has three sons (including twins) and works as a freelance technical writer. She enjoys music, hiking, traveling, and writing poetry and children's books.

Lynel Washington is a native of New Orleans, Louisiana. A former Human Services Counselor, she is now a freelance editor who pays close attention to detail and thrives on creativity. Sharp proofreading and honest feedback are her specialties. Lynel has always enjoyed a love for the written word, and now her career is based on doing what she loves. She can be reached at Lmaria23@hotmail.com.

Connie Watson is a mother and grandmother who lives in Hazel Park, Michigan, with her husband of forty years, Alex. They own Alco Printing Services, Inc., in Royal Oak. Prior to *Chicken Soup for* *the Soul*, she had only written stories for her grandchildren, her journal, and greeting cards for friends and family.

Raymond P. Weaver is in his seventies, retired and lives in Clearwater, Florida. He belongs to a local writers group, and has had numerous short stories and articles published in newspapers and magazines. He is currently looking for a publisher for his first mystery novel. Please e-mail him at raymondellie@aol.com.

Melissa Wenzel and her husband Dan live in Surprise, Arizona, with their twins and cocker spaniel, Hogan. Melissa is a full-time mother to their twenty-one-month-old twin boys, Jonathan and James, and is a part-time public relations manager and consultant. She can be reached at mel_wenzel@yahoo.com.

Maureen Kenny Winick, Ph.D., is a licensed psychologist and director of the Counselor Education Program at Florida International University in Miami, Florida. She is the proud (but tired) mother of four-year-old girl/boy/girl triplets: Jordan, Toby and Samantha. Please e-mail her at kennym@fiu.edu.

Paul Winick, M.D., lives in Hollywood, Florida, with his wife, Dorothy. He practiced pediatrics for thirty years. He has two children and five grandchildren, including triplets. Paul is a full professor of clinical pediatrics at the University of Miami, School of Medicine. This is his fourth *Chicken Soup for the Soul* contribution. He has published a memoir, *Finding Ruth*, and many prize-winning stories.

Helen Zanone has been married eighteen years and is a stay-at-home mother of three. Now that her kids are more independent, writing has become her second career. She enjoys cooking, reading, and painting. Please e-mail her at hzanone@yahoo.com.

Chicken Soup for the Soul

Who Is Jack Canfield?

Jack Canfield is the co-creator and editor of the *Chicken Soup for the Soul* series, which *Time* magazine has called "the publishing phenomenon of the decade." Jack is also the co-author of eight other bestselling books including *The Success Principles™: How to Get from Where You Are to Where You Want to Be*, *Dare to Win*, *The Aladdin Factor*, *You've Got to Read This Book*, and *The Power of Focus: How to Hit Your Business and Personal and Financial Targets with Absolute Certainty*.

Jack is the CEO of the Canfield Training Group in Santa Barbara, California, and founder of the Foundation for Self-Esteem in Culver City, California. He has conducted intensive personal and professional development seminars on the principles of success for over a million people in twenty-three countries. Jack is a dynamic keynote speaker and he has spoken to hundreds of thousands of others at more than 1,000 corporations, universities, professional conferences and conventions, and has been seen by millions more on national television shows such as *The Today Show*, *Fox and Friends*, *Inside Edition*, *Hard Copy*, CNN's *Talk Back Live*, *20/20*, *Eye to Eye*, and the *NBC Nightly News* and the *CBS Evening News*.

Jack is the recipient of many awards and honors, including three honorary doctorates and a Guinness World Records Certificate for having seven books from the *Chicken Soup for the Soul* series appearing on the New York Times bestseller list on May 24, 1998.

You can reach Jack at:

Jack Canfield
The Canfield Companies
P. O. Box 30880 • Santa Barbara, CA 93130
phone: 805-563-2935 • fax: 805-563-2945
www.jackcanfield.com

Who Is

Mark Victor Hansen?

Mark Victor Hansen is the co-founder of Chicken Soup for the Soul, along with Jack Canfield. He is also a sought-after keynote speaker, bestselling author, and marketing maven. For more than thirty years, Mark's powerful messages of possibility, opportunity, and action have created powerful change in thousands of organizations and millions of individuals worldwide.

Mark's credentials include a lifetime of entrepreneurial success. He is a prolific writer with many bestselling books, such as *The One Minute Millionaire*, *Cracking the Millionaire Code*, *How to Make the Rest of Your Life the Best of Your Life*, *The Power of Focus*, *The Aladdin Factor*, and *Dare to Win*, in addition to the *Chicken Soup for the Soul* series. Mark has had a profound influence in the field of human potential through his library of audios, videos, and articles in the areas of big thinking, sales achievement, wealth building, publishing success, and personal and professional development. Mark is also the founder of the MEGA Seminar Series.

He has appeared on *Oprah*, CNN, and *The Today Show*. He has been quoted in *Time*, *U.S. News & World Report*, *USA Today*, *The New York Times*, and *Entrepreneur* and has given countless radio interviews, assuring our planet's people that "You can easily create the life you deserve."

Mark is the recipient of numerous awards that honor his entrepreneurial spirit, philanthropic heart, and business acumen. He is a lifetime member of the Horatio Alger Association of Distinguished Americans, an organization that honored Mark with the prestigious Horatio Alger Award for his extraordinary life achievements.

You can reach Mark at:

Mark Victor Hansen & Associates, Inc.
P. O. Box 7665 • Newport Beach, CA 92658
phone: 949-764-2640 • fax: 949-722-6912
www.markvictorhansen.com

Who Is

Susan M. Heim?

Susan M. Heim is an author and editor, specializing in parenting, multiples, women's and Christian issues. After the birth of her fraternal twin boys, Austen and Caleb, Susan left her 8-to-5 job as a Senior Editor for a publishing company and has never looked back!

Chicken Soup for the Soul: Twins and More is Susan's fifth published book. Her other books include *It's Twins! Parent-to-Parent Advice from Infancy Through Adolescence; Oh, Baby! 7 Ways a Baby Will Change Your Life the First Year; Twice the Love: Stories of Inspiration for Families with Twins, Multiples and Singletons*; and *Boosting Your Baby's Brain Power*. Susan has two books scheduled for publication in the fall of 2009: *Chicken Soup for the Soul: All in the Family* and *Moms of Multiples' Devotions to Go*. She has many more projects in the works, including a book of devotionals for women. She also hopes to venture into fiction writing in the future!

Susan's articles and stories have appeared in many books, magazines and websites. Susan writes an online column for *Mommies Magazine* called "Loving and Living with Twins and Multiples." She shares her thoughts and experiences about raising children in today's world through her blog, "Susan Heim on Parenting," at www.susanheim.blogspot.com. Susan is also an expert on twins and multiples for AllExperts.com and ParentsConnect.com, and a parenting expert for SelfGrowth.com.

Susan is the founder of TwinsTalk, a website where parents share tips, advice and stories about raising twins and multiples, at www.twinstalk.com. She is a member of the National Association of Women Writers and the Southeastern Writers Association.

Susan is married to Mike, whose ever-present support enables Susan to pursue a career she loves. They are the parents of four sons—two teenagers and twin preschoolers. You can reach Susan at susan@susanheim.com and visit her website at www.susanheim.com.

Chicken Soup for the Soul

Thank You!

We appreciate all of our wonderful family members and friends, who continue to inspire and teach us on our life's journey. We have been blessed beyond measure with their constant love and support.

We owe huge thanks to all of our contributors. We know that you pour your hearts and souls into the stories that you share with us, and ultimately with each other. We appreciate your willingness to open up your lives to other Chicken Soup for the Soul readers. We can only publish a small percentage of the stories that are submitted, but we read every single one, and even the ones that do not appear in the book have an influence on us and on the final manuscript. We strongly encourage you to continue submitting to future Chicken Soup for the Soul books.

We would like to thank Amy Newmark, our Publisher, for her generous spirit, creative vision, and expert editing. We're also grateful to D'ette Corona, our Assistant Publisher, who seamlessly manages twenty to thirty projects at a time while keeping all of us focused and on schedule. And we'd like to express our gratitude to Barbara LoMonaco, Chicken Soup for the Soul's Webmaster and Editor; Chicken Soup for the Soul Editor Kristiana Glavin, for her assistance with the final manuscript and proofreading; and Leigh Holmes, who keeps our office running smoothly.

We owe a very special thanks to our Creative Director and book producer, Brian Taylor at Pneuma Books, for his brilliant vision for our covers and interiors. Finally, none of this would be possible without the business and creative leadership of our CEO, Bill Rouhana, and our president, Bob Jacobs.

Chicken Soup for the Soul®

Improving Your Life Every Day

Real people sharing real stories—for fifteen years. Now, Chicken Soup for the Soul has gone beyond the bookstore to become a world leader in life improvement. Through books, movies, DVDs, online resources and other partnerships, we bring hope, courage, inspiration and love to hundreds of millions of people around the world. Chicken Soup for the Soul's writers and readers belong to a one-of-a-kind global community, sharing advice, support, guidance, comfort, and knowledge.

Chicken Soup for the Soul stories have been translated into more than forty languages and can be found in more than one hundred countries. Every day, millions of people experience a Chicken Soup for the Soul story in a book, magazine, newspaper or online. As we share our life experiences through these stories, we offer hope, comfort and inspiration to one another. The stories travel from person to person, and from country to country, helping to improve lives everywhere.

Share with Us

We all have had Chicken Soup for the Soul moments in our lives. If you would like to share your story or poem with millions of people around the world, go to www.chickensoup.com and click on "Submit Your Story." You may be able to help another reader, and become a published author at the same time. Some of our past contributors have launched writing and speaking careers from the publication of their stories in our books!

Your stories have the best chance of being used if you submit them through our website, at

www.chickensoup.com

If you do not have access to the Internet, you may submit your stories by mail or by facsimile. Starting in 2010, submissions will only be accepted via the website. Please do not send us any book manuscripts, unless through a literary agent, as these will be automatically discarded.

Chicken Soup for the Soul
P.O. Box 700
Cos Cob, CT 06807-0700
Fax 203-861-7194

This "support group in a book" is specifically geared to younger teens — the ones still worrying about puberty, cliques, discovering the opposite sex, and figuring out who they are. Meant for middle school students ages eleven to fourteen, stories cover regrets and lessons learned, love and "like," popularity, friendship, tough issues such as divorce, illness, and death, failure and rising above it, embarrassing moments, bullying, and finding something you're passionate about.

978-1-935096-26-9

TEENS books!

Chicken Soup for the Soul

www.chickensoup.com